The McGraw-Hill
36-Hour
Marketing
Course

The McGraw-Hill
36-Hour
Marketing
Course

Jeffrey L. Seglin

McGraw-Hill Publishing Company

New York St. Louis San Francisco Auckland Bogotá
Caracas Hamburg Lisbon London Madrid Mexico
Milan Montreal New Delhi Oklahoma City
Paris San Juan São Paulo Singapore
Sydney Tokyo Toronto

To Nancy,
Who makes life like Section 14 at Fenway—magic.

Library of Congress Cataloging-in-Publication Data
Seglin, Jeffrey L., date.
  The McGraw-Hill 36-hour marketing course / by Jeffrey L. Seglin.
    p.   cm.
  Includes index.
  ISBN 0-07-056062-5 : — ISBN 0-07-056063-3 (pbk.) :
    1. Marketing—United States.   2. Marketing—United States—Case
  studies.   3. Marketing—Problems, exercises, etc.   I. Title.
  HF5415.1.S443   1989
  658.8′0076—dc20   89-8100
                                                      CIP

1234567890   DOC/DOC   895432109

ISBN 0-07-056062-5
ISBN 0-07-056063-3 {PBK.}

*The editors for this book were Martha Jewett and Georgia
Kornbluth, the designer was Naomi Auerbach, and the production
supervisor was Dianne Walber. This book was set in Baskerville.
It was composed by the McGraw-Hill Publishing Company Professional &
Reference Division composition unit.*

Printed and bound by R. R. Donnelley & Sons Company.

*For more information about other McGraw-Hill materials,
call 1-800-2-MCGRAW in the United States. In other
countries, call your nearest McGraw-Hill office.*

Contents

Preface   viii

Study Plan   x

Chapter 1. What Is Marketing?   1

The Setting for Marketing   2
A Working Definition   2
Creation of Utilities   3
The Evolution of Marketing   4
The Marketing Concept   8
CASE STUDY: Putting the Customer First   10
CASE REVIEW   12
LESSON ONE QUESTIONS   12

Chapter 2. Strategic Marketing Planning   13

What Is Strategic Planning?   13
Scope of Planning Activities   13
What Is Strategic Marketing Planning?   16
The Management Process   18
Basic Management Terms   18
The Strategic Environment   20
CASE STUDY: Coke Is It?   20
CASE REVIEW   22
LESSON TWO QUESTIONS

Chapter 3. Marketing Research and Marketing Information Systems   23

The Development of Marketing Research   23
What Is Marketing Research?   24
Types of Marketing Research Applications   25
What Are Marketing Information Systems?   27
LESSON THREE QUESTIONS   31
The Marketing Research Process   32
Marketing Forecasts   41

v

Sales Forecasts   42
Who Does Marketing Research?   45
CASE STUDY: Can "The CELL" Sell?   46
CASE REVIEW   48
LESSON FOUR QUESTIONS   48

Chapter 4. Target Markets, Consumerism, Customers, Demographics, and Psychographics 49

What Are Markets?   49
Marketing Mix   50
Market Definition   53
Business Purpose   53
Target Markets   54
LESSON FIVE QUESTIONS   57
Consumer Buying Behavior   57
Consumer Demographics   58
Consumer Psychographics   69
CASE STUDY: Honda Understands the Market   78
CASE REVIEW   79
LESSON SIX QUESTIONS   79

Chapter 5. The Product 81

New Products   81
Parity Products   82
Augmented Products   83
Product Planning and Development   83
Product Adoption by Customer   84
Product Classification   86
Product Lines   90
Product Positioning   91
Trading Up and Trading Down   91
The Product Life Cycle   92
Product Life-Cycle Length   94
Branding   94
Packaging   98
Labeling   99
Warranties   100
CASE STUDY: Trademark Licensing to Gain Recognition—
            The Natural Choice   101
CASE REVIEW   102
LESSON SEVEN QUESTIONS   102

Chapter 6. Pricing 103

Establishing Price 103
Break-Even Analysis 106
Pricing Objectives 107
Determining Demand 110
LESSON EIGHT QUESTIONS 114
Evaluating Competitors' Prices 114
Pricing Strategies 117
Geographic Factors in Pricing 123
Federal Legislation Affecting Pricing 125
CASE STUDY: What Would You Pay for a Bagel? 126
CASE REVIEW 128
LESSON NINE QUESTIONS 128

Chapter 7. Product Distribution 129

Channels of Distribution 129
Major Channels of Distribution 130
Factors Affecting Distribution 133
Multiple Channels of Distribution 136
Vertical Channels 137
Intermediaries 139
LESSON TEN QUESTIONS 147
Physical Distribution 154
CASE STUDY: Cutting out the Middleman 158
CASE REVIEW 159
LESSON ELEVEN QUESTIONS 160

Chapter 8. Marketing Communications 161

Communications Model 161
The Communications Model in Marketing 161
Promotion 162
The Promotional Mix 163
CASE STUDY: Finding the Right Advertising Look 185
CASE REVIEW 186
LESSON TWELVE QUESTIONS 187

Answers to Lesson Questions 189

Index 202

Final Examination (following Index) 1

Preface

The McGraw-Hill 36-Hour Marketing Course is designed as a self-study course for people who have had little or no formal training in marketing, but find themselves in the position of needing to get a handle on major marketing issues. The book is designed to meet the needs of:

- Business professionals who work with marketing professionals on a day-to-day basis.
- Managers who want to know more about marketing so that they can better understand how their company works.
- Small business owners who need to understand basic marketing concepts in order to run their businesses more efficiently.

The bottom line is that the book is written for any professional or layperson who wants to understand marketing.

Only after years of training and experience can marketing professionals excel in their field. *The McGraw-Hill 36-Hour Marketing Course* does not supplant that experience; it merely gives the professional who may not be well-seasoned in marketing the information needed to become well versed in the basics of the topic.

The book is organized logically, taking the reader through explanations of what marketing is and how it can be used, and through the specifics of what makes the field of marketing tick. Many readers could conceivably read the entire book in a couple of evenings or on a weekend. But you should resist the temptation.

The book is designed as a self-study course. To come away with an understanding of marketing that you can remember and apply, it's important to study the material, rather than skim it.

The lesson plan includes 12 lessons plus a final examination. Each of the 12 lessons has a reading assignment plus a short test and is designed to be completed in 3 hours. The whole course (with the exception of the final) is designed to be completed in 36 hours. Pace yourself. If you don't have available 3 uninterrupted hours for completing a lesson, study as many pages as you can in one sitting, and come back to it. The beauty of a self-study course is that you can proceed at your own pace. The delightfulness of the "36-hour approach" is that it enables you to learn the basics of a rich topic in a relatively manageable period of time. But be forewarned: you'll get no microwave learning techniques here. Learning takes time, and the 36 hours this marketing course is designed to take is well worthwhile.

After you've finished the course, if you want to pursue the field of marketing further, you might turn to some of the more detailed texts and professional books that are available.. Victor P. Buell's *Handbook of Modern Marketing* (McGraw-Hill, New York, 1986), James Myers' *Marketing* (McGraw-Hill, New York, 1986), and William J. Stanton and Charles Futrell's *Fundamentals of Marketing* (McGraw-Hill, New York, 1987) are excellent sources. Among the general publications that are useful for insight into marketing are *Advertising Age, Business Week, Forbes, Fortune, Inc., Journal of Marketing, Sales & Marketing Management, Venture,* and *The Wall Street Journal.*

I would like to thank three editors who blessed *The McGraw-Hill 36-Hour Marketing Course* with their talent. Georgia Kornbluth patiently moved the book through production, adding her insight to the manuscript and making sure the sentences flowed. easily. Martha Jewett, senior editor at McGraw-Hill, guided me through this project. She was instrumental in developing the manuscript and getting me through the times when I was tempted to burden the reader with more material than could be digested in a lifetime, let alone 36 hours.

My wife, Nancy Seglin, who is a business editor with another publisher, took time in her evenings to read the manuscript, suggested changes and improvements, and put up with my grousing about the project when I hit tough spots. She is as much a source of inspiration as she is my saving grace.

Jeffrey L. Seglin

Study Plan

The McGraw-Hill 36-Hour Marketing Course is a self-study course that is designed to give you a broad understanding of the field of marketing. It consists of 36 hours of lessons that spell out the basics and arm you with enough knowledge to work with marketing professionals and understand the language and concepts of the field. It is not meant to supplant the years of experience and study that marketing professionals go through—merely to give you the information you need to be better able to get your own job done. Since marketing touches on so many aspects of business, an understanding of the basics is critical for today's professional.

A few suggestions before you undertake the course:

- Give yourself the time and work space you'll need to concentrate on taking the course. Like any field of study, marketing is full of concepts that may be new to you. You'll need time to absorb the new information.
- Formulate a study plan ahead of time and try to stick to it. Set aside time for two or more study sessions a week, during which you will devote your attention to the course. If you formulate such a study plan and stick to it, you'll be likely to work through the lessons and grasp a solid understanding of marketing basics. But if you leave study time to chance, you'll be more than likely to set the book aside and never get back to it.
- Be prepared to encounter marketing professionals who will disagree with some of the concepts and approaches you'll be learning. The most widely accepted are included here—but, like any field, marketing is full of different interpretations of the same concepts.

The Lesson Plan

Each lesson is designed so that you will need an average of 3 hours to complete the reading selection, the case study, the case review, and the lesson questions. You should feel free to do each 3-hour lesson in any way that is most convenient for your schedule, whether in one 3-hour sitting or in a few shorter time periods. Suggested answers to all the lesson questions appear at the end of the book.

Follow the specific guidelines below for the individual lessons.

Lesson One. Read Chapter 1, What Is Marketing? Read the case study and answer the case review questions. Then take the Lesson One test at the end of the chapter. You may feel that you would be able to complete this lesson in less than the 3 hours allotted, but take the full time to read and review the text, the case study, the case review, and the lesson questions. As you look back over the chapter, you should feel that you have a firm grasp of the material covered.

Lesson Two. Read Chapter 2, Strategic Marketing Planning. Read the case study, consider the case review questions, and take the Lesson Two test at the end of the chapter.

Lesson Three. Read through to about the middle of Chapter 3, Marketing Research and Marketing Information Systems, up through the section entitled "Marketing Information Systems Operations." Review the material, and then take the Lesson Three test on pages 31 and 32.

Lesson Four. Finish reading Chapter 3, beginning with the section entitled "The Marketing Research Process." Read the case study, consider the case review questions, and review the material. Then take the Lesson Four test at the end of the chapter.

Lesson Five. Read Chapter 4, Target Markets, Consumerism, Customers, Demographics and Psychographics, up to the end of the section entitled "Ultimate Consumers versus Industrial Users." Review the material and take the Lesson Five test on page 57.

Lesson Six. Finish reading Chapter 4, beginning with the section entitled "Consumer Buying Behavior." Review the material. Read the case study and answer the case review questions. Take the Lesson Six test at the end of the chapter.

Lesson Seven. Read Chapter 5, The Product. Review the chapter. Read the case study and answer the case review questions. Then take the Lesson Seven test at the end of the chapter.

Lesson Eight. Read Chapter 6, Pricing, up to the end of the section entitled "Demand Curves." Review the material. Take the Lesson Eight test on page 114.

Lesson Nine. Finish reading Chapter 6, beginning with the section entitled "Evaluating Competitors' Prices." Review the material. Read the case study and answer the case review questions. Take the Lesson Nine test at the end of the chapter.

Lesson Ten. Read Chapter 7, Product Distribution, up to the end of the section entitled "Manufacturers' Sales Branches and Offices." Review the material. Take the Lesson Ten test on page 147.

Lesson Eleven. Finish reading Chapter 7, beginning with the section entitled "Retailing Intermediaries." Review the material. Read the case study and answer the case review questions. Take the Lesson Eleven test at the end of the chapter.

Lesson Twelve. Read Chapter 8, Marketing Communications. Review the material. Read the case study and answer the case review questions. Take the Lesson Twelve test at the end of the chapter.

The Final Examination. Review the material in the book by going through each chapter and reviewing the lesson tests. Take the final examination. It may take you up to 2 hours to do a thorough job on the test. Send your exam into McGraw-Hill for grading. (Instructions appear at the beginning of the final examination.)

1
What Is Marketing?

For many years, professionals and laypeople have confused marketing with selling. But the field of marketing encompasses far more than just the act of selling. In fact, selling is but one of the many areas that make up the discipline of marketing.

Marketing is a very broad concept. As defined by the American Management Association (AMA), it is "the process of planning and executing the conception, pricing, promotion, and distribution of ideas, goods, and services to create exchanges that satisfy individual and organization objectives."[1] In lay terms, marketing involves everything that it takes to get a product off the drawing board and into the hands of the ultimate customer.

The concept of exchange is integral to marketing. Marketers use exchange as a means to satisfy needs and wants. *Exchange* is the process of trading something of value (e.g., money, time, or goods) to someone who voluntarily offers you in return something of value (e.g., ideas, goods, or services) that you want.

There are other methods of satisfying needs or wants that individuals or corporations can use if they desire. One method is to make something that satisfies their need or want; another is to steal what they need or want. But when we discuss marketing, exchange is at the heart of the process of satisfying needs and wants.

[1]"AMA Board Approves New Marketing Definition," *Marketing News*, Mar. 1, 1985, p. 1.

The Setting for Marketing

For marketing to occur, three distinct factors must exist.

1. *Marketers.*   These might include:
   - Business entities
   - Political parties
   - Not-for-profit organizations

   Marketers might also include any other firm or individual trying to exchange services, ideas, or goods.

2. *The goods, services, or ideas being marketed.*

3. *Potential markets.*   These would include not only the end user or buyer of goods but also those who are affected by or play a role in what is being marketed.

For example, an art museum's market would include not only the patrons who attend its galleries, but also:

- The foundations and corporations which provide funding
- The neighboring community which might be affected by the museum's activities
- The artists whose paintings hang in the galleries

A Working Definition

Marketing can be used to mean a variety of things, including the following:

- *Economists* may think of marketing chiefly as the movement of goods and services from those producing them to the consumers who will be using them—a process through which supply and demand are matched to fulfill the needs of a society.

- *Business firms*, which, like economists, see promotion and distribution as a function of marketing, also see marketing as the method that helps them design and price the product or service they are offering to the consumer.

- *Consumers* add still another dimension to the role of marketing. They are the ultimate beneficiaries of the products and services produced by businesses. Consumers can use these products and services to fulfill tasks and improve their quality of life.

- *Not-for-profit organizations* in today's society are also using marketing to build awareness of social issues and instill social change.

"Marketing" can be defined broadly. In effect, if the American Management Association definition is to be accepted, we all have to market ourselves in our daily life, perhaps in business life to our supervisors or prospective employers, or in family life to our parents or spouses. If we want to successfully promote an exchange that satisfies our objectives, we must go through the process of marketing ourselves. We develop the product, which is ourselves; establish a price, which may be a salary or an allowance; use promotional tools by employing appropriate communication skills; and satisfy distribution by being in the right place at the right time. Once we have marketed ourselves successfully, we provide after-sales service to assure our audience that we truly stand behind what we were marketing.

Business firms act similarly. Whether they are marketing a telephone system, teacups, or tanks, they first strive to develop the right product or service. They then establish an appropriate price, choose the appropriate location in which to market their product, and use promotional skills to sell their product or service to individuals or business firms.

Business professionals may glibly toss off the comment, "Everything comes down to marketing." And if we look at marketing carefully, such a glib saying can really be taken as a truism—a self-evident truth—for marketing plays a role not only in business but in all aspects of life.

That should not diminish the important role marketing plays in business. Measured in money, an average of almost 50 cents of every dollar a consumer spends at a retail store goes directly toward covering marketing costs.

Creation of Utilities

Marketing is indeed important. That it helps to create four types of utilities and support a fifth is testament to this observation.

A *utility* is that feature in something that causes it to be able to satisfy needs and wants. The four types of utilities created by marketing—time, place, possession, and image—as well as form, which marketing helps to support, attest to marketing's importance in both business and society.

Form utility, or "production," as it is referred to in business, consists of the changes that make a product more valuable than it had been before. When lumber is made into paper, form utility results. When paper is printed and bound into books, these acts too result in the creation of form utility. Form utility is not marketing, but rather production. But marketing may impact form utility as a result of marketing research that might indicate a variety of production issues—e.g., what weight, design, typeface, quantity, color, or fabric a product should be.

When prospective customers have a product or service readily available to them, it is the result of the creation of *place utility*. When customers have the product available to them when they want it, *time utility* has been created. When a customer buys a product or service, *possession utility* is created.

Books printed and bound in July in Westport, Massachusetts, have little value to a man living in Grand Forks, North Dakota, who wants to buy a book for his wife for her birthday in January. The marketing efforts that result in getting the books to a Grand Forks bookstore add value to the books: the marketing activities create place utility. Because the bookstore fulfills another marketing activity by housing the books from July to January, time utility is created. The man has the book available to him when he wants it. When, in January, the man has the ownership of the books transferred to him by buying the book, possession utility is created.

Image utility is created when someone attaches a high value to a product or service offered. People attach emotional or psychological value to products or services for a variety of reasons, including a business firm's or individual's reputation, or perhaps the prestige associated with a given product or service provider. As a result of marketing techniques including advertising, promotions, and public relations, image utility can be created. Image utility is much more subjective than the other utilities that marketing can help to create, because different things have different levels of prestige or value to different people. A dress designed for office wear may be seen as prestige fashion by a 45-year-old banking vice president, whereas her 18-year-old daughter may see the same dress as totally inappropriate or worthless.

The Evolution of Marketing

While marketing may seem integral to the success of every business today, it has not always been that way. Only when a society reaches the stage of having satisfied its production and sales needs does it pass on into a marketing-oriented phase. In fact, while many business firms have passed from a production-oriented to a sales-oriented to a marketing-oriented phase, and some are now increasingly moving into a social-oriented phase, some firms never manage to get out of one of the earlier phases of marketing. It is only when a company reaches maturity that it passes beyond the earlier stages.

When a society is in the early stages of industrialization, business forces focus on providing products that fill the basic needs of the members of that society. For the most part, individuals' needs are similar in nature, and their discretionary income is small. When the industrialized society begins to mature, many things begin to happen. Mass production results in a lower cost for goods being produced, and the income of workers producing those goods typically rises. The focus shifts from a desire to just secure goods to a desire for variety and volume. Money becomes available, and competing companies begin to form. Discretionary income continues to rise. New market segments develop. As a whole, society becomes more affluent. Individuals in society no longer want just those products that meet their basic needs. They begin to desire services that include everything from education to investment management. (See Figure 1-1.)

Production-Oriented Phase

From the latter part of the 1800s to around 1920, U.S. business firms were basically production-oriented. Engineering and production departments typically wielded the greatest influence over product decisions. During this phase, the following conditions prevailed:

- Business firms produced products that filled society's basic needs.
- Suppliers of products determined what the public demanded by perceiving the public's needs.
- The limits of manufacturing typically dictated product design and product variety decisions.
- Production and financial executives set the price for goods.
- The sales department's chief role was to sell whatever products the firm could produce.

During a production-oriented phase, management does not focus on marketing, but instead spends its time looking for ways to increase the number of products it can produce at the lowest possible costs. Companies may try to build a better black box than competitors, but little at-

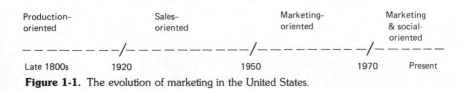

Figure 1-1. The evolution of marketing in the United States.

tention is addressed to marketing issues since the belief is that individuals will buy well-made, fairly priced products. Elaborate marketing efforts to induce customers to buy are deemed unnecessary.

During the production-oriented phase, sales departments are made up of sales managers who supervise a sales force that simply sells the products being made. Marketing departments as they are known today do not exist in the production-oriented phase of society.

Sales-Oriented Phase

From roughly 1920 through 1950, U.S. business firms passed through a sales-oriented phase. Discretionary income rose (except during the great depression in the early 1930s), and individuals began to insist on having available a variety of different products. Competition among firms increased and distribution channels were broadened to meet public demand.

The seeds of modern marketing in the United States were planted after World War I. *Surplus* and *overproduction* began to be economic factors in the country. Since 1920 (with lapses that occurred because of shortages during World War II), the supply of products available in the United States has outdistanced the demand for them by consumers. When supply outpaces demand, a *buyer's market* is created, in which buyers can pick and choose the best products to meet their needs among the many available on the market.

The sales department's role in business firms gains importance during the sales-oriented phase. Product design and pricing decisions, however, are still usually relegated to the manufacturing department. But since mass-production lines are turning out products faster than ever before, the success or demise of many companies rests on the shoulders of their sales forces. The sales force must be able to sell the products in a business's inventory to the consumer. Since building better black boxes does not assure the sale of those black boxes, the importance of sales and promotional efforts grows during the sales-oriented phase.

The prestige of the sales force in business firms grows during the sales-oriented phase. But during this phase, salespeople often begin to use high-pressure tactics to sell their products. The hard-sell tactics of a crafty salesperson, whether one who is going door-to-door or one who is selling in a store, ultimately result in a tarnished image for salespeople in general. Innocent selling and marketing professionals are often chastised for the actions of other companies guilty of employing hard-sell tactics in the market today.

During the sales-oriented phase, producing goods is no longer a difficult issue. The selling of products grows in importance. A slowdown in selling results in production cutbacks, which in turn can trigger recessionary periods in the economy.

Marketing-Oriented Phase

The marketing-oriented phase of business in the United States occurred roughly between 1950 and 1970. Discretionary income rose dramatically after World War II, as did the demand for more products and services. More and more individuals began to own cars, which allowed them to travel greater distances to and from work. Suburbs developed. The life cycle of products shortened dramatically. Market segmentation and complexity became the order of the day. As shopping patterns changed, businesses had to adapt their distribution channels to meet consumers' needs.

A marketing-oriented phase is marked by a noted shift from the hard-sell tactics common in the sales-oriented phase to the goal of satisfying customers' needs and wants and achieving a profitable volume of sales. Marketing, rather than selling, becomes the business firm's priority. Production people can no longer dictate to discriminating customers what they should buy, nor can sales forces sell products that fail to meet consumers' needs and wants.

To help align company product or service offerings and market demand, marketing departments are established in business firms. These departments, which are typically headed by marketing managers or vice presidents of marketing, receive increased importance. Sophisticated approaches to marketing issues are developed, and the marketing manager takes on responsibilities that in earlier phases of the business were the domain of other departments and department managers. Inventory control, warehousing, pricing decisions, product promotion, distribution channel management, input into product planning decisions, and other functions now come under the marketing manager's purview.

No longer does the manufacturing or engineering department rule the roost. Professionals in the marketing department are assigned the task of analyzing the needs and wants of the market and synthesizing this information for the research and development, engineering, and manufacturing departments of the firm.

As the role of marketing becomes more and more important, marketing departments begin to have significant input into business strategy decisions that address how firms will adapt to changing markets. As a result, marketing departments begin to play an important role in both short-term and long-range planning for the business firm.

Many business firms in the United States now are in the marketing-oriented phase.

Social-Oriented Phase

Largely as a result of social and economic conditions that arose in the United States in the 1970s and 1980s, businesses have begun to temper their marketing-oriented philosophies with a concern for social issues. As our society evolved, it became more and more apparent that a marketing-oriented philosophy could not always address issues related to society at large. A business firm that strove to meet the needs and wants of the individual in the marketplace, as well as the firm's need for profits, did not necessarily ensure that issues such as poverty, environmental concerns, and resource management would be sufficiently addressed.

As legislature begins to address these concerns and the United States makes stabs at adopting a national policy, businesses in turn respond by addressing not just the needs of the individual consumer but also the needs of society as a total entity.

While a marketing-oriented philosophy still lies at the core of most modern business policies in the United States, more and more marketing decisions are being weighed against the impact they will have on society. Sometimes this impact results from businesses' adherence to restrictive legislation. At other times it reflects a responsible management policy that is responsive to social concerns.

The social-oriented phase may be viewed as both a survival strategy addressing concerns about dwindling supplies of natural resources (e.g., energy, clean air) and a human-focused strategy to provide not just material goods but also products and services that help to ensure a better quality of life. The resulting shift from materialism to humanism requires that firms address issues that are brought to the surface by concerns for the environment, market disapproval, or legislative rulings. As society becomes more affluent, its demands shift from products to services.

Most firms today are still in the third—marketing-oriented—phase in the evolution of marketing. Few have deigned to progress into this fourth, most advanced phase.

The Marketing Concept

The third phase in the evolution of marketing—the marketing-oriented phase—is referred to as the "marketing concept." Many people place the birth of the concept back in the 1950s, when the chairman of General Electric Company declared that the company would be organized around the customer. Today, when a business firm adopts the marketing concept, it indicates not only that it has adopted a customer orientation but also that it has established a corporate structure that includes a marketing executive heading up a division in the firm that handles the marketing functions within the organization.

The marketing concept was not developed to give away the store to the customer. Rather, it assumes that a satisfied customer results in greater profits to a business. It is not the desire of businesses which have adopted the marketing concept to give customers what they want by selling goods or services below cost. In fact, one of the results of the adoption of the marketing concept has been a shift in emphasis from sales volume to sales profitability. The marketing manager realizes that profits ensure the survival of the company, and that therefore a combination of serving the customers' needs and maintaining healthy profitability is the course of businesses which have adopted the marketing concept.

At the heart of the marketing concept are these basic tenets:

- *Customer orientation* should be the aim of business operations and planning.
- *Profitable sales volume,* not just sales volume, should be a business's goal.
- *Organizational coordination* should exist between marketing activities and all other functions within a business.

The marketing concept clearly differs from the selling concept, which preceded it in the sales-oriented phase of the evolution of marketing. The marketing concept at its core holds that businesses exist, economically and socially, to fulfill consumers' wants and needs and, over the long term, to make a profit. On the other hand, the desire to sell a product that the business has made is at the heart of the selling concept. Rather than matching consumer demand, the business seeks to make consumer demand match the products it has produced. (See Figure 1-2.) With the introduction of the marketing concept in American businesses came not only the introduction of a consumer orientation but also the establishment of marketing divisions within businesses. These divisions were entrusted with the duty of helping all other parts of the company become more aware of consumer demands.

Because the marketing concept can affect all business decisions, including top management decisions, most businesses that adhere to the concept have a marketing executive high up in the corporate structure who oversees all the marketing functions of the business, as well as a marketing staff that carries out specific marketing functions within the firm.

Implementation of the marketing concept in medium-size and large firms depends on more than just paying attention to the trappings of the marketing concept. A business must not only establish marketing as an integral part of its organizational structure but also make sure that this emphasis is more than just a titular formality. To succeed under the

Selling concept	Marketing concept
1. Product is emphasized.	1. Customers' wants and needs are emphasized.
2. Company first makes the product, then figures out how to sell it.	2. Company first determines customers' wants and needs, and then figures out how to make and deliver a product to satisfy those wants and needs.
3. Management is sales-volume-oriented.	3. Management is profit-oriented.
4. Planning is short-term-oriented, in terms of today's products and markets.	4. Planning is long-term-oriented, in terms of new products, tomorrow's markets, and future growth.
5. Business stresses needs of seller.	5. Business stresses wants of buyers.

Figure 1-2. The selling concept versus the marketing concept. Adapted from William J. Stanton and Charles Futrell, *Fundamentals of Marketing*, 8th ed., McGraw-Hill, 1987, pp. 11–12.

marketing concept, businesses must be prepared to devote their full efforts to meeting consumer demand and maintaining profitability.

To achieve this goal, top management must buy into the marketing concept. Of course, marketing managers do not have to be the heads of companies. But chief executives, no matter what discipline they come out of, must be market-oriented in order for the marketing concept to succeed within a business.

Case Study

Putting the Customer First

You'd think that the company that would spring first to mind when you think of high technology leaders would be the one that has led the market in technological advances in the computer industry. Well, IBM may be a technological leader in the 1980s, but back in the 1950s and 1960s when it was busy building its market share in the business computer market, such was not the case. In fact, experts generally agree that IBM had not been a technology leader for some time. One securities analyst told *The Wall Street Journal*, "For a long time everybody felt that IBM was the best marketer of computers but that they didn't have the best technology."[2]

Thomas J. Peters and Robert H. Waterman, Jr., observed in *In*

---

[2] James A. White, "IBM Is Aggressively Claiming Widening Lead in Technology," *The Wall Street Journal*, July 30, 1982, p. 23.

Search of Excellence that IBM "is hardly far behind the times, but most observers will agree that it hasn't been a technology leader for decades."[3] Compared to many of its competitors, including such stalwarts as Honeywell, Control Data, and Univac, IBM came up short because of its obsession with the technological features of its products, in the view of many experts.

So how has IBM managed to maintain its lead in the industry? Namely, by focusing on another obsession: *providing customers with products and services that result in increased efficiency, productivity, and profitability.*

In the 1950s and 1960s, IBM focused more on supporting its client companies' efforts to install and operate business computers efficiently than it did on preparing its customers to put their own work into the computers and to make their own equipment changes when necessary. The result for IBM involved both a great cost and a great time commitment, as would any drive to get computers operating efficiently in a large business firm. But IBM was committed to serving its customer base, so it took the following steps:

• Trained computer programmers to go into its client companies.

• Provided systems engineers who went to the businesses to help them decide what types of work the computers should handle and how best to handle the work on the computer.

• Developed simplified computer programming languages that made the task of programming ultimately easier for the client company.

This commitment to helping customers improve their effectiveness seems to have paid off. When Prudential Insurance Company bought more than 700 computers from IBM in the 1950s, IBM reportedly spent more than $1 million of its own on equipment and personnel time to ensure that Prudential's computers worked efficiently for the client's needs. More than 30 years later, Prudential still uses primarily IBM computer equipment.

IBM's 65 percent market share of the mainframe computer market today attests to both its leadership role in technology and the high quality of its equipment. But while IBM has now taken a role as a technology leader, it continues to be customer-driven. It focuses on what its computers can do to fill its customers' needs and wants. Peters and Waterman argue that IBM's "dominance rests on its commitment to service."[4]

As quoted in the *Wall Street Journal* article mentioned above, a consulting firm president told the reporter, "IBM doesn't introduce technology for technology's sake. They have a business plan, and if the technology doesn't make sense with that, they put it on the shelf."[5]

---

[3] Warner Books, New York, 1982, p. 157.

[4] Ibid.

[5] White, op. cit.

Like IBM, many other marketing-oriented companies in the United States have seen fit to put their customer's interests ahead of improving their own technology for technology's sake alone. These firms which adhere to the marketing concept use their marketing research to find out:

- What products and services their customers want
- How the firm can best make or provide these products or services
- When their customers want the products or services
- How the company should promote its products or services

Adapted from James H. Myers, *Marketing*, McGraw-Hill, New York, 1986, pp. 18–20. Additional sources include: Thomas J. Peters and Robert H. Waterman, Jr., *In Search of Excellence*, Warner Books, New York, 1982, p. 157; and James A. White, "IBM Is Aggressively Claiming Widening Lead in Technology," *The Wall Street Journal*, July 30, 1982, p. 23.

CASE REVIEW

1. How has IBM fitted the marketing concept into its corporate philosophy?
2. What are some of the reasons for IBM's continuing dominance of the computer market?

Lesson One Questions

1. What is an exchange?
2. For the marketing process to occur, what three factors must exist?
3. What is a utility?
4. How many utilities does marketing create?
5. How can marketing impact form utility?
6. What are the four phases in the evolution of marketing?
7. Where are most companies in the United States on the marketing evolutionary scale today?
8. What is the marketing concept?
9. What are the three basic tenets at the heart of the marketing concept?
10. How does the marketing concept differ from the sales concept?

2
Strategic Marketing Planning

What Is Strategic Planning?

When a business attempts to formulate a plan that provides it with a direction and focus for the future, that plan is called a "strategic plan." The business evaluates its resources and capabilities and decides how it should plan for opportunities in the future.

The process of strategic planning involves matching a company's resources with the marketing opportunities that will exist for the company in the future. Strategic planning involves the entire company and consists of coming up with a long-term plan for the company's future.

Strategic planning has become more important as larger businesses have been faced with increased competition. Just as adherence to the *marketing concept* had previously forced a company to focus its attention on the customer, *strategic planning* also forces the company to focus its attention. But strategic planning goes beyond the marketing concept by insisting that the business focus its attention on all external factors that may affect the company. Strategic planning by no means replaces the marketing concept. Under strategic planning, the marketing concept simply becomes one of many factors that management seriously considers in its planning process.

Scope of Planning Activities

Long-range planning within a business usually involves top management professionals who consider issues that affect the future of the overall company—such as expansion of staffing and product lines. Long-range planning may involve creating a plan for 3 to 25 years or more.

Short-term planning can usually be performed by lower-level managers, who make decisions about such things as advertising campaigns or sales quotas for the salespeople. The process of strategic planning involves:

- Developing a mission statement for the business
- Setting objectives for the business to meet its goals
- Planning with and evaluating strategic business units (SBU)
- Choosing the strategies that allow the business to meet its goals

Strategic planning is affected not only by the external environment a business faces but also by its internal resources, including:

- Production facilities
- Cash-flow needs
- Research capabilities

Develop a Mission Statement for the Business

To be able to plan strategically, a business must first define its mission. Some firms are able to do this by examining their mission statements to see whether they have remained appropriate since they were first written. But the vast majority of businesses have failed to make an initial formal statement of their mission in business.

These businesses have failed to answer the following questions:

- Given our resources and expertise, what business are we now in?
- What business should we be in?

If these questions are not answered clearly, then the managers within a business may find themselves working with different senses of the true mission of the company. As a result, formulating strategic plans that work is impossible.

The mission statement for a company should be succinctly stated in writing. In addition to helping management focus on the same objectives, the mission statement can also become a useful public relations tool, carrying the message of the business to the public.

The mission statement of a company should not be so broad that it conveys nothing about what the company does. A mission statement such as "Where Quality Controls" is much too broad and is more of a slogan or tag line than a mission statement. On the flip side, the mission statement should not be too confining. To say that the mission of a company is "To make sheet-metal products" is too narrow.

Hudson Industries, a metal and electronic fabrication company located in Hudson, New Hampshire, uses the tag line "Where Quality Controls" on its corporate brochures, but its mission statement is much more defined. It reads in part:

> Hudson Industries is one of the largest and most technically advanced manufacturing support companies in New England. Our 280,000 square feet of manufacturing area, and 100,000 square feet for warehouse and distribution are ideally designed to manage all sheet metal and electronic product fabrication needs. As the industry leader, we have the sophisticated technologies to produce either individual product pieces or complete products. Quality engineering and an exceptional quality control program are the keys to Hudson Industries' success.

Today, a company's mission statement will often incorporate its marketing objectives. As a result, companies like Hudson Industries explore the needs of their customers that they can satisfy and incorporate these into their mission statements.

Set Objectives That Will Enable the Business to Meet Its Goals

After a business has written an appropriate mission statement, it should decide what objectives it needs to meet to reach its goals and fulfill its mission. These objectives can be used as guides for management at all levels of the business and can be a means against which to measure the company's performance.

Planning with Strategic Business Units

Because some businesses have such large and diversified product or service offerings, it often becomes impractical or impossible to strategically plan for the entire business. Instead, for the sake of efficient planning and management, many large companies divide their operations into major product or market divisions, known as *strategic business units (SBUs)*.

An SBU may be:

- A company division

- A group of products
- One major product offered by a company

To be considered an SBU, the division (or product group) should:

- Be in a business distinctly different from the rest of the company's divisions or products
- Have its own mission statement
- Have its own competitors
- Have its own management and financial responsibility
- Have its own strategic plan

A company should be careful not to have too few or too many SBUs. If there are too many, the company may find the burden of so many separate units—each with its own planning, management, and operating responsibilities—overwhelming. If there are too few, strategic planning remains ineffective and the original purpose of the SBU is defeated. The average number of SBUs within the largest U.S. industrial firms is 30.

Once a corporation has set up its SBUs, the business can be examined as a portfolio consisting of separate business units. One of the goals of strategic planning becomes to evaluate the performance of each of these SBUs. The evaluation is known as *business portfolio analysis*.

The end result of business portfolio analysis is to examine each SBU and to determine:

- Its effectiveness within the overall corporation
- The changes that can be made to improve its effectiveness
- The role it should play in the company

The company can look at each SBU and determine how to allocate funds to it. Which SBUs provide the biggest payback potential if money is invested? Which are no longer an effective part of the corporation and should be dropped? Which should be retained but not at the expense of a heavy investment from the overall corporation? The business portfolio analysis helps management to make these decisions.

What Is Strategic Marketing Planning?

Once a business has developed an overall strategic business plan, it should turn its attention to developing a *strategic marketing plan*. The strategic marketing plan details the marketing objectives of a business firm that fit in with the overall strategic objectives of a company.

The strategic marketing plan is important because, among other things, it typically can help the business focus on the most profitable market segments and market opportunities available. Because marketing professionals are so familiar with this territory, they can often pass on the information to others in the business.

The strategic marketing plan lays out:

- How a business will spend its marketing resources
- What target markets will be aimed at
- How the company's marketing mix will be developed to meet those target markets' needs

In large companies, it is often necessary to go beyond the development of one strategic marketing plan to come up with marketing plans for separate divisions, product groups, or even individual products. These individual marketing plans should mesh with the overall strategic plan of the company by aiming for the same basic objectives.

Every company will approach strategic marketing planning differently. A basic approach, however, is to:

- Identify marketing opportunities and objectives.
- Select target markets and evaluate market demand.
- Position the product or service.
- Set measurable quantitative goals.
- Develop the marketing mix.
- Prepare the annual marketing plan.

Depending on size, product offerings, and concerns of management, companies differ in how they approach the strategic marketing planning process. The order of events also varies from company to company.

The annual marketing plan is a 1-year plan developed to serve as a master marketing plan for a company, covering all the marketing activities the business will perform for the year. Some companies prepare marketing plans for even shorter periods than a year. The annual marketing plan:

- Lists the objectives of the marketing effort
- Pinpoints the target markets

- Details the strategies that will be used to attract those target markets including the marketing mix being used

- Identifies how much money is available to perform these marketing tasks

The Management Process

Companies must do more than write up a strategic plan to succeed. The role of management is to plan, implement, and evaluate the effectiveness of the strategic plan and the marketing system. Management evaluates how well the people within a business have done in attempting to reach their objectives for being in business.

When applied to the marketing function, management includes planning a marketing program, implementing that program, and then evaluating its effectiveness. Planning the program involves developing a marketing program that matches the needs of the company and addresses the needs of the target market. Implementing the plan requires hiring the people and carrying out the programs as designed. Management then evaluates the effectiveness of the marketing program and develops its future strategic marketing plans based on the evaluation: what worked and what didn't work in the past.

Basic Management Terms

An *objective* (or *goal*) is something that is sought as an end result, something that is the object of one's planned efforts. For any type of planning to be effective, objectives must be spelled out clearly. We must know what we are trying to achieve by carrying out a plan. When a strategic business plan or a strategic marketing plan is developed, the objectives of the plan should be stated in writing for two reasons: first, to make sure that there is no confusion among managers about what the real objectives are, and second, to make sure that the overall efforts of the business are set on the same goals.

Strategy is a term borrowed from the military that is used to describe the overall planning of large-scale operations. A strategy involves the plans through which an organization hopes to reach its objectives. Companies may have similar objectives but use a different strategy to reach their objectives—or may have different objectives but use similar strategies to reach them.

Tactics, on the other hand, are the specific means through which strategies are to be carried out. Tactics are more specific, task-oriented actions than are strategies. Tactics are also usually more relevant to short-term goals, while strategies encompass the big picture, or long-term goals.

A strategy might be to attract a teenage audience. The tactics used to attract this target market might include advertising in teen-related publications, advertising on teen-watched television shows, or sponsoring teen-attended events. When Sue Fitzgerald wanted to attract an audience for her mail-order T-shirt business, Boomerang, she chose to advertise on the rock-music video station MTV and in the classified advertising section of *Rolling Stone* magazine. Both were ideal vehicles for reaching the young market for which her products were designed.

If a company's strategy were to motivate a sales force, the tactics might be to run incentive-based contests, or to increase bonus pay as an incentive for sales.

Tactics must complement the strategy they are being used to carry out. Anything less would prove futile. For example, if the strategy were to attract a teenage market, it would make no sense to spend money to advertise in *Modern Maturity* magazine or other publications geared to adults.

Obviously, then, companies should find themselves with far more tactics than strategies. If the opposite is the case, then it is likely that tactics have been misidentified as strategies.

Strategies are usually developed by upper management in a business, while tactics are carried out by middle or lower-level management as a method of meeting the objectives of the desired strategy.

A *policy* is a plan adopted by a business that serves as a guide to indicate the decisions and actions that business will make. All levels of a company will be affected by a policy. Policies usually indicate that there is a standard procedure for dealing with specific situations such as retirement, educational requirements for job positions, and discount scheduling.

A company's objectives are what it has succinctly stated that it wishes to achieve within a given period of time. Strategies are the broad methods through which it hopes to achieve these objectives. Tactics are the specific methods it plans to use to fulfill the strategy. Policies are an overall blueprint or a set of rules and guidelines that management expects personnel to follow in the course of seeking to achieve objectives.

Take the example of a maker of packaged rice products. The mission of this business is to market high-quality rice products to a market of consumers and institutions (restaurants, hospitals, and so on). One of its major objectives is to increase its national market share for rice products by 2 percent within a 3-year period. The primary marketing strategy is to increase promotional efforts to half the metropolitan areas in which this company is not the leading manufacturer. Specific tactics might include a targeted radio advertising campaign and a local newspaper coupon-advertisement campaign. Company policy might prohibit cutting prices other than through use of store coupons, which would mean that the business would be limited in how far it could go to achieve a higher market share.

The Strategic Environment

Marketing can be affected by both internal and external factors. Strategy is often looked at as use of internal methods to respond to external factors. A company might have control over its internal methods but little control over the external environment in which it is marketing its goods and services.

The external environment might include such factors as:

- The economy
- Market size
- Market trends
- Competition
- Available distribution channels
- Available technology
- Government regulations

The internal environment might include such factors as:

- Company resources
- Company organization
- Marketing and management approach

Case Study
Coke Is It?

Atlanta, Georgia, is a Coca-Cola city. Driving into the city, you can see corporate headquarters looming prominently on the horizon. A few miles away, at Emory University, Coca-Cola's presence is felt by virtue of the hefty dollars it has poured into the university. For years, Coca-Cola's success in the marketplace was as constant as its presence in Atlanta.

That success was built on a basic strategy: sell one product to industrial users (bottlers, soda fountains, and restaurants) in the form of Coke syrup, and one product to the consumer market in the form of Coca-Cola, packaged in the famous 6.5-ounce green glass bottle. For more than 80 years, Coca-Cola's strategy resulted in its domination of the soft-drink market. Coca-Cola became America's drink.

In the 1970s, however, Coca-Cola had to reevaluate its strategic marketing planning. As a response to more competition in the soft-drink marketplace, a growing concern about caffeine and weight control, and the consumer's desire for variety in soft drinks, Coca-Cola decided to roll out several new soft drinks—Tab, Caffeine-free Coca Cola, Diet Coke, Caffeine-free Diet Coke, Cherry Coke, and Diet Cherry Coke. This strategy allowed Coca-Cola to address the needs of various market segments and to meet its competition head-on. Some of these products were rolled out with much fanfare and great market acceptance. Diet Coke, for example, hit the market in 1982 with an advertising blitz and regional unveilings that made it almost an instant hit. Diet Cherry Coke, released to the consumer market 4 or 5 years later, did not receive the same blitz, but it did meet with consumer approval, as witnessed by some users hoarding six-packs of the drink in their refrigerators when the product was first being tested in Manhattan and other cities.

At the same time, Coca-Cola began to experiment with packaging strategies more than ever before by offering Coke products in 12-ounce bottles and cans, and in 1-, 2-, and 3-liter bottles, as well as in other containers.

Coca-Cola's strategic plan was working, from both a corporate and a marketing viewpoint. But then, just as the world was beginning to truly believe that "Coke Is It," as the advertising slogan proclaimed, something curious happened. After pouring more than $4 million and 4.5 years into research and development, Coca-Cola decided to make a strategic move, announced in April 1985: it was going to introduce a new Coke and take the old Coke formula off the market.

Its studies had convinced it that this was the correct strategic marketing move to make. The strategic planning change came 1 year shy of Coca-Cola's hundredth anniversary. Consumers apparently wanted a sweeter drink than the old Coke, and the new Coke was designed to brilliantly tap into that market and meet its needs.

But after many years of success in introducing and marketing new products, Coca-Cola's strategic planning had gone awry. Consumers began to complain. Some boycotted the new Coke. Others formed groups demanding that the old Coke be brought back to the market.

For months Coca-Cola held firm in spite of the protests. After all, its strategic marketing plan called for the elimination of the old Coke since consumer demand had been determined to be for its new Coke product. Finally, however, Coca-Cola management acquiesced in July 1985, bringing back the old Coke and calling it Coca-Cola Classic. The old Coke sold along with the new Coke and other Coca-Cola products. The strategic plan may have determined that consumers wanted a different soft drink, but when the reality hit, consumers let Coca-Cola know how they really felt.

What management hadn't calculated in its strategic planning was the mystique and loyalty that accompanied the Coca-Cola drink.

Adapted from William J. Stanton and Charles Futrell, *Fundamentals of Marketing*, 8th ed., McGraw-Hill, New York, 1987, p. 39. Additional source: Thomas Oliver, *The Real Coke, The Real Story*, Random House, New York, 1986.

CASE REVIEW

1. Why did Coca-Cola change a strategic marketing planning that had worked for more that 80 years?
2. Why did Coca-Cola's plan to eliminate the old Coke fall flat on its face? What did Coca-Cola fail to take into account in its strategic marketing planning?

Lesson Two Questions

1. What is a strategic plan?
2. How does strategic planning go beyond the marketing concept?
3. What four steps are involved in strategic planning?
4. What is a mission statement?
5. What are strategic business units (SBUs)? Why were they developed?
6. What is business portfolio analysis? What is its end result?
7. What is a strategic marketing plan?
8. What should an annual marketing plan include?
9. What is the difference between strategy and tactics?
10. What is a policy?

3

Marketing Research and Marketing Information Systems

The Development of Marketing Research

The era of modern marketing research in the United States was ushered in by the appointment in 1911 of Charles Coolidge Parlin, a onetime Wisconsin high school principal, to manage the Curtis Publishing Company's newly formed commercial research division. Other corporations began sensing that marketing research could help them also to understand how their products or services could best satisfy the marketplace.

United States Rubber Company hired Dr. Paul H. Nystrom in 1915 to manage its marketing research. And in 1917, Swift and Company hired Dr. L. D. H. Wild of Yale University as its economist. Along with Dr. C. S. Duncan, who published the first book on marketing research in 1919, Parlin, Nystrom, and Wild were pioneers in marketing research, a field that was to become increasingly important to businesses.

It would be years before marketing research would develop the sophisticated methods it commonly employs today. In fact, most early marketing research consisted of little more than descriptive studies of the marketplace. Prior to World War II, scientific sampling methods for marketing research had not been developed. And computers and databases certainly were not as readily available as they are today. Behavioral scientists had not yet come into the picture to develop sophisticated data collection techniques.

With major corporations making commitments to marketing research departments, the area was certainly gaining importance. But in the 1920s and 1930s, marketing research activity was still relegated to a minority role in a company's activities. During this period in the United States, the total amount spent by businesses on marketing research added up to only several million dollars.

As the marketing concept, which placed the customer at the heart of a company's marketing efforts, gained more and more acceptance, so too did the concept of marketing research. In the late 1940s, marketing research began to be seen more and more as a critical tool for use in business operations. By the 1980s, it has been estimated, more than $1 billion was being spent on marketing research activities in the United States.

Overall, the business dollars budgeted for marketing research still account for less than 1 percent of sales and are minute compared with the amount spent on research and development of new technologies and products. In fact, very few companies with sales of less than $10 million have a full-time marketing research department. It is unusual, however, for companies with sales greater than $500 million not to have a marketing research department.

The amount of money spent on marketing research varies from industry to industry. Logically, consumer goods manufacturers spend more on marketing research than do industrial goods manufacturers. And advertisers whose job it is to reach customers spend more on marketing research than do consumer goods manufacturers.

What Is Marketing Research?

Marketing research is the gathering, recording, and analyzing of data that relates to a specific problem in marketing products or services. While this definition implies a systematic approach to marketing, marketing research is often performed as a *reaction* to a problem that occurs. Marketing research efforts, therefore, often are undertaken for specific projects that have set beginning and ending points. In contrast, *marketing information systems*, discussed later in this chapter, provide continuous marketing information that enables marketing professionals to plan for future events.

Types of Marketing Research Applications

Market and Economic Analysis

Market analysis involves analyzing market-segment factors to determine the *market potential* of a given product or service. The marketing researcher gathers data and analyzes the factors that affect possible sales in a given market segment. The *economic analysis* is also used by marketing research departments to determine:

- How actively a company should market in a given market segment
- How much money it should invest in marketing to that segment
- How much it may have to produce to fulfill the needs of the market segment

Economic analysis often involves *economic forecasting*, which analyzes and attempts to forecast developing market trends and demands.

Product Research

Marketing research departments conduct *product research* for a variety of reasons, including:

- Measuring potential acceptance of new products
- Finding improvements or additions for existing products
- Making changes or improvements in product packaging
- Determining acceptability of a product over a competitor's product

When a new product is being developed, marketing research departments will often use *product concept testing* to see how customers might react to the new product. Typically, before a business invests in the development of a prototype for a new or improved product, it will have its marketing researchers verbally describe or visually depict the prospective product to a group of potential customers in the target market.

Once a product has been accepted during the concept-testing stage, the business may move on to develop a prototype of the product. The marketing research department may then conduct *product use tests*, in which potential customers—be they industrial users or consumers—are given the new or modified product to try. Consumers may be given a new type of hot breakfast cereal to try at home so that the marketing researcher can test the product use among families; industries may be given a new type of telephone system to test in their offices so that the marketing researcher can receive management's evaluation of the system and see how the new product works in a field test site.

After product concept and product use tests are completed, businesses may decide to use *market tests* before they go full-throttle into the marketplace with their products. These market tests allow the business to see how the product is accepted in various market segments before it is rolled out to the mass market, and before the business invests in a full-blown release of the product. While test marketing is viable for producers of products that do not involve millions of dollars in production costs for production facilities, it may be cost-prohibitive for businesses producing large, expensive goods. Soap detergent is easily test-marketed for a relatively inexpensive price tag; the cost of test marketing jet airplanes, on the other hand, is not cheap.

Pricing Research

Marketing research can be used to evaluate the acceptability of product or service prices in the marketplace. While businesses must price their products to make enough money to cover production and operating costs, often the formula they use for achieving a given profit margin causes them to price their products or services above or below acceptable market levels.

Pricing research activities conducted by marketing researchers to determine buyers' perception of price and quality factors in a given product can be used to determine acceptable price levels that will allow businesses to achieve desired profits and gain market share. Marketing research can help to determine acceptable price levels. Because of the competitive marketplace, however, businesses frequently do not have the time to conduct an elaborate pricing research study; therefore, they often enter the marketplace without conducting one.

Advertising Research

Advertising can be a costly endeavor for businesses. To determine the potential effect their advertising might have on a target audience, businesses often conduct research into the content, the media, and the effectiveness of advertisements before they invest heavily in the advertising campaign.

Content research measures how the desired content comes across to an audience sample (a limited number of people). If the advertisement is pretested, a sample audience may be asked questions after being shown a television commercial or after viewing a layout of a print advertisement. If the advertisements are tested after they have appeared in various media, customers may be asked what they remember about the particular advertisements and how they reacted to them. By pretesting and posttesting customers, marketing researchers can determine whether the desired message is getting across in a positive manner.

Media research involves finding the best mix of media with which to hit a target audience. Marketing researchers may evaluate market studies of various media outlets (e.g., A. C. Nielsen for electronic media, or W. R. Simmons and Company for print media). By researching the media, marketing researchers can determine how best to allocate marketing dollars to hit the desired market.

To perform *advertising effectiveness research*, businesses must state what marketing objectives they hope to accomplish with their advertising efforts before they roll out the advertising campaign. Marketing research must be done prior to the advertising campaign so as to have something to measure the results of the advertising against. If a business is trying to increase customer awareness of one of its more overlooked products, then it must determine, before the advertising campaign begins, how well-known that product actually is so that the business will be able to measure how well advertising increases awareness.

Sales Research

When a marketing research department conducts a *sales analysis*, it studies customer records and other available data to determine where marketing opportunities lie among potential target markets. *Selling research*, on the other hand, analyzes the approach used by the person selling the product or service to determine whether the sales presentation is effectively piquing the interest of customers and allowing them to understand the product. The selling research can determine:

- The kinds of *collateral materials* (e.g., brochures, charts, lists) that work best to sell the product

- The percentage of sales that are closed in a sales call

- Other aspects of the selling process that show what methods have been most effective with the target market

What Are Marketing Information Systems?

A *marketing information system* is a system providing a continuous flow of marketing information that management can use to make marketing decisions. Such a system is called a "decision support system" by many businesses.

The marketing information system is made up of data that can be generated, stored, and retrieved for use in the marketing decision-making process. Unlike marketing research, which may address marketing problems on a project-by-project basis as a problem occurs, a marketing information system provides a means through which management of a business can plan for the future based on collected data. It can help marketing professionals to prevent foreseeable problems, as well as solve them when they do occur.

The information collected in the marketing information system comes both from within a business and from outside data sources. Since extensive database management is required, marketing information systems are marked by their use of computer technology and personnel who are capable of dealing with this technology. Because of the advances in technology and the drop in the prices of computer hardware and software, most businesses today find marketing information systems to be not only useful tools, but also affordable ones.

A well-designed marketing information system lets a business keep track of all potential marketing-related information that can possibly be used in the marketing decision-making process. Using the marketing information system, business management and marketing professionals can assess the performance of products, salespeople, and marketing efforts in the marketplace.

The positive impact of marketing information systems may be more blatantly felt in larger businesses where the sheer volume of information is massive. But it has equal value for smaller companies because it enables a more efficient analysis of marketing information.

An effective marketing information system allows the marketing professional not only to store data but also to determine the appropriate data to store, to find out how to gather the data, to learn how to use the appropriate quantitative analysis to process the data, and to determine what systems are necessary to store the data for future use.

The Relationship between Marketing Research and Marketing Information Systems

Opinions on the relationship between marketing research and marketing information systems differ. Some professionals see marketing information systems simply as a computer-oriented expansion of traditional marketing research methods. Others suggest that the two areas are distinct in nature, except in that both focus on information used in making marketing decisions.

Typically, if a business has no formal marketing information system, its marketing research department will have to play a larger role in gathering, sorting, and analyzing marketing information. In businesses that do have a marketing information system, marketing research is often viewed as one component of this system.

Where Does Marketing Information System Data Come From?

The sources of data for a marketing information system are broad. They may include:

- Accounting records within the company that detail sales volumes, shipping records, profit margins, product costs, overhead costs, levels of inventory, and orders from new customers
- Sales call reports filled out after salespeople have made their calls on potential and active customers
- Available published data, including the competition's prices, sales, and profits; the characteristics and size of a target market; the competition's marketing efforts; and changes in the overall marketplace
- Trade association reports
- Government-published data
- Data purchased from marketing research companies

After all this data is collected, it is then organized in a logical format and placed into a database stored in the business's computer system.

Types of Marketing Information Systems

There are three basic types of marketing information systems, as follows:

- Data banks
- Statistical banks
- Model banks

All three can help marketing professionals make decisions about the marketing efforts of their businesses.

The *data bank* is an extensive computerized collection of raw data. Marketing professionals can call up (request) desired pieces of information from this data bank. The computerized data bank will typically instruct users on how to retrieve, store, and collect data to be included in the data bank itself.

The *statistical bank* lets marketing professionals work out "what-if" scenarios using the information available in the marketing information system. Based on past information stored in the marketing information system, they can evaluate what effects various marketing efforts will have on their sales.

The *model bank* lets the marketing professional determine what the best solutions to marketing problems might be, based on information stored in the marketing information system. Models can help the marketing professional make basic marketing decisions, including:

- Inventory control methods
- Media purchase decisions
- More elaborate analysis of why a particular segment of customers has switched brands or changed its attitude about a given product or service

Model banks can be purchased from outside vendors or prepared by in-house operations researchers.

Design of a Marketing Information System

The five basic parts of any marketing information system are:

1. *Hardware—the physical mechanism that holds the marketing information system's data.*   In most businesses this is a computer, but hardware can include something as simple as a filing cabinet that holds marketing information, if a company has no electronic data system set up. The hardware also includes:
   - Modems
   - Printers
   - Monitors
   - Anything else that lets the user retrieve the data stored in the marketing information system

2. *Software—the operating programs that let the user instruct the computer to retrieve desired information.*   Software is also used to instruct the computer to do calculations, and to generate statistical analyses, possibly including regression or correlation analyses.

3. *Information—the data stored in the marketing information system that can be used to make marketing decisions.*

4. *Procedures—the methods a user can use to gather, retrieve, and analyze data in the marketing information system.*

5. *Personnel—the people whose function it is to keep the marketing information system up-to-date and functioning.* Among the job titles included might be:

- Programmers
- Systems analysts
- Computer operators
- Researchers
- Statisticians
- Managers who oversee the operation

Marketing Information Systems Operations

The Quality of Data. The expression "garbage in, garbage out" certainly holds true with marketing information systems. The primary factor determining the effectiveness of a marketing information system is the data which is inputted into the system. Since not every piece of marketing data is relevant for marketing decision making, all of it should be screened for appropriateness before being inputted into the system.

The data that *is* inputted should contain an abstract that says what that particular piece of data includes, so that users will not have to read through an entire file of information if much of it is irrelevant for their needs. *Abstracts* are terse descriptions of the information that include highlights of the data, the source of the data, the group from which it was derived, when it was collected, and how to access it in the computer system.

Where the abstract allows the user to quickly grasp the content of a piece of information, the *index* in the marketing information system enables the user to access the data he or she is looking for. The information in the marketing information system is identified in the index by key words or phrases, which the user can call up to access information.

Lesson Three Questions

1. What is marketing research?
2. What is marketing analysis used for?
3. What is an economic analysis in marketing research?
4. What are product concept tests? Product use tests?
5. What does content research measure in advertising?

(Continued)

6. What can a marketing researcher achieve by pretesting and postesting an audience exposed to a particular advertisement?

7. What is the difference between sales analysis and selling research?

8. What is a marketing information system?

9. What are the three basic types of marketing information systems? Describe them.

10. What are the five basic parts of any marketing information system?

The Marketing Research Process

The marketing research process can be broken down into five major steps:

1. Define the marketing objective.

2. Design the marketing research study.

3. Collect the necessary data.

4. Analyze and interpret the collected data.

5. Present the findings of the marketing research study to company management.

Defining the Marketing Objective

Marketing researchers should always clearly define the goal of their marketing research project: what they hope to accomplish or learn from the research. The objective is often to solve a problem, but another frequent objective is to identify potential marketing opportunities for the business. Businesses often design a marketing research project around these two objectives: solving problems and identifying opportunities.

The objective of the marketing research should be stated in broad terms so that the researcher will not study too narrow a field of information, thereby eliminating potential solutions or opportunities. As the marketing research proceeds, the researcher can begin to narrow the focus of the research project.

Designing the Marketing Research Study

The plan for carrying out the marketing research study is called the *marketing research design*. It details how the marketing research will be approached: what types of data are going to be collected, where the data will be collected from, and how the data will be collected.

Before a business invests in a marketing research project, however, it may want to conduct an informal investigation to determine whether or not an elaborate project would be worthwhile. Before designing an elaborate plan, marketing researchers often conduct a *situation analysis* and an *informal investigation* to better focus the problem solution or opportunity to be identified by a marketing research project.

Situation Analysis. In a situation analysis, marketing researchers gather information about a business entity from library materials and from interviews with business officials. The purpose is to get a sense of the situation in which the problem exists by analyzing the business, the market, the competition, and the type of business being done.

The situation analysis can help the marketing researcher to better focus the objective of the marketing research and perhaps to arrive at hypotheses that the business wants to test. These hypotheses should be proved or disproved in the process of the marketing research project.

Informal Investigation. In situation analysis, researchers get information from within the company. In the informal investigation, they go a step further by getting information from outside the company. The researcher talks to competitors, customers, advertising professionals, distributors, vendors, and anyone else outside the company who can help to shed light on the objective of the marketing research project.

By conducting an informal investigation, researchers can determine whether a formal marketing research project is warranted. Once the informal investigation has been completed, and if the researcher determines that a further study is necessary, the marketing research project is designed.

Designing the Marketing Research Project

One of the first things a marketing researcher must do in designing a marketing research project is to determine what information is needed and what the sources of information should be. In this step, researchers decide whether to use primary or secondary data, or both, in the marketing research project.

Primary data is data gathered specifically for the project at hand. *Secondary data* is data that already exists because it was collected for a different purpose. When marketing researchers observe whether or not people read unit pricing labels on supermarket shelves, they are collecting primary data. When they rely on information published by the Bureau of Labor Statistics of the U.S. Department of Commerce, they are using secondary data. It is most often much cheaper and quicker to use secondary data, if available, for a given project. Researchers should exhaust the sources of secondary data available to them before they begin the time-consuming process of collecting primary data.

Sources of secondary data are numerous and include:

- Documents within the business's library
- Government publications
- Public or college libraries
- Trade associations
- Marketing research firms
- Advertising agencies and media
- Professional associations

Since secondary data has not been collected specifically to meet the marketing research project's objective, researchers must take care to assure that the data is as accurate as possible, with no inherent biases or consistent errors.

Once researchers collect the needed information from available secondary sources, they should turn their attention to primary sources. Three methods of gathering primary data are frequently used in marketing research, as follows:

- Survey
- Observation
- Experimentation

Survey. Using the *survey method,* a researcher gathers data by interviewing a *sample* of people selected from a larger target market group.

One of the advantages of the survey method of collecting primary data is that the researcher has access to the original source of information. There are drawbacks, however. Surveys may be expensive and time-consuming, may contain errors or biases in the survey questionnaire, and may be plagued with respondents who refuse or are unable to answer questions truthfully.

The three major options available for conducting surveys are personal interviews, telephone interviews, and mail interviews. Variations of these three are also discussed below.

Personal Interviews. Of the three options available for conducting surveys, *personal interviews* are obviously the most flexible, because the researcher or interviewer can adapt questions to fit the specific situations that develop. If respondents do not answer questions appropriately, the researcher can probe for more specific answers. The researcher can also observe the respondent's characteristics, a feat that would be impossible using mail or telephone survey methods. One of the drawbacks of the personal interview, however, is that the interviewer may allow his or her own biases to influence the interview process.

While personal interviews typically provide the best quality and volume of data, they are often cost-prohibitive and time-consuming. As a result of the rising costs and other problems related to house-to-house personal interviews, researchers have begun to employ a method called the *shopping-mall intercept method,* in which researchers interview consumers who are shopping or walking through shopping malls. The researchers conduct the interviews in offices or cubicles in the mall known as "central-location testing facilities." This method saves both time and money, as compared with the personal interview process.

The *focus group* has also been a popular alternative to the personal interview. In the focus group, typically 4 to 10 people meet with the researcher or interviewer, who asks broad questions designed to stimulate conversation among the consumers about a given product—how and for what purpose they use the product, what they like and dislike about the product, how they would react to changes or to introduction of new products, and what they would like the product to do that it doesn't already do. Follow-up questions are then asked to further analyze consumers' views.

Focus group participants may be all members of the same organization or may be recruited randomly. Focus groups work on the premise that, by brainstorming, consumers force one another to think about and discuss aspects of the product which they might not expound upon in a one-on-one interview. Researchers, by listening to a somewhat freeflowing discussion, can determine what is foremost in customers' minds about the product or company.

Telephone Interviews. *Telephone interviews* are typically less time-consuming than personal interviews and less costly than personal or mail interviews. Telephone interviewers can conduct the survey from a central location, where a bank of telephones has been installed, by calling the targeted market sample to ask the desired questions.

Modern technology has advanced telephone interviewing to the point that random-dialing machines, recorded interview messages, and automatic response storage is now possible. *Wide-Area Telephone Service (WATS)* has become widely available, cutting down on the cost of telephone interviews. An advantage of telephone interviews is that they can be timely measures of what the consumer is doing in the home at the time of the call—what food is in the cupboard, what show is on the television or radio. But a drawback is that they must be short and (with the exception of the random-dialing approach) can only be directed at those consumers who have telephones and whose telephone numbers are listed. In terms of quality of responses, the telephone interview does not compare with the personal interview, but it surpasses the mail interview.

Mail Interviews. To conduct a *mail interview,* a researcher sends a questionnaire to a customer. The customer fills it out and sends it back to the researcher. The process is not affected by the interviewer's biases since he or she never talks directly with the customer. The method is less costly than personal interviews. Often a respondent will give a more truthful answer to an anonymous questionnaire than he or she might to a researcher doing the interviewing in person.

One of the biggest problems of doing mail interviews is finding a good mailing list to use—a list that hits the market sample the researcher wants to have fill out the questionnaire. The percentage of returns can also be a problem: it may be very low and thus not give the researcher enough of a sample to make the research an accurate reflection of the target market. If not enough customers respond to the questionnaire, it will suffer from a *nonresponse bias.* Often, researchers face the problem of getting customers to respond to the questionnaires. They have tried to increase response rates through a variety of methods, such as sending follow-up questionnaires, sending questionnaires via first-class mail, and including some kind of incentive for responding. Sometimes the incentive is monetary; other times it takes other forms. When U.S. Sprint surveyed its business users, for example, it offered the incentive of a travel alarm clock to those who completed and filled out its questionnaire.

Observation. When researchers use the *observation method* to collect data, they observe the respondent doing something. No interviewing is involved until perhaps after the action has been completed and the researcher wants to follow up. The researcher may, for example, observe the father of a toddler buying juice in box containers rather than small cans and then ask the consumer why he made that choice of packaging.

Researchers may use a personal or a mechanical observation method. The personal observation might take the form of posing as a customer to see how a given product is displayed or moved in a store. The mechanical approach might involve using a turnstile to count the number of customers who enter a building through a particular entrance.

Supermarkets have begun to use electronic scanning devices, which not only help improve inventory control, but also allow researchers to make observations about buying patterns and choice selections. The observation method also makes use of interactive computer services (how many key hits a given feature gets), two-way mirrors, and cable television. In recent years, television has sought to increase interaction by allowing viewers to telephone in requests on a special number. This technique was highly successful when NBC allowed viewers to vote on their favorite *Hill Street Blues* episodes to determine which ones would be shown in the show's final season on the air.

A big advantage of the observation method is that the researcher can observe how the respondent actually acts in a specific setting, rather than relying on the respondent's recollection of how he or she acted. The observation method removes biases that may exist in the survey method.

One drawback of the observation method is that it cannot assess the customer's motive for acting in a particular manner. Another is that it gives researchers no way of knowing the person's socioeconomic status or family situation.

Experimental Method.   Of the three methods of collecting data, the *experimental method* is considered the strongest. When researchers use the experimental method to gather data, they set up a controlled experiment in which they try to simulate real market situations. By analyzing the results of this smaller-scale experiment among a market sample, researchers can use the results to develop a market program to hit the larger target market. One of the more positive aspects of the experimental method is that it is the only one of the three methods of collecting data that makes use of actual market situations.

To use the experimental method, a business may produce a few product samples that will be given to employees or customers to try.

When a business does decide to use the experimental method to do test marketing, it must:

- Establish a control market, in which all market factors are kept constant.

- Establish at least one test market in which one of those market factors becomes a variable.

The variable is typically some aspect of the product or service that the business wants to test. The variable could involve any one of the four aspects of the marketing mix: product, price, promotion, and distribution. By keeping the product constant in the control market and changing one of the variables in the test market, a business can find out whether the change has any influence on the customer's buying pattern.

One of the big problems with test marketing is finding two markets that match in every aspect except for the one variable being tested. Controlling the variables is also often difficult. Because of the planning and time that go into executing the experimental method, it can become cost-prohibitive for some businesses.

More and more businesses are opting to use less expensive alternatives to test marketing, such as a controlled environment in which a simulated market test is performed using fewer respondents. Businesses may perform some sort of market testing in a laboratory setting or use computerized information available from electronic scanners in supermarkets that indicate customer buying patterns. (See Figure 3-1.)

When the survey or observation method is used, the researcher must prepare standard forms on which the necessary data can be recorded. Most problems that arise in personal, telephone, or mail surveys result from poorly prepared questionnaires. The marketing researcher must

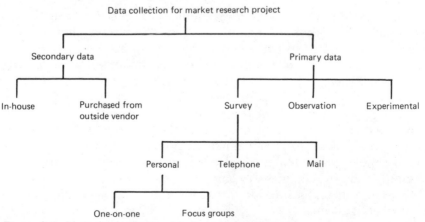

Figure 3-1. Methods of collecting data for marketing research.

prepare the questionnaire or data collection form so that the amount of bias, confusion, or annoyance caused to the respondent is kept to the barest minimum.

To ensure that a questionnaire does not suffer from any of these flaws, it should be pretested on a small group of people who share the characteristics of the market segment which is to be questioned. This process should alert marketing researchers to any potential problems with the questionnaire.

Planning the Sample. Not everyone in the target market is surveyed. Researchers must determine what *market sample* they wish to use. The sample must be representative of the overall behavior patterns of the entire target market.

Sampling involves randomly selecting a sample—a smaller number of items from a *universe*—from a larger number of items, with the premise that the characteristics of the sample will be proportionately the same as the characteristics of the universe. It is critical to the marketing research process that the sample be accurately chosen, in order for the results to have any validity.

To survey a market sampling, marketing researchers must define:

- The number of respondents they want to include in their ultimate sample

- The part of the overall population they want to sample

- The frame of reference they want to use as source material to get the names they want to use (mailing lists, phones books, census records, etc.)

- The method of sampling they want to use—random or nonrandom

The sample must be large enough to be representative of the entire universe. It must proportionately include the same types of units as found in the universe.

There are many different types of sampling techniques that marketing researchers can use. Among the most common are:

- *Simple random samples.* Each unit in the sample is chosen from the overall universe.

- *Area samples.* A variation of simple random sampling that is often used when getting a full list of the universe is cost-prohibitive.

- *Quota samples.* Unlike random sampling, in quota samples not every unit in the overall universe has the same chance of being selected for the sample. Marketing researchers determine which characteristics occur in the universe. They then choose a sampling that exhibits those same characteristics in proportion to how much they occur in the larger universe.

Simple random samples and area samples are examples of *probability samples* (random samples). In a random sample, the units are selected so that each unit in the overall universe has the same probability of being chosen for the sample. Quota samples are an example of a *nonprobability sample* (nonrandom samples). They are also examples of *stratified samples* (sometimes called "layered samples"). The randomness disappears because the sample is forced to be proportionate in some characteristic.

The advantage of random sampling is that its results can be mathematically measured. Quota sampling depends on the judgment of the researchers designing and choosing the quota sample. The results of a quota sampling cannot be mathematically measured for exactness.

In addition to simple random samples, area samples, and quota samples, other types of sampling methods include, but are by no means limited to:

- *Systematic.* This method involves choosing every *n*th name or unit from a given universe.

- *Stratified.* As with the quota sample, this method involves dividing the total universe of names into groups sharing similar characteristics and then randomly drawing names from each group.

- *Cluster.* This method involves selecting a natural grouping of people to sample, and either interviewing everyone in that cluster or randomly selecting members of the cluster to interview.

Collecting the Necessary Data

While the collection of the necessary data chiefly involves carrying out the marketing research process that has been carefully designed, it is easier said than done. The collection of primary data by survey, observation, or experimentation requires that the data gatherers be trained well enough to get the desired information without influencing the respondents or biasing their responses. Because data gatherers are often part-time employees and because their work is being done in the field at a variety of locations, it is often impossible to consistently monitor their performance. It is critical, however, that the marketing management use the resources necessary to ensure that data collection is done professionally and accurately. Otherwise the results of a potentially time-consuming, costly marketing research project will be worthless.

**Analyzing and Interpreting the Data,
and Presenting the Findings of the
Marketing Research Project to
Management in a Written Report**

As the marketing research project nears completion, the researcher analyzes and interprets the data collected and presents a report of the findings to management. While an oral report can be given to management, it should be followed up by a more detailed marketing research report. There is no standard format for such a report, but for it to be useful to management it should include a summary at the beginning of each section, highlighting the findings and how they relate to the original objective and hypotheses of the marketing research project. Sections of the report might include:

- *A summary of the overall marketing research project.*
- *A restatement of the objective of the marketing research project.*
- *The design that was ultimately used for the marketing research project.*
- *What data was collected and the methods that were used to collect it.*
- *What was ultimately discovered as a result of the marketing research project.* Both the findings and supplementary data from the marketing research project should be included in the report.
- *What actions management might take based on the findings of the marketing research project.*
- *What the project was unable to accomplish.*
- *Appendices containing a detailed explanation of the methodology and types of analyses used, and tables including data findings.*

Marketing researchers may want to follow up to see whether their recommendations were acted upon.

Marketing Forecasts

As part of its marketing research function, a company must forecast the demand for a product or service. Forecasting market demand for a product involves estimating both how many sales a company expects in the overall marketplace and how many sales it expects within each segment of that marketplace.

The company may express its product or service in terms of a *market factor* which relates to an item in the marketplace that may be measured quantitatively and in relation to the demand for the product. When this market factor is expressed as a percentage of the marketplace, it is referred to as a *market index*.

Forecasting then involves estimating two factors:

- *Market potential.* The total market within the industry for the product or service.

- *Sales potential (or market share).* The specific company's estimate of how much of that market it can capture.

Industry experts refer to the "market potential" for television sets and the "sales potential" for a particular company's television sets.

Sales Forecasts

To successfully set budgets and plan for operations, a company should prepare a sales forecast for at least 1 year ahead, so that it will have an idea of how it expects its products or services to sell and how well actual sales measure up to expectations. Many companies review sales forecasts at regular intervals (1- or 3-month periods) to see how closely actual performance matches the original forecasts. The sales forecast figures are generally also reviewed as a regular part of yearly financial reporting.

In some industries, particularly those with heavy barrages of seasonal sales activity, such as fashion and toys, sales forecasts for less than 1 year may be used.

Once a company arrives at its sales forecast, that forecast becomes the underlying control in all aspects of operations as well as budgeting, financial planning, and other company needs that are dictated by sales volume. Sales forecasts also indicate how many employees and how much material will be needed to produce the appropriate amount of product.

Sales forecasts are done to arrive at approximate sales figures for a specific period of time, using a particular marketing plan designed by a company. While many companies prepare a sales forecast with little market background, it is generally more accurate if the company takes into account the market potential and sales potential for a product or service.

Methods of Forecasting Demand

The top-down method and the buildup method are two basic approaches companies use to forecast sales.

The *top-down method* (sometimes called the "breakdown method") involves (1) forecasting overall economic trends to determine the industry's market potential for a product and (2) measuring the market share the firm is already getting. The company then uses these figures to arrive at a sales forecast for the product.

Using the *buildup method,* a company estimates the future demand for a product within particular segments of the overall marketplace. To get an overall sales forecast, it then adds together all these individual segment forecasts.

Accurately predicting future market demand for a product is no easy task. Marketing professionals use a variety of techniques to predict the future. Among the more widely used are:

- Market-factor analysis
- Customer-intention surveys
- Test marketing
- Past sales analysis
- Trend analysis
- Sales-force composite

A brief description of each of these methods follows.

Market-Factor Analysis.   The premise underlying *market-factor analysis* is that if we can ascertain the behavior of specific market factors, we will be able to predict the future demand for a product or service—that there is a relationship between some market factors and future demand. Once we determine what these market factors are, we can determine future sales by monitoring these factors.

The difficulty is determining which factors affect product demand. The fewer the number of factors we determine as having an effect on future sales, the better. An unwieldy number of factors increases the likelihood of false conclusions.

Direct derivation and *correlation analysis* are used to predict future sales based on related market factors.

Direct Derivation.   Direct derivation is a simple method of market-factor analysis that can be used to predict future market demand based on specific market factors. Consider the case of the house-painting firm that wants to know the market potential for house-painting jobs in 1991. The principal market factor is the number of houses in existence in 1991. Next the professional would estimate how many houses are apt to be due for a paint job in 1991. If the assumption is made that all houses require new paint jobs every 5 years, then all houses that become 5 years old during 1991 are part of the potential market for paint jobs. The housepainter can determine how many houses will be 5 years old in

1991 by checking local registries to see how many building permits were issued in 1986. The housepainter might also decide to see how many houses became 10, 15, or 20 years old (multiples of 5) in 1991 since they too might likely belong to the potential market. The number of houses reaching these ages might give a rough idea of the potential market for housepainting in 1991. Since not all homeowners have their houses painted every 5 years, the figures for the potential market will, of course, be estimates.

Correlation Analysis. *Correlation analysis* is another type of market-factor analysis, but here a mathematical correlation is drawn between the market factor and the potential sales of a product. On a scale from 0 to 1, correlation analysis uses past sales and market-factor history to measure the relationship between the two sets of data. The direct derivation method, on the other hand, always assumes a 1.0 correlation between market factor and sales potential, but such a perfect relationship rarely occurs.

Forecasters can use correlation analysis to measure the correlation between a variety of market factors and the sales potential of a product. To be assured of relative accuracy, at least 20 sales periods should be measured.

Correlation analysis may be more accurate than derivation analysis, but it is also more problematic, for two reasons:

1. It assumes that the market factors had the same effect on the sales during all the sales periods measured (which is not always a safe assumption to make).

2. Since correlation analysis is a relatively difficult mathematical procedure, the function must often be handled by statistical professionals who understand the procedure.

Customer-Intention Surveys. Sales forecasting is also done by *customer-intention surveys*—surveying a group of prospective customers to see whether or not they would buy a given product at a specific price. Surveying customers' buying intentions is often not enough, however, since it is more important whether these customers will actually act on their intentions and buy the product or service. Customer-intention surveys are therefore probably most accurate when the product in question is not a mass-merchandise product and therefore large groups of prospective buyers needn't be surveyed to make the survey accurate. The buyers who should be surveyed are those who do indeed have a history of backing up their intentions with an actual purchase.

Test Marketing. *Test marketing,* as discussed earlier, involves testing the product or service in a specific segment of the marketplace. Using the results of this test, the company estimates what the product or service's sales potential or market share would be for a larger marketplace.

Companies often use test marketing to decide whether or not there is a large enough market for a new product they plan to introduce, or whether specific features of a product help its overall sales. Test marketing can be very costly, but it provides a company with accurate sales figures representing people who actually bought the product rather than those who simply said they would.

Past Sales Analysis.   *Past sales analysis* bases forecasts on past histories. Retailers will often use this method of analysis to improve year-earlier sales figures. Unless market conditions remain constant, however, basing sales forecasts on past sales can give very inconsistent results.

Trend Analysis.   *Trend analysis* takes past sales analysis a step further by using statistics to predict a long-term sales trend or to predict sales for the short term—several months. It does this by applying a seasonally adjusted index to sales. For example, if a business sells 100 widgets in the third quarter of a year, and the fourth quarter historically has proven to be 75 percent better in sales, the business owner makes the assumption that 175 widgets will sell during the fourth quarter.

Trend analysis shares the weakness of past sales analysis in basing future forecasts on past sales history.

Sales-Force Composite.   The *sales-force composite* method of market-factor analysis involves gathering estimates from the entire sales force for sales in their particular regions during the period in question. The total of these individual forecasts makes up the sales forecast for the company. The sales-force composite is an example of the buildup method of market demand forecasting.

When a sales force is well-versed in its product, the sales-force composite can be a very effective method of forecasting sales. It is particularly useful in forecasting sales of big-ticket items—an area in which salespeople generally have a solid handle on their prospective customers. The sales-force composite would probably be more effective in forecasting sales of automated teller machines than in forecasting sales of razor blades.

Who Does Marketing Research?

Typically, an in-house professional who fills the role of marketing research manager reports to the top marketing executive or to top management. In-house marketing researchers are well-informed on the data available to them within the business itself.

If a company decides to go to outside help in conducting marketing research projects, there are a number of marketing research firms to which they can turn. Research and consulting firms are eager to perform such tasks for companies. Other outside agencies that can be turned to for marketing research information include trade or professional organizations that provide marketing research data to member organizations. While these outside firms may not have the insight and knowledge of in-house policies and data available, they are typically well-trained marketing research professionals who may be able to share the experiences of others with similar marketing research problems to whom they have provided consulting sevices.

Case Study
Can "The CELL" Sell?

When Camera Equipment Leaders Ltd. (CELL)—a fictitious company—was ready to introduce a new piece of equipment for professional photographers, it wanted first to make sure that the target market would buy the product.

CELL had been a small manufacturer of professional photography equipment for 12 years. Its product engineers developed a prototype for a rechargeable power-cell battery that was 2 inches thick, 4 inches wide, and 7 inches long. It weighed 2.5 pounds. They called the new product "The CELL," seeking not only to offer an attractive new product to the professional photography market but also to capitalize on some name recognition it had generated over the years for its quality product offerings. "The CELL" would hang from a professional photographer's belt and be attached via a 2-foot cable to the camera. Plugging "The CELL" into an electrical outlet for a few hours would recharge it, so that it could then be attached to the camera and produce 450 flashes before another recharging became necessary.

The broad objective of the marketing research project was to determine whether or not CELL should add "The CELL" to its line of products. The marketing researchers broke down the problem into several parts to make it more focused. Namely, the company wanted to know:

- Whether there was a market demand within its target market of professional photographers for a product like "The CELL"
- Whether that target market indeed wanted "The CELL"
- What extra attributes the target market might want the product to have

- How CELL should distribute "The CELL" to the marketplace
- Whether or not developments in technology in the next 2 to 3 years might eclipse the attractiveness of a product like "The CELL"

The marketing researchers conducted a situation analysis by scouring the library for background material and interviewing CELL management at length. Their situation analysis resulted in developing several hypotheses, including:

- That there was indeed a market demand for such a product as "The CELL"
- That the company should distribute the product through camera shops and other retail outlets to reach the largest possible market
- That technology was not advancing so rapidly that new research and development at competing firms would make "The CELL" obsolete in the foreseeable future
- That competition would not be a major factor in the success or failure of "The CELL"

After analyzing the situation and getting a handle on the marketing problem, the researchers decided to proceed with their marketing research project, by conducting a series of informal investigations.

The researchers talked with many people—including professional associations and potential distributors—about the potential market for "The CELL". They were pleased with what estimates for a potential market showed and decided to proceed with marketing research.

Before designing and implementing a full-blown research project, the researchers continued their informal investigation by talking to 20 professional photographers in 5 different locations to get their reactions to "The CELL". The photographers all generally liked the product and had suggestions for improvements or modifications to the prototype.

As the next step in the informal investigation, the marketing researchers talked on the telephone with a dozen or more potential distributors of "The CELL." When these retailers were asked whether they would stock "The CELL," their reaction was overwhelmingly negative. When the marketing researchers attended a professional photography trade show to get a sense of what the competition was doing, they got the same negative reaction from potential distributors. What the marketing researchers also learned at the trade show was that four major camera manufacturing companies in the country were all developing competing products and that foreign competition was also expected to compete directly with "The CELL."

At this point in their informal investigation, the marketing researchers reported their findings to management at CELL. Management decided that—before an extensive marketing research plan was designed or implemented—it was best not to market "The CELL."

The marketing researchers had completed their job: They had defined their marketing objective and performed a situation analysis and informal investigations to determine whether further marketing research needed to be done to examine the hypotheses posed. And in this instance the company had decided, on the basis of the marketing research, that no further research was needed.

Adapted from William J. Stanton and Charles Futrell, *Fundamentals of Marketing*, 8th ed., McGraw-Hill, New York, 1987, pp. 67–69.

CASE REVIEW

1. What was the advantage to CELL of performing a situation analysis and informal research for its new product?
2. Did CELL give up too quickly on the product? Facing the same negative responses, how would you have proceeded?

Lesson Four Questions

1. What are the five major steps of the marketing research process?

2. What is the purpose of a situation analysis?

3. What is the survey method of gathering primary data for marketing research?

4. What is the observation method of gathering primary data for marketing research?

5. What is the experimental method of gathering primary data for marketing research?

6. What does market sampling involve?

7. What is a random (probability) sample?

8. What is the top-down method of forecasting sales?

9. What is the buildup method of forecasting sales?

10. What is the difference between market potential and sales potential?

4

Target Markets, Consumerism, Customers, Demographics, and Psychographics

What Are Markets?

The term *market* can be used in a variety of ways. As an adjective, it is used as a modifier, as in:

- Market research
- Market demand
- Market segment

Market also can be used as a verb, to indicate everything that is involved in making a sale of a product or service. For example, we can say that Andersen *markets* its windows to building contractors as original equipment and to homeowners as replacements.

As a noun, *market* can have two meanings, as follows:

1. *A place where exchanges occur—where goods and services are exchanged for other goods and services or, in today's economy, for money.* Stock markets, flea markets, and farmer's markets are all

examples of this noun definition of market. There are also retail markets for goods as well as wholesale markets.

2. *A prospective group of buyers for a given product or service.*   It is this definition that is most often used by marketing professionals when they talk of markets for their products or services. This market should be the focal point for an organization's management when it is making marketing decisions.

A market, then, is the overall *demand* for a product or service by buyers or prospective buyers over a given period of time. The term "home market," for example, describes all the buyers and prospective buyers who will either buy or consider buying a home this year. Because this definition of "market" reflects a demand for a product, the words "market" and "demand" are sometimes used interchangeably, or the phrase "market demand" may be used to indicate the same concept.

To define the term "market" a bit more precisely, it is people or groups of people with needs to satisfy, money to spend fulfilling those needs, and willingness to spend money satisfying those needs. A *need* is the lack of something that is required, wanted, or useful. In the market demand for any given product or service, the following three factors come into play:

- People or groups with needs to satisfy
- The purchasing power of these people or groups
- The buying patterns and behavior of these people or groups

Marketing Mix

The *marketing mix* consists of the four inputs that should lie at the heart of an organization's marketing efforts. Traditionally, the four elements listed below have been referred to as "the four P's" of the marketing mix.

1. Product
2. Price
3. Place
4. Promotion

More specifically, the four variables of the marketing mix are:

1. Product or service offerings

2. Pricing structure

3. The distribution system (getting the product or service "in place")

4. Promotional activities

These four variables are the heart of an organization's marketing system. While the labels vary, the concept of the four P's is a generally accepted alliterative device for remembering the four variables of the marketing mix.

Product

To manage the product variable of the marketing mix, management must devise strategies for developing and adding new products or services, adapting or refining old ones, and taking other steps to ensure that market demand is met. Product decisions will also involve questions about branding, packaging, product or service features, and other items affecting the product or service offering.

Price

Management of the pricing variable of the marketing mix involves making appropriate decisions about the base price for products and services. This might include developing discount schedules, assessing freight and shipping costs, and handling other pricing variable issues.

Place

Management of the distribution variable of the marketing mix involves choosing the distribution channels through which the right product can reach the right market at the right time. It also involves developing a distribution system that ensures that the movement and physical handling of these products gets them through appropriate channels. Marketing intermediaries are often an uncontrollable factor, but marketing professionals' correct choices about distribution can influence the smooth functioning of this variable.

Promotion

Management of the promotion variable of the marketing mix involves informing members of the public about a product or service and convincing them that the product is appropriate for their needs. Major examples of promotional activities are as follows:

- Advertising
- Sales promotion
- Publicity
- Personal selling
- Direct mail
- Telemarketing

The four variables of the marketing mix are interrelated. Decisions made in one area of the marketing mix usually will have an effect on another area. An organization's management can have a great deal of control over its marketing mix, both through its marketing department and through other departments. But there are also outside forces that exert some element of control. This is particularly evident in the distribution variable of the marketing mix because, for distribution, the organization must rely on outside intermediaries.

There are many variables at play even within the parameters of the four variables of the marketing mix. A company, for example, must decide how many products it will produce or what combination of promotional activities will be best to use in marketing the product or service. From the wide array of choices available, a company must eventually, however, select a marketing mix combination that

- Addresses issues raised by its marketing environment
- Satisfies the targeted market
- Meets the organizational and marketing goals of the overall organization

The concept of the marketing mix works for both profit and not-for-profit organizations. For example, the marketing mix for a publicly funded, not-for-profit radio station might include the following items:

- *Product.* Programs of musical and informational content that provide both musical appreciation and insight into current events.
- *Price.* Free, with occasional pledge drives to raise contributions for support.
- *Place or distribution.* Through the local public radio affiliate. No middlemen, or intermediaries, are used.
- *Promotion.* Advertisements in the media telling about the forthcom-

ing programs; signs in public areas; an on-air advertising campaign to solicit contributions.

An effective marketing mix will involve use of various organizational resources to handle the product, price, distribution, and promotional variables. The ultimate marketing mix will depend on the organization's goals and the industry in which it operates, as well as how it has positioned itself in the marketplace and the competition it faces from other firms offering the same products or services.

Market Definition

Market definition is the measurement of the characteristics of an organization's actual or prospective buyers. If they have an understanding of the size and nature of the market, marketing professionals can plan their organization's products or services to meet the market's needs.

Knowledge of market definition also helps marketing professionals to develop advertising campaigns that can capture the approval of the target audience.

Two basic areas that are measured by market definition are:

1. *Who are the buyers and prospective buyers, both in number and in demographic and psychographic makeup?* ("Demographic makeup" includes population characteristics reported by censuses, including such information as sex, age, income, education, occupation, family size, religion, and race. "Psychographic makeup" includes the target or prospective market's psychological characteristics, including a buyer's lifestyle and self-image, and how he or she wants to be perceived by other people.) Marketing professionals will also want to have an idea of the makeup of their competitors' markets.

2. *How do the buyers and prospective buyers buy?* This kind of study may vary widely in content, depending on the company's needs.

Business Purpose

Giving the buyer and prospective buyer the product or service they want is not enough to ensure an organization's profitability. To succeed, a seller must also have a defined *business purpose* (or *business charter*), that is, the desire to create a market for the kind of products or services the company is able to provide—called the "company resources." A combination of financial, technical, marketing, management, and people skills creates the types of products or services a company is able to provide to the market.

Market opportunity also plays a part in developing a business purpose. An organization matches its technical and marketing abilities with the opportunity to serve market needs. Financial and management abilities determine how quickly an organization can develop these market opportunities. To successfully develop a business purpose, an organization must both recognize the potential for market expansion and realistically plan within the capabilities and resources available at the organization.

Organizations must not define their business purpose so broadly that they fail to serve any market well. They also must not get so absorbed in their own technology that they are blind to changing market demand.

The managers of a wood-stove manufacturing firm may be thinking too narrowly when they define their firm's business purpose as providing wood stoves for the homeowner. They may be using too broad a definition, however, if they define it as generating energy for the masses. A more contained business purpose, such as providing home heating, not only keeps the managers more focused but also might help them evaluate the possibility of marketing other products that make use of alternative sources of energy before the wood-stove market becomes saturated or competitors begin to take a stronger share of the market.

Target Markets

A *target market* is that segment (or segments) of the market to which an organization has chosen to direct its primary marketing efforts. Organizations generally identify their target markets as those which will have the largest potential or opportunity for successful marketing of products or services.

Target markets must be identified and chosen before an organization can effectively establish its marketing goals. To define markets or potential markets, organizations must decide what strategy to use in selecting a target market. They can use various approaches. Two of the more common approaches are as follows:

1. *Market aggregation.* When using a market aggregation strategy, organizations view the market as an entirety, as one large, aggregate market.

2. *Market segmentation.* If, on the other hand, an organization views the market as being composed of several smaller segments, it employs a market segmentation strategy, in which it targets one of the segments.

Market segmentation is based on the concept that there are groups of prospective product or service buyers in the overall marketplace who share similar characteristics. These people with shared characteristics make up *market segments.*

Market segments are groups of prospective buyers with similar needs who will respond favorably to a given marketing mix, such as:

A particular product design.
A particular price range
A particular supplier
A particular promotional effort

Once an organization identifies market segments, it can concentrate on the parts of the market it can best serve and those which offer the best profit potential. The segment (or segments) identified for a strong marketing effort becomes the organization's target market. The organization will then build its entire marketing effort around serving the needs of that target market.

Breaking Down the Potential Market

One of the more common ways to break down a potential market is to identify it according to the way it ultimately uses the product or service marketed.

The total potential market for any organization can be divided into two broad classifications, as follows:

- *Ultimate consumers*
- *Industrial users*

In addition to these two broad classifications, there are other important potential markets. Two of these, discussed below, are:

- *Government market*
- *International market*

Government Market.   The government market is made up of federal, state, and local government bodies that account for 30 percent of the gross national product in the United States. One of the things that makes the government market unique is the way it buys. A great deal of what the government buys must be purchased under a *bidding system.* The government lists the product specifications of the products it wants to buy, and companies are welcome to bid on the project. The government awards the project to the lowest bidder. If a new product is being developed for which no specifications exist, the government may contract with an individual company to buy the product.

Because the government market is a complex one to deal with, many companies avoid it completely. Those who have mastered dealing with government bureaucracy and the bidding process have found it to be a lucrative source of revenue.

International Market. International markets are another potential target market for U.S. companies. In this market, companies must deal with issues of unknown demographics, foreign politics and trade policies, and, needless to say, language barriers.

But the fundamentals of marketing apply just as well to foreign markets as they do to domestic ones. If a company wants to market internationally, and if it has done appropriate marketing research and is able to meet the needs of its market, there is no reason for it not to succeed in any marketplace.

The main methods used to do business internationally are:

- *Franchising.* Some U.S. franchises, such as McDonald's and Kentucky Fried Chicken, market internationally through company-owned franchises or by allowing businesspeople in foreign markets to become franchisees in their country.

- *Exporting.* Some U.S. firms export U.S.-made goods to foreign countries to sell. They generally do this by directly calling on foreign wholesalers or firms, using exporters in the United States, using importers in foreign countries, or establishing sales offices in the foreign country.

- *Joint ventures.* Sometimes a U.S. company will make an arrangement with a foreign business to market goods in the foreign country. In such instances, each party typically brings some special expertise to the arrangement. One may have capital and technological expertise, while the other has production facilities.

- *Direct investment.* Some U.S. firms will buy production facilities, or controlling interest in production facilities, in a foreign country. Some countries, however, limit foreign ownership, with the result that U.S. companies cannot always own the facility outright.

Ultimate Consumers versus Industrial Users

Customers' reasons for buying products or services are what distinguishes them as either ultimate consumers or industrial users. The distinguishing reasons are as follows:

- *Ultimate consumers* buy a product or service for their own nonbusiness use and are referred to as the "consumer market."

- *Industrial users* include institutional organizations that buy products or services to use either in their own businesses or in making other products or services.

For example, a manufacturer who buys chemicals to use in making pharmaceuticals is an industrial user of that product. Pharmacists who purchase those pharmaceuticals to sell to the public are also industrial users of that product. But an individual who buys the pharmaceutical for home use is an ultimate consumer. The manufacturer and the pharmacist in this example are part of a total market of industrial users who make up the *industrial market*.

Lesson Five Questions

1. What three factors come into play in the market demand for any product?
2. What are the four elements of the marketing mix?
3. What is market definition?
4. What two broad areas are measured by market definition?
5. What is a target market?
6. What is a market aggregation strategy?
7. What is market segmentation?
8. What are market segments?
9. What are four methods of doing business internationally?
10. What is the difference between an ultimate consumer and an industrial user?

Consumer Buying Behavior

A major market factor in developing most products and services is how consumers spend their money—how they buy products and services. Marketing professionals must have a sense of *consumer spending patterns* and the motivational factors that go into their decision making process. Two broad areas of study, discussed below, that can help marketing professionals understand and predict consumer buying behavior are:

- Demographics
- Psychographics

Consumer Demographics

The earliest and still the most widely used approach to segmenting consumer markets is based on demographic characteristics. *Demography* is the statistical study of human populations in terms of the following characteristics:

- Size
- Growth patterns
- Density
- Distribution
- Other vital statistics

Demographic studies analyze the following population characteristics, which can be objectively measured:

- Total number
- Age
- Geographic location
- Ethnicity
- Marital status
- Family size and structure
- Education
- Occupation
- Birth rates
- Death rates

Some of the facts statistically measurable by demographics can play a more important role in marketing decisions than others. Among these are:

- Population size and growth rates
- Population location
- Age composition
- Sex

- Household size and structure
- Income and expenditures
- Family life cycle

Population Size and Growth Rates

While the overall population of the United States is always increasing, the rate at which it increases varies from one time period to another. The period beginning just after World War II, for example, witnessed one of the greatest population growths in the country's history. But by the 1960s and 1970s, that population growth had slowed down significantly. Table 4-1 depicts how population in the United States has grown and is projected to grow from 1975 through 2000.

Organizations can use this information about population growth to make a variety of marketing decisions. For example, a demand for the following goods and services is typically associated with new families which have young children:

Baby food

Baby clothing

Toys

Single-family homes

Station wagons

Home appliances

Looking at the information presented in Table 4-1, a marketing professional might conclude that during the late 1980s and 1990s, not as large a number of new families will be formed as were formed in the period after World War II. If this holds true, then demand for the

Table 4-1. Projections of Total U.S. Population, 1975–2000

Year	Population	Percentage change
1975	213,032	
1980	221,651	4.0
1985	232,271	4.8
1990	243,004	4.6
1995	252,241	3.8
2000	259,869	3.0

SOURCE: U.S. Department of Commerce, Bureau of the Census, March 1979, p. 8.

goods and services listed above may not be as high. There will continue
to be a market demand for these products since millions of new babies
will be born. But there may not be the same demand as there had been
during the earlier so-called baby-boom years ranging from 1946 to
1964, when the pace of population growth was at an all-time high.

The slowing down of population growth since the 1960s has affected
both public- and private-sector industries. Elementary school enroll-
ments have dropped, demand for beds in maternity wards of hospitals
has slowed, and many colleges have struggled to keep their doors open
in the face of a dwindling pool of applicants.

Population Location

Marketing professionals can glean a variety of information from demographic statistics such as the census population projections shown in Table 4-2. They can see the range of projected population increases in various regions of the United States, ranging from a low of 8 percent
growth in the middle Atlantic to highs of 61.4 percent growth in the
mountain region, and 47.9 percent in the south Atlantic region. These
projections suggest that the population is continuing to move west and
south (to what is referred to as the "sunbelt"), as it has been doing over
the past 20 or 30 years.

Marketing departments, particularly those with a national sales scope,
can view each region of the United States as a potential *market segment*
for their goods and services. The importance of understanding and
keeping abreast of population growth in various regions of the country
is important to marketing professionals because buyers and potential
buyers in a given region have a tendency to have similar buying behavior.

What can marketing professionals learn from this population-growth
information? To begin with, they can shift the bulk of their advertising
budgets away from campaigns in the regions that are growing slowly
and into those that are rapidly increasing. They can also develop products and services that are particularly well-suited to buyers and potential
buyers living in the warmer sunbelt region, and can use or develop distribution systems that are conducive to serving that year-round market.
As the western and southern populations continue to grow, marketing
professionals may find larger market demand for products ranging
from patio furniture and casual clothing to barbecue and other products associated with the outdoors.

Farm Population.   As regional population shifts, so too does the U.S.
farm population, which has been decreasing for many years. Whereas 1
out of 6 people in the United States lived on a farm in 1950, the num-

Table 4-2. Population Projections in the United States by Region, 1970–2000

Region	Year	Population, millions	Percentage increase, 1970–2000
New England	1970	11.8	
	1980	12.3	
	1990	13.7	
	2000	14.6	23.7
Middle Atlantic	1970	37.2	
	1980	36.7	
	1990	39.1	
	2000	40.2	8.0
East north central	1970	40.3	
	1980	41.7	
	1990	44.8	
	2000	47.0	16.6
West north central	1970	16.3	
	1980	17.1	
	1990	18.1	
	2000	18.8	15.3
South Atlantic	1970	30.7	
	1980	36.9	
	1990	41.1	
	2000	45.4	47.9
East south central	1970	12.8	
	1980	14.6	
	1990	15.1	
	2000	15.9	24.2
West south central	1970	19.3	
	1980	23.7	
	1990	24.7	
	2000	27.0	39.9
Mountain	1970	8.3	
	1980	11.7	
	1990	12.1	
	2000	13.4	61.4
Pacific	1970	26.5	
	1980	31.8	
	1990	38.1	
	2000	37.6	41.9

SOURCE: U.S. Department of Commerce, Bureau of the Census, March 1979.

ber had dwindled to 1 out of 40 by 1980. The buying power of the farm market, however, has not been completely obliterated. Industrial markets for farm equipment remain viable, as do consumer markets for goods and services.

Suburban Growth.   While the farm population dwindles, the metropolitan areas of the country are not absorbing all the population shift. Instead, areas on the outskirts of the metropolitan areas—the suburbs—have been growing. Over the past 40 years, as more and more middle-income families have moved to the suburban areas, the racial, cultural, and ethnic mixes of the cities have changed. As a result, the markets in these areas have also changed considerably.

Over the years, the suburban market has presented new marketing opportunities for businesses. In addition to a growing demand for single-family homes in these areas, there has also been a demand for products and services that are closely tied to home ownership, such as:

Home maintenance products

Lawn mowers

Lawn-care services

Because of the lack of public transportation in many suburban areas, ownership of one and two cars per family is not uncommon. Also indicative of the market is an increased demand for home entertainment products.

As the suburbs have grown and prices have increased, marketing professionals have begun to notice a growing trend to move to what some marketing observers call "exurbia"—areas just beyond the suburban areas. As this has been happening, the rapid growth of the suburban population has slowed somewhat and the country's smaller cities and rural areas have picked up steam in population growth.

Metropolitan Statistical Areas.   The U.S. government has established a geographic hierarchy of metropolitan areas that marketers can use to measure their potential markets. This government classification is composed of three groups of metropolitan areas, as follows:

- Metropolitan Statistical Area (MSA)
- Primary Metropolitan Statistical Area (PMSA)
- Consolidated Metropolitan Statistical Area (CMSA)

All told, these three account for 75 to 80 percent of the U.S. population and retail sales. For marketers, these areas are geographically concentrated target markets that have excellent sales potential for many products and services.

The Metropolitan Statistical Area is the basic unit in this metropolitan area structure. The U.S. government has identified 335 MSAs. There are two ways in which a geographical area can qualify as an MSA, as follows:

1. If it consists of a central city with a 50,000-plus population
2. If it consists of a general urban area of 50,000 and has a total metropolitan population of at least 100,000

MSA boundaries may cross state borders. The boundaries are drawn around county lines. The counties in the MSA must be socially and economically integrated, and almost all employment must be in areas other than agriculture.

The Primary Metropolitan Statistical Area is the same as an MSA, except that it is a component of the CMSA, a giant urban center. There are 78 PMSAs identified by the U.S. government.

The Consolidated Metropolitan Statistical Area is made up of a group of closely related PMSAs. It is a *megalopolis*—a region made up of several large cities and their areas in close enough proximity to be considered an urban complex. The center of each CMSA is a very large city, such as New York, Los Angeles, or Chicago.

Age Composition

The growth and shift in location of the population may sometimes be difficult to predict. Its age composition, however, can be predicted with greater accuracy. By keeping abreast of growing numbers in a given age group, organizations can better target their products to the needs of larger potential markets.

Table 4-3 shows the changes that have occurred and will occur in the age composition of the United States from 1970 through 2000. Because of the post-World War II baby boom, the number of 45- to 54-year-olds

Table 4-3. Age Composition Changes in the U.S. Population, 1970–2000

1970–1984	Age	1985–2000
−1%	Under 22	23%
49	22–34	−14
35	34–44	32
−4	45–54	60
16	55–64	7
36	65 and over	17

SOURCE: U.S. Department of Commerce, Bureau of the Census, *Statistical Abstract of the United States*, 1980.

will increase by almost 60 percent from 1985 to 2000, while the number of 22- to 34-year-olds will decrease by 14 percent. This baby-boom market has a profound effect on marketing in the United States. As the group begins to accumulate more and more wealth, its level of disposable income increases. Because of its size, it represents one of the largest target age groups and thus dictates the types of products and services that will be offered. As the group continues to mature and build families, it continues to need larger homes, cars, and education facilities for its children.

Similarly, the projected 17 percent increase in the elderly market suggests another market-segment opportunity. As members of the population grow older, it is true that some of them live at relatively low levels of income. But a large number also begin to have a great need for services such as financial management and a desire to take advantage of recreational or vacation-oriented services.

The market of young people under age 22 is also projected to grow by 23 percent from 1985 to 2000. This presents additional marketing opportunities. While the very young have little disposable income, they can influence parental purchase decisions. Parents spend billions of dollars a year on this age group to keep them fed, clothed, and educated. And, as these youths reach their teenage years, they themselves begin to have money to spend. Organizations often direct promotional programs directly at this age group. Apple Computer, for example, very wisely targeted the college market for its personal computer products. Because many college students had been trained on Apple Computers, they felt inclined to purchase them when they graduated and entered the work force.

Sexual Composition

The sex of the potential buyer is also a factor marketing professionals must consider in their marketing analysis. Products that continue to lend themselves to use by only one or the other sex include:

Makeup

Dresses

After-shave products

Neckties

But because sexual stereotypes are breaking down, many of the traditional buying patterns attributed to sex are changing. With more and more women returning to the work force, women no longer always have primary control of household purchases such as food or convenience items. Nor do men exclusively make what were once stereotypical male purchases, such as automobiles or tools for household use. The lines of sexual buying patterns in these areas are starting to be blurred.

For those products that still have one sex as their chief target market, however, marketers should keep abreast of changes and developments in the product and the user that would change receptivity to the product.

Household Size and Structure

Because some products are sold to families or households, it is important for marketing professionals in organizations selling products ranging from household appliances to food condiments to be aware of shifts and changes in household size and structure in the United States.

The U.S. Department of Commerce projects that, between 1970 and 1990, there will have been a 20 percent increase in the number of households in the United States, but that, as the number of children under 18 decreases and the number of single-individual households increases, the number of people per household will decrease from 3.1 to 2.5.

Because the total number of households will increase, there will continue to be a demand for typical household products. But because these households will be smaller, companies will have to alter their marketing strategies. Perhaps more two-person servings or smaller containers of food will find their way to supermarket shelves. As more and more families have two full-time wage earners, appliances that make food preparation and household maintenance simpler and less time-consuming may find larger markets.

Income and Expenditures

Knowing consumers' *spending patterns* can help marketing professionals plan products and services to meet the needs of the consumer market. The distribution of income can help researchers to determine how large various target-market income groups are in the country.

To get a grasp on how the market is segmented in terms of buying power, marketing professionals can look at how income is distributed by percentage of households at various income levels. Table 4-4 shows the dramatic increase in the percentage of affluent households—those with incomes of $40,000 and above. This rise in the number of affluent households from 1980 to 1995 may have resulted from a number of factors, including:

Table 4-4. Household Income Distribution, 1980–1995

(In 1982 Dollars)

	Percentage of households				Percentage change
Annual household income	1980	1985	1990	1995	1980–1995
Less than $10,000	23	22	21	20	−13
$10,000–19,999	26	25	22	21	−19
20,000–29,999	21	20	19	17	−19
30,000–39,999	14	14	14	14	0
40,000–49,999	8	9	10	10	+25
50,000 and up	8	10	14	18	+125
Total	100	100	100	100	

SOURCE: *American Demographics*, April 1984, p. 50.

- The increase in the number of Americans falling into the age groups of 25 and above
- The increase in the number of two-wage-earner families
- The distribution of inherited wealth among more people

The number of women entering the work force has had a significant impact on the increase in household income. During World War II, millions of women entered the work force. After the war, many remained there. As a result, the composition of the work force began to change. When inflation rates hit double digits in the 1970s, many women who had been full-time homemakers entered the work force to help maintain their families' standards of living. And many other women continued to work in their chosen professions after marrying.

Marketing professionals are wise to pay attention to this increase in dual-income families. Working couples need more timesaving products and services for the home and, if there are children, more services such as day care and home cleaning. More of a family's money is spent on clothes for work than if there were only one wage earner.

The consumer market in the United States has experienced stellar growth in household income since 1960. From 1960 to 1985, disposable income grew from $350 billion to about $2.8 trillion, an increase of 700 percent.

Overall, many households in the United States are projected to have more buying power in terms of real dollars (Table 4-4), than would have been thought conceivable 20 or 30 years ago. While the percentage of households at poverty level has fallen, there is still a significant number of poverty-level households in an increasingly affluent society.

The amount of household income has a direct effect on how money in that household is spent. U.S. Department of Labor studies of consumer expenditures suggest:

- As household income rises, there is an increase in the number of dollars spent in various product categories. Lower-income households spend a larger percentage of their income in certain product categories, such as food.

- As the household income rises, the percentage of money spent for food as a percentage of total expenditures decreases.

- In middle- and high-income households, the percentage of income spent on household maintenance (e.g., housing and utilities) stays fairly constant.

- In each household income group, the percentage of income spent on medical and personal care stays around the same.

- In low- and middle-income households, the percentage of spending on automotive products and services has a tendency to increase as income increases in these categories. That percentage then drops somewhat in higher-income categories.

These generalizations, drawn from Department of Labor studies, are not, of course, ironclad rules. But they do give marketing professionals information to use in developing their products or services to match the needs of target markets.

Family Life Cycles

Another demographic factor that affects buying behavior is the life cycle or stage of the family at a given time. William Stanton and Charles Futrell[1] identify six stages in a typical family cycle, as follows:

1. Bachelor stage: young, single people
2. Young married couples with no children
3. Full nest I: young married couples with children
4. Full nest II: older married couples who still have dependent children
5. Empty nest: older married couples with no children living with them
6. Older single people, still working or retired

---

[1]*Fundamentals of Marketing*, 8th ed., McGraw-Hill, New York, 1987.

Stanton and Futrell also identify two alternative stages:

1. Divorced people without dependent children
2. Young or middle-aged people with dependent children—single parents

Marketing professionals can use these family life cycles to help identify various target markets, realizing that the needs of young married couples vary significantly from those of full nesters, and also from those of couples with empty nests. Young unmarried people may spend large percentages of income on clothing and recreation, while those in the full nest I stage may begin to focus more on furnishings for the home. By the time they reach the full nest II stage, the family priorities shift to educational needs, as well as food and clothing expenses. The empty nesters who are still working and older working single people provide a handsome target market, since they typically have more discretionary income than do families in earlier stages.

Other Demographic Bases for Market Segmentation

Singles and Young Unmarried Couples. Two market segments that are growing rapidly and that provide valuable market opportunities for business are:

- Single people living alone
- Young unmarried couples living together

The 1980 U.S. Census suggested that 25 percent of all households consisted of one person. This market segment has an impact on housing size, restaurant offerings, leisure-time activities, and even food portion offerings in grocery stores.

While the number of young unmarried couples of the opposite sex living together increased dramatically and reached 2 million couples by 1984, a fourfold increase since 1970, these households still only account for about 2 percent of total U.S. households.

Other demographic factors also can be used as bases for market segmentation. These include:

- Education
- Religion
- Ethnic heritage
- Occupation

All these factors can come into play when a market segment makes choices about consumer products.

Consumer Psychographics

While there is no universally accepted definition for the term *psychographics*, it is most commonly used in marketing to describe people's:

- Activities
- Interests
- Opinions
- Motives
- Personalities
- Personal values
- Attitudes
- Lifestyles

All these have a profound influence on people's *buying patterns*.

The term "psychographics" is often used by marketing researchers to encompass the psychological variables and personal values that can affect a buyer's or potential buyer's decision making. Marketers can use psychographic information to market their goods and services, designing promotional activities or product features to match their target market's psychographic needs.

Motivation

A *motive* is a need that is stimulated and seeks to be satisfied. *Needs* become motives when they are stimulated or aroused.

Before anybody buys anything, a motive is involved. Motives involve a need or drive that causes someone to take action. To be successful, marketers must try to uncover prospective buyers' underlying motives for buying a company's products or services.

Motives can be grouped into two broad categories:

- *Biogenic needs.*   These include needs for food and physical comfort, and arise out of physiological states.
- *Psychogenic needs.*   These include the need for appreciation and self-esteem, and arise out of psychological states.

Abraham H. Maslow's theory of motivation identifies a hierarchy of five levels of needs,[2] arranged in the order people try to satisfy them. These needs are as follows:

1. *Physiological.* Need for food, drink, clothing, sex.

2. *Safety and security.* Need for protection and order.

3. *Belongingness and love.* Need for affection and acceptance.

4. *Esteem.* Need for self-respect, prestige, status.

5. *Self-actualization.* Need for self-fulfillment.

Maslow held that people meet the needs on one level before they move on to the next. In reality, however, most people seek to satisfy needs on various levels of Maslow's hierarchy simultaneously. By recognizing people's various needs along the motivational hierarchy, product and service marketers can seek to fulfill the needs their prospective buyers experience.

Perception

Using *perception*, people receive stimuli through the five senses, recognize the information given in the stimuli, and proceed to attach some meaning to the stimuli. *Perception* is how we interpret stimuli. *Selectivity* is the process that continually occurs that allows us to limit the stimuli we attach meaning to.

In marketing, if your product did not fall within the selectivity and perception of a potential buyer, that buyer would fail to see your product as an option. Marketers, however, cannot blanket the country trying to address everyone's range of perception. Instead, they try to pinpoint the needs and desires of their target markets, and they attempt to run ads in appropriate media or to have their products carried in appropriate stores to hit the selective perception range of the prospects.

Learning

In addition to motivational forces, people also change their behavior based on previous experiences. This process is called "learning." If they can understand consumers' learning process, marketers can unlock the key to their buying behavior. Two major learning theories that may

---

[2]Abraham H. Maslow, *Motivation and Personality*, Harper & Row, New York, 1954, pp. 80–106.

help the marketing professional to understand how buyers think are *stimulus response theories* and *cognitive theories*.

Stimulus-Response Theories.　The *stimulus-response theories* hold that people respond to some stimulus in a behavior, particularly when that behavior is *reinforced* with a satisfying of the needs when a correct response is given and *penalized* when a correct response is not given. Four factors are integral to the stimulus-response process:

1. *Drive (motive)*.　A stimulus that requires satisfaction.
2. *Cues*.　Weaker stimuli that determine when, where, and how the response behavior will occur. (A radio advertisement or price cut at the local store would be a cue.)
3. *Response*.　The behavioral reaction to the drive and the cues.
4. *Reinforcement*.　The process of making the response rewarding.

If a person responds in a given way and finds it to be satisfying, he or she will make the connection between the cue and the response. Reinforcing the appropriate behavior causes learning to occur; habitual behavior develops.

In marketing, the stronger a customer's habit of buying a given product, the harder it is for competing marketers to change that customer's behavior. Only after the behavior ceases to be rewarding will the customer be able to develop new behavior patterns based on cues and reinforcement given by a competing company.

Cognitive Theories.　*Cognitive theorists* believe that learning is not as machinelike a process as stimulus-response models would suggest. Rather, they hold that learning is a process influenced by attitudes, beliefs, and understanding of how to reach a goal. Cognitive theories hold that habitual behavior patterns result from a combination of being perceptive and being goal-oriented.

Personality and Psychoanalytic Theory

Sigmund Freud, the father of psychoanalysis, believed that the mind consisted of three parts:

- The *id*, where basic, sometimes inappropriate, drives exist
- The *superego*, which acts as a conscience, developing moral stan-

dards and placing a check on instinctive, sometimes inappropriate drives

- The *ego,* which acts as a control center, achieving a balance between the drives of the id and the constraints of the superego

Psychoanalytic theory and personality studies have made it clear to marketers that sometimes the measurable economic or demographic patterns existing in a target market do not get at the heart of the potential buyer's actual reason for buying something. Successful marketers have realized that they must seek to appeal not only to buyers' hopes or fears but also to their moral conscience, which rationalizes the purchase.

Attitudes and Beliefs

An *attitude* is a person's tendency to act in a certain way or to hold an emotion or feeling about something. Attitudes affect consumers' buying patterns. They are formed by gathering information from:

- Past experiences with a product or concept
- Information passed on from their reference group

It is difficult to measure attitude. Often, marketing researchers will resort to directly questioning potential buyers about products or services to be marketed. Respondents will be asked to respond on some sort of scale in their reactions. They may be asked to rate the service they received or the features of a product.

When a marketer attempts to change consumers' attitudes about a product, the process is often called *repositioning.* But it is hard to change buyers' attitudes. To sell a product, a marketer can choose between (1) trying to change buyers' attitudes to get them to buy a product and (2) changing the product to match the customer's attitude. The latter course is typically much easier.

There are three parts to attitudes:

- *Beliefs.*   What the buyer thinks about the product or service.
- *Evaluations.*   Judgments which are made about a brand or product based on the buyer's beliefs about its features.
- *Tendency to act.*   Whether the customer is likely or not likely to buy the product.

Potential buyers with positive evaluations of a particular brand or product are more likely to buy it than those with unfavorable evaluations.

High-Involvement Purchases. When potential buyers are about to make a *high-involvement purchase* (such as a car or stereo system), their attitudes play a large role in their purchase behavior. Fearing that they may make a wrong decision, potential buyers will seek information about the product they are considering buying. This information helps to form the *beliefs* they will hold about the product. They then *evaluate* the product and determine whether or not they like the product. Their evaluations will or will not result in a *tendency to act* to purchase the product.

Low-Involvement Purchases. *Low-involvement purchases* often do not involve the same evaluation process that high-involvement purchases do. The customer may examine only a few of the product's features before making the purchase. Marketing professionals try to let the potential buyer know about their product's benefits by making it easy to make the evaluation in the store. If the buyer is pleased with the product after purchasing it, the stimulus to buy it has been rewarded. As a result, an attitude can often be developed about the product *after* the initial purchase.

Lifestyle Influences on Buying Behavior

Lifestyle can be defined as what people do with their financial, social, and economic resources. Barry Wine, a restaurateur in Manhattan, knows lifestyle. When he was looking for a way to cater to some of his clientele—the ones who did not want to bear the burden of hefty checks for a five-course meals at a four-star restaurant—he opened the Casual Quilted Giraffe. The restaurant serves appetizer-size portions of meals and allows patrons to "graze" through the menu rather than eat a big meal. Rather than spend almost $140 at one of Wine's upscale restaurants, grazers can get away with spending $40 for smaller portions of gourmet delights. In his first year of business in 1986, Wine took in $3.5 million. By catering to the lifestyle of this particular target market, Wine has been able to build a successful offshoot to his more expensive restaurants.

Activities, interests, and opinions are all reflected in a person's lifestyle choices. While there are no universally accepted categorizations of lifestyles, researchers have developed *psychographic profiles* that are designed to measure people's *attitudes, interests, and opinions (AIO)*. These characteristics can be used to identify cohesive market segments made up of people with similar AIOs.

Marketing professionals typically determine a market's AIOs by using questionnaires. Once they identify similar AIOs in a target group, marketers can use the information to target specific market segments with shared AIOs.

Another study of *values and lifestyles (VALS)* placed consumers in nine distinct lifestyle segments, as follows:

- Survivors
- Sustainers
- Belongers
- Emulators
- Achievers
- I-am-me
- Experiential
- Socially conscious
- Integrated

Some businesses have successfully used VALS research to identify a particular segment of the market they wanted to go after for a product or service offering. But like personality, lifestyles are often difficult to measure in quantitative terms. And even when lifestyles are measurable, many organizations may find it cost-prohibitive to reach the desired market.

Cultural Influences on Buying Behavior

Culture is defined as the overall behavior patterns, arts, beliefs, institutions, and other human-produced works that are characteristic of a community or a people. Cultural influences are perhaps the broadest influences on buyer behavior.

Values within a culture are widely accepted and passed on for generations. As a result, younger members of a culture inherit attitudes about products or brands or how a particular product should be purchased.

Subcultures.   Subcultures exist in large numbers in the United States. Once a subculture contains enough people, it becomes an attractive market segment that warrants distinct marketing campaigns. Blacks and Hispanics account for the largest ethnic subcultures in the United States. According to Selling Areas-Marketing, Inc. (SAMI), the black population, consisting of 26 million people, and the Hispanic population, consisting of 15 million people, account for about 20 percent of the country's total population. Together, they spent $145 billion in 1980, up from $20 billion in 1960.

Social Class

Potential buyers are often more influenced by the *social class* to which they belong than they are by income alone. In the United States, marketing researchers recognize that social classes exist, and for marketing planning purposes, they typically break these classes into six categories, as follows:

1. *Upper-upper class.* Accounts for about 0.5 percent of the U.S. population. The members have social prominence and often have inherited their wealth. Behaviorally, these people have security of social position, reflected in such things as elite private club memberships and private prep schools and colleges for children. They spend considerable amounts of money, but are not flamboyant, tending to wear conservative clothing and choosing elegance over flashiness at social gatherings.

2. *Lower-upper class.* Accounts for about 2.5 percent of the population, and consists of people who typically have worked their way to riches rather than inheriting them. Behaviorally, members have social mobility and are college-educated but not necessarily at the most elite schools. They spend money on products that reflect their success in society and fall into the category of those who indulge in *conspicuous consumption*, letting others know about their social status.

3. *Upper-middle class.* Accounts for about 12 percent of the population, and consists of businesspeople and professionals who have been moderately successful. Behaviorally, they are motivated by their careers, are highly educated but did not attend prestigious schools, are demanding with their children, and have a wide variety of cultural interests. They spend money on quality goods and want to be perceived as fashionable without being showy.

4. *Lower-middle class.* Accounts for about 30 percent of the population, and consists of the average American. Behaviorally, these people work hard and strive to do well at work and in society. They typically are white-collar workers—salespeople, teachers, office workers—and conform to social norms. They spend money on their home, which is typically their most valuable possession. They are sensitive to price fluctuations and rely on media and product literature to inform them about

products. They buy commonly available rather than flamboyant or un-usual products.

5. *Upper-lower class.*   Accounts for about 35 percent of the popula-tion and is sometimes referred to as the *working class.* Behaviorally these people are typically blue-collar workers and have little expectation of social mobility. They live in smaller homes in less desirable areas of a city or town and are loyal to brand products.

6. *Lower-lower class.*   Accounts for about 20 percent of the popula-tion, and is made up of unskilled workers and the unemployed. Typi-cally, the members of this class are poorly educated with low incomes. They buy on impulse and do not seek out product information or de-termine quality before they buy; as a result, they sometimes pay too much money for inferior goods.

Reference Groups

A *reference group* is a group of people who influence an individual's at-titudes, values, and behavior patterns. When a potential buyer goes to make a purchase, he or she is much more likely to be influenced by word-of-mouth advertising from a member of his or her reference group than by any other form of advertising.

A reference group may be a group someone belongs to, such as:

A family

An athletic team

A social organization

Or a reference group may be a group that someone desires to become a member of.

Reference groups serve a variety of purposes. Among the most prev-alent are:

- *Informational.*   To get information about a product or service (or anything, for that matter), most people will seek out an accessible, credible source.

- *Utilitarian.*   To get the respect of their peers, most people will at-tempt to act in concert with others in their reference group.

- *Value-expressive.*   The reference group places members in close psy-chological proximity to others, which most people find comforting.

To successfully influence potential buyers, marketing professionals must identify the reference groups to which these buyers belong, and must also influence the *opinion leader* of that group to believe that the product or service is worth purchasing. All reference groups have such a leader, who is capable of influencing others in the group to take action.

Buying Habits

Marketing professionals must pay close attention to three things when attempting to understand potential buyers' buying habits:

- *When* the potential buyer buys a particular product or service, which can influence an organization's seasonal marketing schedules, pricing strategies, and product introductions
- *Where* the potential buyer decides to buy a product, whether it is in the home or in the place of purchase
- *How* the potential buyer buys a product or service, whether it is, for example, through catalogs or at one-stop department stores

Most organizations make sure that their marketing mix is directed toward building brand loyalty in customers. *Brand loyalty* occurs when a buyer habitually buys the same product. To achieve this goal, marketers must make sure that their product or service continues to meet the needs of customers so that they do not become disenchanted with the product or service.

The Decision-Making Process in Buying

When potential buyers are deciding whether or not to buy a product or service, they go through a problem-solving approach that consists of the following five steps.

1. *They recognize an unsatisfied need.* A family needs a new washer and dryer, for example.
2. *They identify methods to attain satisfaction of that need.* They can purchase a freestanding washing machine or dryer or a portable stacked unit.
3. *They evaluate the alternatives.* They consider the pros and cons of one option over the other, evaluating space and cost considerations as well as washing and drying capacity.
4. *They make a purchase decision.* They buy the portable stacked unit.
5. *They exhibit postpurchase behavior.* They worry about whether or not they bought the appropriate washer and dryer for their needs.

Buyers do not necessarily go through all steps on their way toward the final purchase. They may decide anywhere along the way to call off the purchase altogether. Most likely, they go through all five steps only for first-time or big-ticket purchases.

Often, purchases are made based on responding to aroused needs in ways that have been rewarding in the past. Sometimes buyers have always bought a particular appliance brand and have always had good experiences with it, so they continue that pattern. When that product or service or its price changes dramatically, buyers may then break their pattern and work through the five stages of the purchasing decision-making process once again.

Case Study

Honda Understands the Market

How does a company know it is reaching its target market when it enters a new marketplace with its product? Before developing a marketing strategy, marketing professionals must find out as much as they can about what people in their target market want and think. Only when they understand consumer behavior can they discover how and why people go about making a purchasing decision.

When a Japanese company, Honda Motor Company, Inc., which had already achieved great success in Japan, wanted to penetrate the motorcycle market in the United States, it had to do so in a way that addressed the needs of consumers in the American market. The company knew that its product—motorcycles—was superior, but it was also keenly aware that the U.S. market differed greatly from the Japanese market. At the outset, company officials did not have a clear understanding of American consumers, but they did know that if they approached the market inappropriately, success in capturing a big share of the U.S. motorcycle market would be elusive.

American Honda Motor Company, Inc., Honda's American affiliate, hired Grey Advertising, which proceeded to do marketing research to find out what U.S. consumers' perceptions about motorcycles were. Good news did not abound. What marketing professionals at Grey found was that people associated motorcycles with socially unacceptable norms. When they thought "motorcycle," they thought of Hell's Angels, or hoodlums, or other stereotypical images of sociopaths blazing a trail of trouble through society. To successfully penetrate the market, American Honda had to overcome this perception.

American Honda was marketing four-stroke street bikes that had a much bigger market segment in the United States than did two-stroke off-road bikes. But it had to convince that market that it wanted motorcycles at all.

A series of advertisements carrying the tag line "You meet the nicest people on a Honda" was developed by Grey. One ad showed marching-band members in uniform, one carrying her French horn while riding a Honda in front of the rest of the band. The rest of the ads in the series also depicted young, "all-American" types, which implied that if it was OK for these people to ride motorcycles, then it was OK for the rest of American youth as well—if they wanted to.

The response was great. Millions of young people in the United States bought Honda motorcycles. Honda and motorcycles became firmly entrenched on American turf. Because it took the time to understand its market—the American youth—Honda acquired more than 50 percent of the motorcycle market in the United States.

Adapted from James H. Myers, *Marketing*, McGraw-Hill, New York, 1986, pp. 183–184.

CASE REVIEW

1. How did Honda combat the negative image motorcycles had in the United States market?

2. Based on what you learned in this chapter, how else might Honda have tried to influence this market?

Lesson Six Questions

1. What is demography? How is it used in marketing?

2. What are the three groups of metropolitan areas classified by the U.S. government?

3. What does the term "psychographics" describe?

4. What is a motive?

5. What are biogenic needs? Psychogenic needs?

6. What are Maslow's five levels of human needs?

7. If a product did not fall into the selectivity and perception of a potential buyer, what would this mean for the product?

8. What is repositioning?

9. What is a reference group?

10. What three things must marketing professionals pay close attention to in trying to understand prospective buyers' buying habits?

5
The Product

A *product* can be defined broadly as a tangible or intangible item offered for sale or barter to individuals or institutions. *Services*, which also are marketed by organizations, are activities, accommodations, benefits, or other similar actions that are offered for sale or barter to individuals or institutions, or, in some cases, as an additional benefit when a product is sold.

Product and service benefits are designed to meet the needs of a target market. Rather than simply buying a tangible product, customers buy something that satisfies a need. When businesses market products, they often market *product benefits* that can meet customer needs rather than just marketing the physical product itself.

Products are distinct from one another. Each has its own unique characteristics. If the physical characteristics of a product are changed, the result is the creation of another, different product. Marketers often make changes in order to establish a new product or to appeal to a new set of potential customers.

When the effects of caffeine became a concern for many consumers, for example, cola companies created new products by changing cola drinks that previously had contained caffeine. This presented a new marketing opportunity, enabling companies to attract a new market segment.

New Products

How can a business determine when it has developed a truly new product? There are many types of new products that a company can choose to market. For instance:

- *Unique products* are products that have never been offered before. Unique products may have been newly developed to meet a market need that has never been fulfilled before, or they may meet needs that have been met before but do it in an innovative way that is more attractive to the customer.

  Examples include a low-calorie butter or margarine substitute for diet-conscious consumers, and the Manhattan City Key calculator developed and marketed by Computerized Information Technologies, Inc. Robert Blumenblatt and Klaus Kurzina invented this credit-card-sized calculator that not only functions as a traditional calculator but also helps lost New York City visitors find out where they should be going. The user punches in the desired address, and the calculator names the cross streets nearest to that address. Selling for about $20 to $30, the Manhattan City Key calculators began selling briskly at upscale stores like Fortunoff and Bloomingdale's shortly after their introduction to the market in 1987. By fall of 1987, this unique product was selling at a rate of 100 calculators a day.

- *Replacement products* are not unique to the marketplace, but do meet needs differently from products already on the market. An example is a laundry detergent packet that not only goes into the washer but also acts as a fabric softener when placed in the dryer with the clean laundry. Or a cereal company may begin to package its cereal in resealable packaging, unlike other cereal foods on the market. *Imitative products* may not be unique and may not meet customers' needs differently from other products. They may be simply a company's entry into a new market with a product it has never manufactured before.

Parity Products

Parity products are competing products that customers perceive to be similar. Parity occurs because companies try to keep up with one another in making new improvements to the product. When everything new under the sun has already been added to a product to make it better, it is often difficult for manufacturers to add anything new to make their products stand out from those of competitors.

When products reach parity, businesses must use other methods to achieve *product differentiation*, which is anything that makes customers perceive one company's products as different from those of other companies. For this reason, marketing professionals strive hard to differentiate a product early on in its market growth, hoping that by the time it reaches parity with similar products, customers will have developed a product preference and buying patterns will be unlikely to change.

Augmented Products

Augmented products are products that consist of something extra that is provided to the product buyer—something that goes beyond what is normally expected when such a product is purchased. The augmented-product approach may be used with many products. It is a difficult approach, however, to use effectively with consumer convenience goods, since consumers who buy these products do not anticipate a need for additional services. When they buy a frozen dinner, for example, they hardly expect the seller to give them verbal cooking instructions. Nor would they expect a seller of shampoo to give a demonstration of the proper method for rinsing hair. Consumer convenience goods are products that typically reach parity with competitive products and are difficult to augment to attract significantly new numbers of purchasers.

Product Planning and Development

Before a business introduces a new product to the market, it should define how that product will fit into the company's management and marketing objectives. The objective might be to introduce a product that would help the company to maintain its market share, or to maintain the company's reputation for unique product developments. The goal of introducing a new product also might be to help the company reach specific profit goals or break into a new market.

After a company has established what its new-product goals are, it can proceed through the product-development process. At each stage of the product-development process, a business can decide whether going on to the next stage would make sense, based upon what they have learned about the product up to that point.

There are six stages in the product-development process. The first three stages combined make up what is called *concept testing*, which involves pretesting the product idea before it is actually manufactured. The six stages are as follows:

1. *Producing new-product ideas.*

2. *Evaluating new-product ideas.*

3. *Business analysis.* If the new product idea makes it to the business-analysis stage, a business proposal is developed for the product. Product features, market demand and profitability estimates, and a development program for manufacturing the product are all discussed in the business analysis.

4. *Product development.* In the product-development stage, the product is actually made into a physical object. Specifications are drawn up, and a prototype or samples of the product are made. The product is tested to see whether marketing such a product to potential customers is feasible.

5. *Test marketing.* The product is tested in small target-market segments to determine whether or not it makes sense to commit the money necessary for a full-blown marketing campaign. As the test marketing is being done and results of the testing are studied, changes or variations may be made in the product. After all the testing has been completed, business management has to decide whether or not it makes sense to make the product commercial.

6. *Commercialization.* At the commercialization stage, the product is produced and marketing programs are developed to get the product to market. By the time the product reaches this point, the company has decided that it is worth marketing. Competitive factors begin to have an impact on the survival and success of the product.

Some products are easier than others to develop, test-market, and produce. When William Taylor, for example, found that pecan shells gave his barbecued meals a better taste, he was convinced that he had a hit on his hands. Taylor buys the pecan shells very cheaply from a nut-shelling plant. He took $20,000 in savings and started Wineta, Inc., in Carrollton, Texas. He test-marketed the product and got it bagged and on shelves in Dallas grocery stores. Meeting with success there ($200,000 gross sales in his first full year of operation), he hired food brokers whom he was going to rely on to get his product into the national market.

Product Adoption by Customer

The *customer adoption process* is the procedure potential customers go through when trying to decide whether or not to buy a new product a business has developed. Typically, customers go through the following steps:

1. *Development of awareness.* Potential customers are made aware of the new product.
2. *Stimulation of interest.* They try to get more information about the product.
3. *Evaluation of product.* They use the information they have gathered to try to determine how this product compares with others they have used, and how this product might satisfy their needs.
4. *Trying the product.* Potential customers decide to give the product a try to see how it works. They are not adopting the product outright, but may buy a sample of the new product. Using product samples to get potential customers to try a new product is an effective means of ultimately getting them to adopt the product.
5. *Adoption of the product.* Potential customers decide whether or not to use the new product regularly.
6. *Confirmation of adoption of the product.* After adopting the product, customers try to get reassurances that they have made the correct decision.

Product Adopter Categories

There are five basic categories of product adopters. They are categorized according to when they tend to adopt a new product.

1. *Innovators.* About 2.5 percent of the marketplace is made up of innovators, who are the first customers to adopt a new product. They typically do not rely on the influence of salespeople or word of mouth, but tend to keep abreast of new-product developments on their own through outside sources of information, such as reports and other literature. They tend to be young, affluent, and cosmopolitan.
2. *Early adopters.* About 12 percent of the marketplace consist of early adopters. They tend not to be cosmopolitan like the innovators, but early adopters are opinion leaders within their social groups.
3. *Early majority.* About 34 percent of the marketplace is made up of the early majority—a group that tends to adopt a new product just before the average adopter does. These people tend to be slightly above average in social and financial status, and they rely on adver-

tisements, salespeople, and information provided by early adopters in making their decisions about new products.

4. *Late majority.*   The late majority, consisting of people who are skeptical about new products, constitutes about 34 percent of the marketplace. These customers rely on word of mouth from their peers rather than on advertisements; they typically adopt a new product when it becomes economically prudent or after they have been pressured to do so by their peers.

5. *Laggards.*   Laggards account for about 16 percent of the marketplace. They are the last people in the market to adopt new products. Because they wait so long, laggards are often adopting a new product at the same time innovators have found something new to take its place.

Product Classification

Consumer versus Industrial Products

Two broad categories of products are *consumer goods* and *industrial goods*. Consumer goods are targeted for household use rather than business use. Industrial goods are designed for use as raw materials for producing other products or as means of delivering services through a business. The simplest way to distinguish between the two categories is to determine what end use the product was designed to fulfill.

Consumer Product Classification

Four of the largest categories of consumer products are as follows:

1. *Convenience goods.*   Convenience goods are purchased by consumers with relative ease. Before they purchase a convenience good, consumers know about the product they want to purchase.

Convenience goods, such as household items, are most often comparatively low-priced items that consumers purchase on a regular basis. Typical convenience goods include:

Groceries

Soap

Toiletries

Since consumers use convenience goods regularly, businesses must make sure that these products are distributed efficiently so that the product will be available for purchase.

2. *Shopping goods.* Shopping goods include products for which consumers typically will do some sort of comparison shopping. They might want to compare the quality, price, or design of several similar products before making their final purchasing decisions. Shopping goods would include such things as:

Clothing

Furniture

Major household appliances

Automobiles

Fewer retail outlets are needed for shopping goods because consumers are willing to take the effort to shop around for the product they want. To make comparison shopping easier, product manufacturers may try to get their products into outlets that are in close proximity to other outlets featuring similar products. This technique is most prevalent in shopping malls, where it is easy for the consumer to go from one store to the next to compare similar products.

3. *Specialty goods.* Specialty goods are products for which customers have built up some loyalty. They will go out of their way and perhaps spend a little extra money to find the product they want. Among the specialty goods that consumers will go out of their way to shop for, in order to find their regular brands, are:

Automobiles

Expensive clothing

Stereo sets and equipment

Camera equipment

Sporting goods

Typically, fewer outlets are necessary for specialty goods since consumers will go where they have to, to get the product they want. Retailers for specialty goods are very important to manufacturers, particularly if only one retailer in a geographic area has the rights to sell the product. On the other hand, retailers depend very heavily on manufacturers to supply them with the products that their customers will demand.

4. *Unsought goods.* Unsought goods are consumer products that the customer either does not want or, in the case of a new product, does not yet know about.

Industrial Product Classification

Five of the large categories of industrial products are as follows:

1. *Raw materials.* Raw materials are industrial products that are used in manufacture of other products. Except for packaging to protect them from damage, raw materials have not been processed. Raw materials might include natural materials, such as:

Minerals

Land

Forest products

They might also be agricultural products, such as:

Wheat

Cotton

Fruits

Vegetables

Livestock

Eggs

Raw milk

The marketer who markets raw materials must keep in mind that there is only a finite supply of raw materials available. Typically, there are only a few large producers of raw materials. The products must be classified, graded, and transported to the industrial user. Because of these factors, plus the typically low per-unit cost of raw materials, middlemen are kept to a minimum in the distribution process. Often the raw materials are sold directly by the producer to the industrial user. Because of the limited supply of raw materials, users must take precautions to ensure that they will have these materials available to them when they need them. To do so, they may contract well in advance to purchase quantities of the product. Some industrial users even opt to purchase the raw material provider.

Because there are only a few large providers, advertising is not frequently used to generate product awareness. Because the raw materials are used in other products, there is little product differentiation or branding of any sort. Pricing, quality, and meeting specifications are the factors that play a major role in an industrial user choosing which provider of raw materials to use.

2. *Fabricating materials and parts.* Fabricating material and parts have already been processed and actually become a part of the finished

product. Fabricating materials will undergo further processing (e.g., pig iron will be processed into steel, wool yarn woven into material, yeast baked into bread). Fabricating parts require no further processing and are assembled directly into the product (screw machine parts into machinery, microchips into computers). Industrial users typically purchase large amounts of fabricating materials and parts well in advance of when they need them, so that they will be assured of a ready supply when they manufacture their products. Typically, sales are made directly from producer to user, but a very small user may go through a middleman for distribution of the fabricating material or part.

3. *Installations.* Installations include the industrial products that are expensive, large equipment. The following are examples of installations:

Warehouse buildings

Train engines

Generators for operating plants

Mainframe computers

Buses for a bus company

Because of the size and expense of the installation, the fact that in many cases each installation is made according to customer specifications, the servicing required before and after the sale, and the high caliber of salesperson needed to sell the installation, every installation sale is of crucial importance to the manufacturer. Sales are usually made directly from the installation producer to the user.

4. *Accessory equipment.* Accessory equipment is used for an industrial firm's operations. Unlike installations, it does not have a great impact on the user's scale of operations. Accessory equipment may last longer than operating supplies, but it does not last as long as installations. It does not become part of the product being produced by the industrial firm, but may include such equipment as:

Typewriters

Forklifts

Power tools

Middlemen are often used to sell accessory equipment, but when a large order is placed or the equipment has a very high value, a direct sale from the equipment producer to the industrial user may be made.

5. *Operating supplies*. Operating supplies, like consumer convenience goods, are purchased easily by the end user, are low-priced, and do not have a long life. They help the industrial firm to operate, but they do not become part of the finished product. Here are some examples of operating supplies:

Heating fuel

Lubricating oil

Pens and pencils

Because of their relatively low cost, the wide demand for them, and the small quantities purchased per order, operating supplies are typically distributed through wholesalers. There is not much brand loyalty from one operating supply to the next, and price thus becomes a big factor in purchasing decisions.

Product Lines

A *product line* is a group of related products or services offered by a business to its customers. Often when a product line has been successfully expanded into the market, a business will diversify and offer other product lines.

Product lines consist of closely related products that may:

- Meet similar customer needs
- Be distributed through similar outlets
- Fall into a specific price range
- Be sold to similar target groups
- Share other similar characteristics

Wearing apparel and tools are both examples of product lines. Businesses offer product lines for many reasons, including:

- Meeting customers' demand for a variety of related products
- Outselling competitors that sell just one competing product by meeting all the needs of a customer rather than just a few
- Generating greater sales volumes by selling more products that can fulfill a customer's needs

All the products and product lines a business offers make up its *product mix*. The product mix may include one product or several product lines. The breadth of a product mix can be measured by how many product lines it carries. Its depth can be measured by how many different models, colors, or sizes are offered.

Product Positioning

There is no widely accepted definition of *product positioning*, but the concept refers to a business's ability to portray an image of its product that compares favorably with competing products in the marketplace. Businesses can position a product according to quality or price, or in relation to competitors, target markets, or a class of products.

Trading Up and Trading Down

Trading up and trading down involve expanding the product line to affect product positioning.

When a business *trades up*, it adds a higher-priced product line, hoping that this new product will help increase the sales of lower-priced items in the same product line. Businesses that trade up may count on the lower-priced items to produce most of their sales revenue and therefore will market these items heavily. Or they may count on the newer, more expensive item to generate more sales volume and may shift the bulk of promotional efforts and dollars to promoting that line. Ultimately, if the new item's sales and profits are good, the business may decide to drop the lower-priced products from the line.

A business *trades down* when it adds a lower-priced product to its line of higher-priced goods. The idea is that a customer who is not able to shell out big dollars for the expensive product may want to buy the lower-priced item because it carries some of the name prestige of the higher-priced product.

The danger with using trading-up or trading-down strategies is that customers may become confused. Or sometimes, a former purchaser of the higher-priced item may decide to go with the lower-priced item, thus taking revenue away from the business.

When a business trades down, it must ensure that the new products, while less expensive, do not the damage the reputation the business had built with its higher-priced goods.

When a business trades up, it must change its image enough to convince a customer that its products are high-quality goods worth the money. The trick is to do this without alienating current customers of the lower-priced line.

The Product Life Cycle

New products are generally believed to pass through a four-period life cycle. The periods are:

1. Introduction
2. Growth
3. Maturity
4. Decline

Figure 5-1 shows the typical life cycle of a product.

Introduction

The introduction of a product to a market involves a full-scale production and marketing program designed to get the product to the potential customer. This period in a product's life cycle can last from weeks to years. The product may be new or may be an enhanced version of an existing product.

The period typically involves high costs and net losses. If there are any profits, they are usually very low. Sales of a product that is being introduced to the market normally are slow. The failure rate for products is high during this period. The product manufacturer has to survive until the product gains some market acceptance.

If the product is unique to the market, there may be little competition. Competing companies may enter the market with similar new

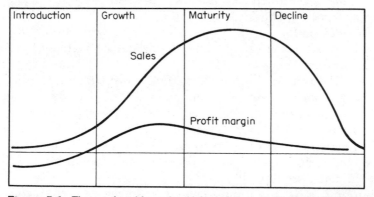

Figure 5-1. The product life cycle. *(Adapted from V. P. Buell,* Marketing Management: A Strategic Planning Approach, *McGraw-Hill, New York, 1984, p. 421.)*

products, but they typically will wait to see how well it does, particularly if it is untested in the marketplace. The marketing effort during this period is designed to create a desire for the product itself, not for the particular brand the company may be offering.

Growth

During the growth period, sales and profits begin to rise. Competitors enter the marketplace with their version of the product, often based on reactions to the originating company's product. If the outlook for profits is great, many competitors will enter the market.

Sellers begin to emphasize their brand of product rather than the product itself. New distribution outlets are created and the price of products may begin to come down during this period, in part because of economies of scale.

Toward the end of the growth period, profits may begin to diminish.

Maturity

In the first part of the maturity period, a product's sales continue to increase, but not as quickly as they did in the growth period. Sales then begin to level off, and profits decrease for both the producer and the seller of the product. Competition becomes intense, and producers that have been making it only marginally drop out of the market.

Producers may spend more on advertising and promotional efforts to maintain their market share. Often a business can stimulate a product's life during the maturity period by enhancing the product with new features, running intensive promotional campaigns, or experimenting with special pricing.

Decline

During the decline period of a product, sales and profits decline, and many businesses drop out of the market. There is a shakeout period, after which the surviving businesses make a small profit on their products.

As sales decline, cost control becomes crucial. During this period, a business's management has several options. It can:

- Enhance the product

- Evaluate the efficiency of production and marketing programs
- Weed out the unprofitable products from the product line (which could decrease sales, but increase profits)
- Run out the product by cutting all costs as much as possible so that profitability will be high until the product must be removed altogether from the market

Business management must establish a strategy, or a plan for when production and marketing of a declining product should stop. Once the decline in sales and profitability has advanced to the ultimate stage, ceasing production may become the only option.

Product Life-Cycle Length

A product life cycle can last from several weeks to several decades. As research and development of new technology have been increasing, product life cycles have begun to get shorter, since products become obsolete more quickly. The introduction and growth periods become shorter, and a product can move quickly into the maturity period if competing companies soon come out with copycat products to match the originator's product.

Some products do not go through all periods of the product life cycle. Some, for example, may fail in the introductory or growth period, while others may enter the market when the product has already entered its period of maturity.

Branding

When a name, phrase, symbol, or graphic design, or some combination of these, is used to designate the products or services of a seller, a *brand* has been created. Brands distinguishes competitors' products from one another. The *brand name* is the name of the product or service, and it can be said aloud. The *brand mark* is the symbol or graphic design that is used to identify the product visually. When a brand is given legal proprietary rights to its name, it receives a *trademark*. "Trademark" is essentially a legal term designating a brand name or a brand mark, or both.

Trademark Licensing

The U.S. Trademark Act of 1946 defines "trademark" as "any word, name, symbol, or device or any combination thereof adopted and used by a manufacturer or merchant to identify his goods and distinguish them from those manufactured or sold by others."

Companies are increasingly using trademark licensing, a branding strategy that entails granting permission to other firms for use of a trademark. A trademark owner grants another company the right to use its name, characters, typeface, or other trademarked aspects of the product on its own line of products. For example, McDonald's and Coca-Cola have both done this for lines of clothing. Jim Henson has licensed rights to use his Muppets characters in a variety of products, from toys to magazines. Charles Shulz has sold the licenses to his Peanuts characters for years. The list of trademark licensing arrangements is a long one.

Trademark licensing can be profitable for trademark owners since they incur no costs other than legal fees involved in setting up agreements. They also gain a great deal of promotion for their own products. Using a trademark to introduce a new product to the market is a method for companies to gain market penetration relatively fast. To launch a new product from scratch would be a costlier task for a company than buying the right to use a well-known trademark on its product.

Brand Classification

Brands can be classified according to who owns them. The possibilities include:

- The producers of the product
- The distributors who bring the product to market

The term *national brand* is sometimes used to indicate a producer's brand, while *private brand* is used to indicate a distributor's brand.

Branding is used for a variety of reasons—among which are to help customers identify desired products or services and to help customers know what they will be getting when they purchase the product or service again in the future. Producers or distributors can also use brands to advertise their products and to help customers differentiate their product from a competitor's.

When a seller of a product decides to brand a product, he or she is making the commitment to advertise that brand and to maintain a level of quality control that ensures a consistent product. When a manufacturer's run of a branded product doesn't meet traditional quality standards, it is typically sold through a different channel of distribution, such as an off-price outlet store.

What's in a Brand Name?

A good brand name should perform the following functions:

- Give the customer some idea of the product or service benefits.
- Be simple to say and recall.
- Be distinctive.
- Be broad enough that it can be applied to new products as they are added to the product line.
- Be worded in such a way that it can be legally registered and protected under federal and state regulations.

Sometimes brand names become so well known that the brand name is substituted for the *generic* name of the product. Some examples include:

Linoleum

Aspirin

Cellophane

Nylon

Originally these were trademarks that only the producer was licensed to use.

Brand names can also become generic when the trademark expires or when no generic name is available for the public to use in describing a product. The latter occurred in the case of shredded wheat.

From time to time a company will promote its product so heavily that its trademarked name begins to be used to describe the product in general. Brand names like Xerox and Kleenex are not generic, but people have begun to use them as if they were. If a company wants to keep the public from using its brand name as a generic name, it will sometimes use the company name along with the brand name, or along with the generic name for the product.

Brand Strategies

Brand strategies can fall into two broad categories: manufacturers' strategies and middlemen's strategies. In this context, "middlemen" includes both retailers and wholesalers.

Manufacturers' Strategies. Manufacturers have the choice of either branding their own products or allowing their middlemen to put their own brand names on the manufacturers' products. Companies that take the former course are typically large enough to support the advertising campaign that must go along with building brand recognition and loyalty.

Some businesses that manufacture fabricating parts and materials for industrial use brand their products, particularly if they are replacement parts that are ultimately used in consumer goods. By branding its windows, for example, Andersen Company has attracted not only a primary market of housing contractors, but also a secondary market of homeowners who might wish to replace windows in their homes.

Middlemen's Strategies.   A middleman may decide to carry only manufacturers' branded products or to carry its own branded products along with the manufacturer's products. Most middlemen (wholesalers and retailers) will not choose to take the latter route, since the task of promoting their own brand along with a manufacturer's brand becomes too overwhelming.

The margins on manufacturers' brands may be lower for the middleman, but the products most often move more quickly than the middleman's own brand would. The result of marketing just the manufacturer's brand can increase overall profits.

Middlemen may decide to market their own brand along with a manufacturer's to have more control over the product. If they choose to take this route, they can sell their branded product at a discounted price. By placing their own brand names on products, middlemen can differentiate their products and undercut the pricing of national brands.

Manufacturer and Middleman Branding Strategies.   Businesses that sell more than one product can use a number of branding strategies to market their products, including the ones listed below.

1. *Use the same family or brand name on each product.*   The *family brand strategy* has several advantages. Companies can introduce new products to a line and have the potential customer already be aware of the brand. The reputation of the brand can spread as new products are added to the line. The demand for consistent quality control among all the brands using the family brand name is great. As more products are introduced under the family brand name, it may become increasingly difficult to differentiate new products from existing ones in the product line.

2. *Use a separate brand name on each product.*   By placing a *separate brand name* on each product, companies hope to saturate more of the market with their products. Anheiser Busch, for example, has used the *multiple-brand strategy* by introducing a variety of beers to

the market under different brand names in hopes of saturating the market with its products.

3. *Differentiate products according to quality and use a separate brand name on each group.*

4. *Use a combination of the business's trade name and the individual product name.*

Packaging

For a business to effectively market consumer or industrial goods, its product packaging must ensure that the product not get damaged or spoiled. In marketing consumer goods, packaging must also help to sell the product by letting the potential buyer know:

- What it consists of
- How to use it
- How to store it
- How it differs from competing products

   Packaging information might include:

- Product and brand name
- Price
- Promotional message
- Instructions
- Warranty

Packaging Strategies

When a company decides to make all the products in the company's product line have the same or a similar feature in the packaging, the result is called *family packaging*.

   The practice of designing a package that can be reused after the original contents of the package have been used is called *reuse packaging*. A classic example of reuse packaging is jam jars that feature cartoon characters on them and can be used as drinking glasses once they are emptied.

   Multiple packaging involves placing several different products within one container. Test marketing has suggested that multiple packaging can increase the total sales of a product. Common examples of multiple packaging are (1) snack packs of a variety of different breakfast cereals and (2) packages containing multiple ballpoint pens.

Changing the package is often done to try to attract new customers, correct a fault in the former packaging, or make use of new materials as they become available. McDonald's, for example, decided to change the packaging of its hamburgers by shifting from a material that was not biodegradable to one that was. By taking advantage of a new material, the company gained goodwill among consumers who were concerned about the environmental impact of packaging.

Labeling

The *product label* is the portion of a product's packaging that contains information about the product or the product's seller. A *brand label* is the brand name attached to the product packaging. A *grade label* identifies the quality of the product; it may consist of a letter, a number, or another method of indicating the grade. The *descriptive label* lists the contents, describes the use, and lists other features of the product.

Labeling Regulations

Product labeling is controlled by a variety of federal regulatory acts. The ones listed below are worth noting.

- The *Food and Drug Act of 1906* and its amendment passed in 1938, the *Food, Drug, and Cosmetics Act,* dictated how drugs, foods, cosmetics, and therapeutic devices must be labeled. Conditions for safe use and any poisonous contents must be identified on the label.

- The *Federal Trade Commission Act of 1914* and its *Wheeler-Lea Amendment,* passed in 1938, held that unfair competition was not legal and that false or deceptive product labeling was an instance of unfair competition.

- The *Wool Products Labeling Act,* passed in 1940, said that clothing containing wool must be labeled to say what type of wool it contained and what percentage of each type of wool was in the product.

- The *Fur Products Labeling Act* passed in 1951 says that the type of fur used in a product must be identified with its generic name, and that the country the fur came from also must be identified.

- The *Textile Fiber Products Identification Act,* passed in 1958, held that fiber content of all clothing and all household textile products must be identified with a generic description.

- The *Fair Packaging and Labeling Act*, passed in 1966, set mandatory labeling requirements, gave industries the chance to adopt packaging standards that would cut down on the wide variety of weights and measures used, and gave the Food and Drug Administration (FDA) and the Federal Trade Commission (FTC) the right to set packaging regulations when it was determined to be necessary.

In addition to these regulations, the FDA has set labeling standards for processed foods, requiring that their nutritional content be disclosed on product labels. This information must clearly include the amount of protein, fat, carbohydrates, and calories that the product in the package contains. Vitamin and mineral content is expressed as a percentage of recommended daily allowance. The ingredients in the product are listed in order (from greatest to least amount), according to how much of the ingredient is included in the packaged product.

In 1962, a federal law was passed requiring that, in addition to brand names, the generic names of prescription and nonprescription drugs must be prominently displayed in both the advertising and the labels for those drugs. And a law passed in 1977 made it mandatory that the ingredients in cosmetics be listed on the product label.

Warranties

Warranties are designed to give the customer some affirmation that, should a product or service not meet reasonable expectations, he or she will have some recourse. There are two basic types of warranties, as follows:

- *Express warranties.* Traditionally, warranties expressed in written or verbal form were the only ones recognized by courts.

- *Implied warranties.* In an effort to protect customers, particularly in the area of product liability, and as a response to customer complaints, courts have begun also to recognize implied warranties— those that are suggested by the manufacturer but not explicitly stated.

The *Magnuson-Moss Consumer Product Warranty-Federal Trade Commission Improvement Act*, passed in 1975, attempts to improve consumers' rights by insisting that warranties be both comprehensive and comprehensible, so that the consumer is protected and can compare the warranty with warranties of competing brands. Under the provisions of the act, the FTC has the authority to establish rules for warrantied products costing more than $5.

Case Study

Trademark Licensing to Gain Recognition—The Natural Choice

Natural Choice Industries, Inc., had a marketing problem. Founded in 1981, the company was selling just over $5 million worth of fruit juices (averaging just over a 2 percent market share on lemonades and powder mixes) and snack-food items by the end of its fourth year in business. But the powdered-drink industry in the United States alone amounts to more than $800 million in sales a year. How could a small company like Natural Choice compete?

The mainstay of Natural Choice's business—its bread and butter—is supplying generic brands of juices to retailers who can put their own labels on the product. The result has been not only added sales for Natural Choice products but also development of a distribution network of stores willing to stock Natural Choice's own brands.

Rather than take on the entire United States, Natural Choice decided to sell its product in the larger fruit juice markets in the country. By 1986, it had moved its product into eight states—Illinois, Michigan, New York, New Jersey, Pennsylvania, Iowa, Minnesota, and California.

But introducing its own brands in addition to the generic brands it supplied was problematic. The cost of introducing a new brand to the national market and making it into a national brand, the company's founders reasoned, could cost upward of $25 to $50 million, money that Natural Choice did not want to commit to one product. What would happen if the product were not accepted? If it had sunk all its marketing dollars into this one product, the company would be devastated.

Instead, Natural Choice decided to buy license to the trademarks of nationally known cartoon characters and to attach them to its own brand of juices. By paying a fee to the owners of the trademarks, Natural Choice acquired the right to place the characters and their names on the juice labels. Rather than starting from scratch to build national recognition, Natural Choice won instant recognition for its products by using characters such as Pink Panther and Tom and Jerry (licensed from MGM–United Artists), and Popeye (licensed from King Features Syndicate).

To introduce its new products using nationally known trademark characters, Natural Choice plans to spend $2.5 to $5 million to introduce the product nationally. Natural Choice hopes to grow to a $50 million company by its tenth year in business. The strategy is to continue to manufacture products that successfully meet market demand and to consistently introduce new products to the market.

The company figures that half of its product mix will be year-to-year products—those that have stuck nationally.

Even the cost of introducing a product using a nationally known trademarked character is expensive for a small company like Natural Choice. But the company's management reasoned that this strategy was the only way a company of its size could compete and succeed in the marketplace.

Adapted from Jeffrey L. Seglin, *America's New Breed of Entrepreneurs*, Acropolis Books, Washington, D.C., 1986, pp. 245–249.

CASE REVIEW

1. Why is the $2.5 to $5 million Natural Choice is spending to introduce a new product by using a nationally known trademark a good investment?

2. Why would a trademarked product be more attractive to an audience than a generic brand?

Lesson Seven Questions

1. What is a product?

2. What are unique products?

3. What are parity products?

4. What are augmented products?

5. What are the six steps of product development?

6. What are the five categories of product adopters?

7. What is a product line?

8. What makes up a product mix?

9. What are the four periods of a product's life cycle?

10. What is a brand?

6
Pricing

Price, value, and *utility* are related economic concepts.

- *Utility* is the feature of a product or service that gives it the ability to satisfy a customer's want or need. (As discussed in Chapter 1, marketing creates four types of utilities—time, place, possession, and image utility—as well as helping to support form utility.)
- *Value* is a quantitative measure of the product's or service's worth, in terms of its ability to attract something in exchange for it. Usually value is determined in terms of money.
- *Price* is what some individual or organization pays for a product or service. It is the monetary value of a product or service that is set when its utility and value have been determined. It is usually expressed in money terms—dollars and cents in the United States, other denominations in other countries.

Price is one of the four elements (the four P's, as discussed in Chapter 4) of the marketing mix. It is intricately related to the other three elements—product, promotion, and place (distribution). A customer pays a given price for a specific product that has been promoted in a particular way and distributed through a particular channel of distribution. If any elements of the marketing mix change, the price must be evaluated to determine whether it must change as well.

Establishing Price

When a company goes about setting a price for a product, it may use a variety of approaches. Companies will draw from such approaches as those listed below.

- *Cost-plus approach.*   Prices are based on the cost of producing the product plus a desired profit. *Break-even analysis* is a variation of the cost-plus approach.

- *Supply and demand approach.*   Prices are based on estimates of how much market demand there will be for the product, as well as how much of the product will be available. The costs of marketing and production must be determined, in order to use this approach.

- *Competitive pricing approach.*   Prices are based on what competitors are charging for their products or services. When a firm enters the market with a product or service, it may simply match the *market price* that has already been established in the marketplace.

Other factors that should be considered when setting a price include such items as company pricing objectives, marketing mix strategy, possible competitive reactions, pricing strategies, and pricing policies.

After these factors are considered by a company, the actual price can be set. Companies do not have to go step by step through these factors, but at some level of the price-setting decision-making process, they should consider every factor.

Cost-Plus Pricing

Cost-plus pricing is used to establish price based on the cost of producing a product or delivering a service plus a desired amount of profit.

For example, consider that a cabinetmaker builds 10 chests of drawers, incurring a building cost of $5000, plus additional expenses of $250. On this total cost of $5250, the cabinetmaker wants to achieve a profit of 25 percent. The cost plus the desired profit add up to $6562.50. As a result of these findings, the cabinetmaker prices each chest of drawers at $656.25.

Cost-Plus Pricing by Middlemen.   Middlemen—wholesalers and retailers—will often use cost-plus pricing. Retailers, for example, will pay a set price for goods to be delivered to their stores. This is their cost. They will then add on a *markup,* an amount sufficient to cover the costs of selling the goods plus a desired profit. Many retailers will attempt to simplify accounting and bookkeeping by adding the same percentage markup to all goods acquired to be sold. This *average markup* has historically yielded enough money to cover costs of goods and return a desired profit.

Different types of retailers may use different percentage markups, depending on the services they provide, even if they are offering similar goods. Filene's Basement in Boston, for example, a self-service retail clothing outlet featuring tables and racks of off-price clothing, has lower costs and may require a lower markup on goods than would Louis of Boston, a high-fashion, high-service men's clothing store.

Markups are usually given in percentage terms, as a percentage of either the cost of the product or the selling price of the product. To avoid confusion and potential misunderstandings, when expressing markup percentages, the base for the markup—the cost or the selling price—must be made clear. There is quite a difference between a 60 percent markup based on cost and a 60 percent markup based on selling price.

In calculating markup percentages, the basic formula is that the markup percentage will equal the dollar markup divided by either the cost or the selling price of the product, depending on which is used as the base. The formula for calculating markup percentage looks like this:

$$\text{Markup \%} = \frac{\text{dollar markup}}{\text{cost}}$$

or like this:

$$\text{Markup \%} = \frac{\text{dollar markup}}{\text{selling price}}$$

Drawbacks to Cost-Plus Pricing. While cost-plus pricing is a simple method to use in establishing price, it is not without its drawbacks. Critics argue that the cost of goods is certainly a floor upon which a price should begin, but that costs are not the only factors to consider. Using just costs to determine price does not take into account market demand or competitive forces in the industry. Even if a company is fortunate enough to attract a market for goods priced with a cost-plus pricing method, it is possible that had market demand been taken into account, the retailer could have priced the goods higher and achieved a more profitable return.

While the cabinetmaker in the example above used a simple method to arrive at a price, the drawback to this method is the failure to consider that there are different types of costs that might affect the overall unit cost of the product, depending on how many units can be sold. The pricing method the cabinetmaker is using assumes that all the chests will be sold. If not all the chests are sold—market demand may not be as great as anticipated—the unit price will have to be raised in order to cover production costs and meet the desired profit goals.

The cost-plus pricing method, however, is a safe approach because it is a simple way to set company pricing policy and it assures a set amount of profit.

Cost Factors

Market demand and competition may dictate how high a business sets its prices, but costs certainly act as a floor below which a business cannot price its goods and expect to stay in business for long.

Most businesses have several kinds of costs that can be directly or indirectly tied to a unit of output. Costs can also be fixed or variable.

Direct costs that can be traced directly to a unit of product output include such items as labor, raw materials, and sales commissions.

Indirect costs that cannot be traced directly to a unit of product output include such things as production machinery maintenance, rent on a production facility, depreciation on an owned building, research and development, and the costs of maintaining a sales office.

Both direct and indirect costs depend on the production process.

Variable costs increase or decrease depending on the number of product units sold. *Fixed costs* exist whether or not any product units are sold. Most frequently, direct costs are variable costs, while indirect costs are fixed.

Break-Even Analysis

A business can use information about fixed and variable costs, product units produced, and projected sales revenue to determine what the *break-even point* will be on a product—when the revenue it earns will equal the total costs that have been incurred, assuming a given selling price. This technique, called *break-even analysis*, can be used to further project profits that a business will realize after it has passed its break-even point. The business loses money on sales until it reaches the break-even point.

Determining the Break-Even Point

To find the break-even point on a product, the following formula can be used:

$$\text{Break-even point in product units} = \frac{\text{total fixed costs}}{\text{unit contribution to overhead}}$$

$$= \frac{\text{total fixed costs}}{\text{selling price} - \text{average variable cost}}$$

The formula makes the assumption that the total fixed costs remain constant. Because fixed costs actually do not remain constant over the entire life of the product (raw material and labor prices may go up, for example), businesses do a break-even analysis, using various projected total fixed costs to determine the break-even analysis as the product matures. The break-even formula also assumes that the average variable costs will be constant for each unit of product produced.

Like cost-plus pricing, break-even analysis does not take into account market demand or competitive price structures at the various levels of prices. Still, it is a useful tool, enabling management to determine the break-even point on a product unit if the cost and demand factors are fairly stable.

Table 6-1 shows how to determine a break-even point, using a variety of factors.

Table 6-1. How to Compute a Break-Even Point

A Unit price	B Average variable cost per unit	C Contribution to overhead (A − B)	D Overhead (total fixed costs)	E Break-even point (D ÷ C)
$ 50	$25	$ 25	$300	12 units
75	25	50	300	6
100	25	75	300	4
125	25	100	300	3

Pricing Objectives

The pricing objectives that a business sets should mesh well with the management and marketing goals that management has set for the company. Pricing objectives can fit into a number of broad categories, including:

- Profit-oriented goals

- Sales-oriented goals
- Goals designed to meet the status quo

Profit-Oriented Goals

If a business decides it wants to get the maximum profit return it can possibly get, or to meet a target profit return on the expenses it has incurred in manufacturing the product, its goals are centered on profit generation. Profit-generating pricing strategies can be used to meet short- or long-term goals.

Target Return Approach. Middlemen and manufacturers both may have the objective of pricing products or services so that they earn a desired percentage return on their investment in the product or service.

Many middlemen use *target return net sales* as a short-term pricing strategy. They use a percentage markup to price a product, and set the markup so that it will cover anticipated costs and generate a profit for the time period. The percentage of profit may remain constant, but the dollars generated will vary according to how many product units are sold.

Target return pricing is essentially a method of cost-plus pricing and, as such, fails to take into effect variables like market demand and competitive pricing structures. Larger firms which are leaders in their respective industries are more likely than smaller businesses to use a target return-on-investment approach, since their pricing decisions are not greatly affected by their smaller competitors.

Maximize Profits. Pricing to achieve maximum profits is perhaps the most common goal of companies. If profits get too high because of small supplies and large demand, however, economic theory suggests that new capital will be attracted to the marketplace to add to the level of supply. Ultimately, profits will drop off to less frenzied levels.

A goal of maximizing profits works best as a long-term goal. To commit to this strategy, businesses will sometimes be willing to absorb short-term losses. If a business wants to enter a new market with its products, it may benefit in the long run from offering its goods at a low price to attract a customer base. The profit-maximizing goal should be viewed as a strategy for a business's overall product line. Occasionally a business is willing to take a loss on one product to get potential customers interested in other products in the line.

Sales-Oriented Goals

Some businesses price their products with the goal of achieving a set sales volume or market share.

The sales volume percentage increase desired is usually set over a specified period of time—perhaps 1, 3, or 5 years. Sometimes sales-oriented goals run counter to profit-oriented goals. A business may decide, for example, to take a short-term loss on a product by discounting it to gain a lock on the market.

Some businesses have the goal of either maintaining or increasing their market share. Especially when the overall market is growing, a business's market share may be a better indication of its stability than its ability to meet a target return on its investment in a product. Businesses must stay aware of the market as it grows to make sure they maintain their desired market share. If they lose sight of the growth of the market, their share of it could slip away.

Pricing to attract market share is particularly common among manufacturers of consumer packaged goods. Data on market usage and market share is readily available from outside sources.

Status Quo Goals

Pricing goals that fit into the general category of meeting the status quo in the market are less aggressive than profit- or sales-oriented goals. Status quo pricing goals include the following:

- *Price stabilization.* When a large company is a leader in its industry and its product is relatively common, it sometimes seeks to achieve a stable price for its products. Either it or another industry leader will raise or lower prices when it becomes necessary, and other firms will follow suit. Smaller firms typically follow the lead of industry leaders in raising or lowering prices.

  By stabilizing prices, companies set prices that are not so high or low that they will face reprisals from competitors. Reprisals could trigger a price war, in which companies begin to battle each other by offering competing products at lower and lower prices. As a result, companies involved in the price war suffer in their earnings. Price stabilization is used in an attempt to avoid price wars.

- *Meeting competition's prices.* In a number of industries in which products are standardized and industry leaders are established, many firms simply set their prices according to whatever their competitors are charging for the product. Meeting the market price is one of the most common methods of pricing products and services.

Determining Demand

Costs and a desired profit alone cannot be the sole factors a marketing professional uses to establish price. *Market demand* must be used to determine the top levels at which businesses can price their products or services. Estimating market demand is a lot easier for products that are established than for those that are new to the market. Businesses cannot price their products or services higher than potential customers are willing to pay.

Demand is measured as the total amount of product or service bought (in monetary amount or units sold) in a given time period. For marketing professionals to be effective, they must attempt to grasp what market demand for a product or service will be in the future. The future market demand will be affected by a number of factors, among which are how the business uses its marketing mix and what the market and competitive conditions are at the time.

When a business introduces a new product to the marketplace, it is particularly difficult to estimate market demand and establish an appropriate price. But marketing professionals *must* estimate market demand for a product over time.

The volume of sales for a product is most frequently affected by its price: if the price is too high, not as many units of the product will be sold. Before the price can be set, costs must be determined. In large part because of economies of scale, these costs tend to go down as more units of the product are produced.

Gauging Customer Reaction

One method of determining probable demand for a product or service is to conduct *market research*. Potential customers can be asked how likely they are to purchase the product or service at various prices. Potential customers can also be asked what they think the price for the product or service should be.

Marketing professionals can analyze the results of the research to determine whether there appears to be sufficient demand for the product. If the results of the research suggest that customers would be unwilling or hesitant to buy the product at the business's cost-plus price, the company may decide not to introduce the product or service at that time because of insufficient demand, or the product or service may be enhanced to cause its value, as perceived by the target market, to rise.

On the flip side, if the customer shows little or no resistance to the company's projected cost-plus price range, the company may reevaluate the situation, to see whether it is setting too low a price for the product or service.

What Is the Expected Price?

The *expected price* for a product or service reflects the value that potential customers place on that product or service. It is the price the potential customer expects to pay for such goods and services. In market research, potential customers typically will express a range into which they expect the price for a product or service to fall.

Businesses also rely on the reaction of their middlemen—wholesalers or retailers—to the expected price of a product. If the price is considered inappropriate, middlemen may not support the product as much as they would a more appropriately priced product. Because of their experience with similar products, middlemen are often able to give a good reading on what an acceptable price among potential customers would be. Industrial-product producers, for example, may canvass potential customers' engineers by showing them prototypes or blueprints for new products and asking their opinions about appropriate price levels.

Businesses may also use the market research technique of *test marketing* to determine appropriate demand. By testing the product in a few market segments and offering it at a variety of prices, the business can get a feel for an appropriate price range for a product.

Sellers may also design a computerized model that they can use to simulate market conditions and sales responses at a variety of prices.

Demand Curves

Demand curves depict the effect on demand of raising and lowering prices. A positively sloped demand curve suggests that, as prices rise, demand increases. A negatively sloped demand curve suggests that, as prices rise, demand decreases.

Businesses sometimes set the prices on their products too low. Sales may be off if the market expects to pay more for a product than the business is charging. The situation in which a business raises its prices and finds that sales increase is called *inverse demand*: as the price is increased, there is also an increase in the units of product sold. Once a product reaches an appropriate price level, inverse demand stops and the usual demand curve begins. At this point, demand begins to go down as prices go up.

Knowing the Shape of the Demand Curve. Because many businesses have difficulty in determining their *marginal costs* (the cost of selling an additional product unit) and *marginal revenues* (the income received from the sale of the last product unit, referred to as the "marginal unit"), one of the biggest problems they have in setting prices is that they do not know the shape of the demand curve for the product they are offering. Companies that find testing different prices cost-prohibitive because they produce very expensive products face the problem of not knowing the demand curve for their product. Companies producing less expensive consumer goods more often find it affordable to test their products at various price levels to determine demand.

Elasticity of Demand. Changes in prices affect the demand for different products differently. A slight increase or decrease in the price of one product may cause a dramatic increase in demand, while changes in the price of another product may have little or no impact on demand.

Elasticity measures the change in total revenue (price multiplied by the number of product units purchased) that results from a change in the price of a product. By estimating what the total sales revenue will be at a given price, the seller effectively determines the demand curve for a product and its demand elasticity. (The seller can also use these estimates of sales to determine the break-even point on a product.)

Demand for a product is said to be *elastic* when reducing the product's unit price would cause an increase in total revenue or raising the unit price would cause a decrease in total revenue.

Demand for a product is said to be *inelastic* when a cut in the price would cause total revenues to decline or raising the price would result in an increase in total revenue.

An elastic demand curve is illustrated in Figure 6-1. At $9 per unit, 75 units are sold and total revenue amounts to $675. When the price is lowered to $8 per unit, the quantity sold rises to 115 units, and the total revenues increase to $920. But when the unit price is raised to $10 per unit, the number of units sold decreases to 50 units, and total revenue decreases to $500.

An inelastic demand curve is illustrated in Figure 6-2. Again the unit is introduced at a price of $9 per unit and the total number of units sold amounts to 75, with a total revenue of $675. When the unit price is lowered to $8, the the quantity sold increases to 80 units. This increase in the quantity of units sold is not enough, however, to offset the cut in

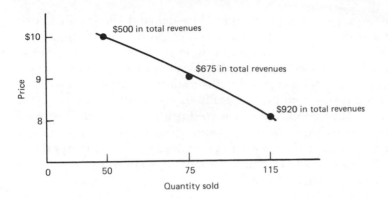

Figure 6-1. Elastic demand curve.

price, reflected in the fact that total revenues decline to $640. When the unit price is raised to $10, the quantity sold decreases to 70 units. But this increase in price does offset the number of units sold, as reflected in the total revenue increase to $700.

A formula that can be used to determine the elasticity of demand is:

$$\text{Elasticity} = \frac{\text{percentage change in quantity demanded}}{\text{percentage change in price}}$$

If the result is 1, than the product is said to have *unit elasticity*. If it is greater than 1, demand is elastic, because the total revenue has increased. When the result is less than 1, demand is inelastic, as reflected in the decrease in total revenue.

A market's sensitivity to the price change of a product is not always known. But when it can be determined, it can be useful to help in pre-

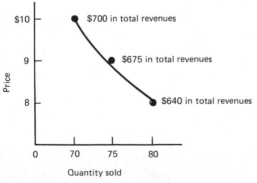

Figure 6-2. Inelastic demand curve.

dicting the impact of pricing changes. The demand for products that are considered necessities (e.g., salt; electric, gas, or oil heating; gasoline) is typically inelastic. If the price of these products goes up or down, the total number of units sold typically does not change all that much. The demand for products that are not considered necessities (e.g., cars, furniture, expensive clothing) is typically more elastic.

For example, lamb chops are considered price-elastic because, even if people prefer lamb chops, cheaper substitutes such as chicken and hamburger are available. If the price of lamb chops increases, the percentage of the decrease in the quantity demanded is apt to be larger than that of the price increase. If the price decreases, the percentage of the increase in the quantity demanded is apt to be larger than that of the price decrease.

Lesson Eight Questions

1. What is price?
2. What is value?
3. What is the supply-and-demand approach to pricing?
4. What is the competitive approach to pricing?
5. Using the cost-plus pricing method, how much would you charge for each unit of a product if your total cost for producing 2000 units was $11,000 and you wanted a 30 percent profit?
6. What is the break-even point on a product?
7. How is demand measured?
8. What does a positively sloped demand curve show? A negatively sloped demand curve?
9. What is inverse demand?
10. What does elasticity measure? When is demand for a product considered to be elastic? Inelastic?

Evaluating Competitors' Prices

Competitors' prices often play a large role in how a company decides to set its own prices. If a price is too much higher than a competitor's, attracting a market share will be difficult; if it is too much lower, a price war may break out, resulting in lower profit margins for both the low pricer and the competitor. The result may be losses for both companies.

When a company puts a product on the market, it usually attempts to compete in a high-, medium-, or low-priced range. Within these ranges, companies compete with one another. A company's prices usually hit some midpoint or average level within each price range. The more established businesses with a higher percentage of market share tend to price at the high end of each of these ranges. As these leaders raise and lower their prices in response to demand or costs, other companies with products in that price range tend to follow suit. When a new company is trying to gain market share, it may price its products aggressively. When this happens, companies within that range have to decide whether or not to respond to the cut in price.

Whether or not a company should respond to a competitor's price cuts depends on a variety of factors, including:

- *Price sensitivity.* When customers' preference for a particular brand of product is not strong enough to keep them from switching to another similar product in response to a price cut, the product is price-sensitive. Such products usually are standard products that are viewed as interchangeable—e.g., gasoline, salt, batteries. On the other hand, when customers will not readily switch from a brand of product, even in response to a price cut, that product has low price sensitivity. These brands are typically quite distinctive, or have qualities that cause customers to build up personal loyalty to the product.

- *Market position.* When a business has a very strong market share, it is not as likely to have to respond to a competitor's price cuts, particularly if one of the weaker competitors in the market makes the price change. A company holding a high percentage market share has the luxury of deciding to hold steady on prices and waiting to see how the market responds to a weaker competitor's cuts. If a leading company makes the price cut, however, the weaker company with a poorer position in the market may have no choice but to cut prices.

- *Price segments served.* In the low- and medium-priced segments of the market, the market may respond more to price than in the higher segments of the market where customers are typically more concerned with the image of the product or its style.

- *Product differentiation.* Typically, producers of commodity-type products must follow the price trends in the industry. The only way providers of this type of product can stray from the prevailing price is to differentiate their products with additional services. Manufactured products may be differentiated by offering special services and en-

hanced designs. Advertising can also be used to differentiate manufactured products. Products that can be highly differentiated are
likely to be least affected by the prices of competing brands.

Types of Competition

Oligopolies.   An *oligopoly* exists when a few product sellers control all
or almost all of the supply of a particular product. These leading companies will protect their market-share position by moving in concert
with one another on price cuts and increases. In an oligopoly, the pressure to respond to price cuts is strong. Because each company in an oligopoly knows that other companies will respond to price cuts, use of
price cuts to gain market share is not very effective.

When costs or market demands change in an oligopoly, price increases or cuts usually are relatively easy to make. The leading company
may decide to change its prices. If it has made the right choice in terms
of demand, others will follow. If other leaders in the oligopoly disagree
with the price change and hold their prices steady, however, the leader
who changed prices may have to rescind its move and set its product
price back at competitive levels within the market.

When a price is raised above the prevailing market level, a sharp drop
in revenues can result. The result is a *kinked demand curve* for that seller's products. To maximize profits, a business in an oligopoly must
price its products at market level. If its goods are priced above market
level, revenues will drop off sharply at some point where demand becomes elastic.

Monopolistic   Competition. *Monopolistic   competition* (sometimes
called "imperfect competition") occurs when there are many sellers for
a product but each tries to differentiate itself enough to give the appearance of offering a product unique in the marketplace. Since their
products are highly differentiated or the companies themselves are separated by geographical distances, these companies do not necessarily
gain or lose market share because of a competitor's price cuts or increases.

Nonprice Options in Response to
Competitors' Pricing

Many companies choose not to respond to competitors' price cuts because, if they responded, their profit margins would shrivel up, and also
because they have in the past often found it difficult to raise prices at a

later date when market conditions changed. Rather than slash prices, companies may decide to use more advertising or provide enhanced service for their products. Once they have exhausted these nonprice options, however, ultimately they may *have* to cut their prices to meet competitors' price cuts.

Quality and Service. When quality and service are not important to potential customers, companies face increased pressure to meet competitors' price cuts. In industrial markets in which products are purchased according to rigid specifications set by government or industry—e.g., lubricating oil, typewriter paper—quality and service are not always major factors in purchasing decisions. As long as the products meet specifications and are delivered when they are supposed to be, industrial customers usually will opt for the lowest available prices.

But for some consumer and industrial goods, quality and service are the major factors (often more important than price) affecting a purchase decision. When health (e.g., hospital equipment), safety (e.g., parachutes), or production (e.g., reliable factory line equipment) issues are at stake, buyers will often weigh quality and service heavily in making purchases. Once a buyer has identified the product or service providers that offer the quality or service level desired, price then may affect the decision-making process about which product to purchase.

Pricing Below or Above Competitive Levels

Discount retailers will often make a conscious decision to price their products below prevailing market levels set by competitors. Usually these retailers are aiming to sell a high volume of low-markup goods in a low-service setting.

When a product producer or retailer reaches a perceived level of prestige in its market, it may decide to charge prices above competitive market levels. Products offered in this context are usually easily distinguished from competitors' products.

Pricing Strategies

A company can pick and choose from a smorgasbord of pricing strategies. Some of the more common of these techniques are skimming, penetration pricing, unit pricing, price lining, leader pricing, bait-and-switch pricing, psychological pricing, and discount pricing. These techniques are described below.

Skimming

Pricing a product high in the expected price range is called *skimming*. This strategy is used frequently when a new product is introduced because a company hopes to quickly recover the money it invested in development costs. If the product is unique, the skimming strategy usually is effective upon initial introduction of the new product because there will be relatively little competition. Since it will take competitors a while to put a matching product on the market, the product innovator can enjoy being alone on the market for some time.

Initially the seller can attract market segments that want the product (e.g., early adopters) and are not price-sensitive. Skimming is used primarily with new products on the market and very often with either consumer or industrial high-technology products. In the market for these products there are often customers who want the product enough to pay almost any price for it. If the company wants to target a higher end of the market, the early stages of the product's life cycle is generally a good period in which to do this.

As competitors introduce their competing products, the initial producer may then decide to lower its prices to attract other market segments. Competitors often will come in under the product originator's price simply to capture a share of the market.

Price skimming gives companies a mechanism whereby they can make correctable mistakes in pricing. If a company introduces a product that is priced too high, it can lower its price to attract an audience. But if the company has introduced the product at too low a price, it may be difficult (because of market resistance) to raise the initial price to cover product and marketing costs.

Price skimming is also a strategy companies can use to keep initial demand for their products manageable until their production capabilities are enhanced to keep up with a larger demand.

Penetration

Penetration pricing is the antithesis to skimming. It is the strategy of setting a low initial price on a product, with the objective of immediately reaching the mass market. Companies will also use penetration later in a product's life cycle to reach the mass market.

When the product has an elastic demand and intense competition is likely to occur, penetration pricing is frequently a more effective strategy than skimming. Low initial pricing may give a company a strong hold on market share that competitors will find difficult to break. It may also cause potential competitors not to enter the market since they may not be able to make their desired profit margins if they match the low initial price.

Penetration pricing is more likely to be used for non-high-technology products that are easily imitated by competitors, such as:

- Food products
- Financial services products
- Clothing products

The disadvantages of penetration pricing are that:

1. A business has to sell more units to reach the break-even point on a product than when using a skimming strategy.
2. A business must commit money to fully develop production of the product before it knows whether or not the product will be accepted by the mass market.

Unit Pricing

Unit pricing is a pricing strategy used by retailers to report price information. While the practice of unit pricing has been used chiefly by supermarkets to report the unit cost of goods per pound, gallon, or some other standard measurement, it is adaptable to other businesses as well. For example, the owners of Happy Harry's Bottle Shop, a wine and spirits store in Grand Forks, North Dakota, decided that when the liquor industry went to metric measurements, comparison shopping was too confusing for the consumer. In 1979, it became the first shop of its kind to unit-price its products on the shelves, showing price per ounce for each product.

The practice of unit pricing grew out of consumers' confusion, resulting from the massive variety of packaging for similar products. It became increasingly difficult to comparison shop for goods, particularly groceries. To combat the confusion, unit pricing (on a label on the shelf holding the product) displays not only the product's package price but a price in some measurement that allows comparison with similar products. What unit pricing cannot do, of course, is to allow the consumer to compare the quality of products.

Pricing Lining

In *pricing lining*, a strategy used by some retailers, a set number of price categories is chosen and then all goods sold by the particular retailer are priced within those categories. A clothing store may offer dresses for $29.95, $49.95, and $69.95, for example. Or consider the example of Larry Smith and Morrie Dym, who started the $5 Clothing Store in southern California in 1981. Every piece of clothing the partners sell in their 30 west coast stores costs $5. By 1987, the partners were grossing around $20 million in sales.

The concept of pricing lining attempts to simplify consumers' buying decisions and to help retailers make inventory purchasing decisions. If prices for goods remain stable, the retailer can continue to offer the same goods within the price categories. If prices for goods rise too much, the retailer may face lessened profit margins and be forced to look for other goods to fit within its pricing lining categories. When these sources are exhausted or market conditions change enough to warrant it, the retailer using the pricing-lining strategy may be forced to abandon the strategy (witness the demise of the five-and-dime store that could offer goods for a nickel or a dime) or to raise its price categories.

Leader Pricing

The *leader pricing* strategy involves a retailer's cutting the prices of a handful of popular items to attract customers. The items offered at special prices are called "loss leaders." The strategy holds that customers will come into the store to buy the advertised loss leader and then will buy nonsale items as well. As a result, the retailer hopes to experience an overall increase in sales volume as well as an increase in net profits.

Many states have laws regulating leader pricing. These laws typically insist that a retailer not sell a product below invoice cost of the product plus freight costs and a required minimum markup, usually 2 percent for wholesale and 6 percent for retail.

Bait-and-Switch Pricing

Bait-and-switch pricing can be viewed as leader pricing gone bad. Retailers will advertise a low-priced product at the low end of a line of products. Customers who consider purchasing this product are given the pitch that it's not a good purchase, and that the product they should really buy is the expensive one in the product line. A good number of customers will ultimately buy the higher-priced model.

In leader pricing, retailers expect that they will sell a number of advertised sale items. The Federal Trade Commission has made it illegal for retail stores operating in many states to continuously employ the bait-and-switch strategy. However, the FTC has no control over retail stores operating in only one state.

Psychological Pricing Strategies

Perception plays an important role in customers' buying decisions. Often price may influence a buying decision because the price, more than the product itself, will indicate something to a customer or to others who see the customer with the product.

Prestige Pricing.   Use of high prices to suggest that a product or service is of high quality is called *prestige pricing*. The high price not only suggests superior quality but also gives the purchaser of the product the prestige of owning it. Examples of such products include:

Rolex watches

Gucci luggage

Lincoln town cars

Ferraris

Odd-Even Pricing.   A strategy employed by some companies is *odd-even pricing*. Retail consumer companies in particular often price their goods with prices ending in an odd number, because they believe consumers will respond more favorably to such prices. Some studies indicate that four out of five products sold in retail stores feature prices ending in a 5 or a 9. Retailers believe that potential customers will respond more favorably to 79 cents than to 80 cents, and more favorably to $59.95 than to $60 because the first prices in each category are perceived as being much less. Theoretically, instead of scrutinizing the entire price, the customer will react mostly to the first number on the price tag.

There are no studies that conclusively show that prices ending in odd numbers increase the units of product sold or the overall sales volume of a retailer. Even so, the strategy is widely used.

Discounts

Often companies will offer *discounts* or *allowances* off the *base price* (the list price or the unit price of a product where it is produced or resold). These discounts will most often be offered on the condition that a specific quantity is purchased, that cash is paid, or that the buyer does some marketing services for the product provider.

Quantity Discounts.   When sellers want to get potential buyers to buy large amounts of product, they will often offer *quantity discounts* off the list price of the product. Such a discount can be based on the unit or dollar size of the buyer's purchase.

Industrial product companies are big users of quantity discounts. The discount may reflect some of the economies of scale the seller can use in shipping large orders. Quantity discounts might also result in buyers' keeping larger inventory of products, thus reducing inventory costs for sellers.

A *noncumulative discount* is based on a one-time order for a quantity of a product. This discount strategy encourages large orders.

A *cumulative discount* is based on the total volume purchased by a buyer over an agreed-upon period of time. The strategy is used to build a relationship between buyer and seller in which the buyer becomes closely dependent upon the seller. By buying more, the customer gets more of a discount.

Trade Discounts.   *Trade discounts* (also called "functional discounts") are given to buyers who perform some type of marketing service for the seller.

A product manufacturer, for example, could quote a wholesaler a retail list price of $750 with trade discounts of 45 percent and 10 percent. This would mean that the retailer would pay the wholesaler $412.50 ($750 minus 45 percent) and a wholesaler would pay the manufacturer $371.25 ($412.50 minus 10 percent). It works like this:

1. The product manufacturer gives the 45 and 10 percent discounts to the wholesaler.

2. The wholesaler passes the 45 percent discount on to the retailer and keeps 10 percent for fulfilling the role of wholesaler.

The 45 and 10 percent trade discounts do not add up to a total discount of 55 percent. The second portion of the trade discount is calculated on the sum remaining after the previous discount has been taken.

Cash Discounts.   A discount given to a customer for paying a bill within a specified period of time is called a *cash discount*. After trade and quantity discounts are figured and a net amount due is arrived at, a cash discount may be calculated.

For example, assume that after other discounts have been calculated, a buyer of a product owes $550. On an invoice dated January 18, the buyer is offered the terms "2/10 net 30" (sometimes written "2/10, n/30"). This means that, by paying the bill within 10 days after the invoice date (that is, by January 28), the buyer may deduct a discount of 2 percent, or $11. If the buyer does not pay the bill by January 28, the entire bill must be paid within 30 days of the invoice date (by February 17).

There are three parts to a cash discount, as follows:

1. The percentage discount being offered
2. The time frame for which the discount is offered
3. An indication of the date after which the bill becomes overdue

Within different industries there are traditional cash discount combinations.

Cash discounts are used to encourage industrial buyers to pay cash instead of using credit. For consumer goods, most companies charge customers the same amount whether they pay cash or credit, although in recent years some gasoline companies have begun to offer discounted rates to consumers who use cash instead of credit cards.

Seasonal Discounts. Firms which produce products for which the demand is high during a particular season may decide to offer a *seasonal discount* to buyers during the off season. These discounts, which might be 5, 10, or 15 percent off regular prices, serve to fulfill the following functions:

- Keep cash flow running during a company's off season.
- Run production lines more efficiently.
- Keep inventory from building up.

Forward Dating. *Forward dating* is a combination of a cash discount and a seasonal discount pricing strategy. The buyer buys and is delivered goods during the off season, but doesn't have to pay for the goods until the season begins. A manufacturer of ski jackets might decide to fill wholesale and retail orders in summer months, but date the invoice October 1, with terms of 2/10 net 30, as of October 1. If the manufacturer can keep the plant running during the summer months, production can be spread out over the year. The wholesalers and retailers do not have to pay their bills until after the season has started and they have begun to receive cash for sold merchandise.

Geographic Factors in Pricing

When pricing goods, sellers have to figure the cost of delivery of goods to a buyer. A number of delivery cost arrangements are possible, including the following:

- The seller pays all costs.
- The buyer pays all costs.
- The two parties split the costs.

FOB Point-of-Production Pricing

In *FOB (free-on-board) point-of-production pricing*, the buyer pays all the transportation costs. The seller quotes the buyer a selling price from the point of production. This practice is also called either "FOB mill pricing" or "FOB factory pricing." With this method of pricing, the seller pays only the expense of loading the product to be shipped to the buyer.

For the seller using the FOB pricing strategy, the same net profit is realized for all sales of similar numbers of goods. The buyer's price will depend upon the added delivery costs.

The FOB pricing strategy can have distinct marketing implications for a company, since it makes it difficult for competing firms outside the region to offer the same rates as a firm inside a region. It also limits the probability that a company's marketing efforts will be successful if the buyer is far away from the region where the products originate.

Uniform-Delivered Pricing

The *uniform-delivered pricing* (sometimes called "postage stamp pricing") strategy is one that quotes the same delivered price to all purchasers regardless of where they are located and what actual shippings are. The sellers' net revenues will vary for each sale, depending upon the transportation charges for delivery of the product.

Uniform-delivered pricing is often used when the transportation cost of delivering a product accounts for only a small portion of the costs of that product. Some retailers use uniform-delivered pricing as a service to their customers in an effort to strengthen their position in the market.

Zone-Delivered Pricing

A *zone-delivered pricing* strategy divides the market in which a seller sells goods into broad regional categories. Within each of these categories the same charge is made for delivery. The price results from use of an averaged cost for all the deliveries to buyers in that region.

Freight Absorption Pricing

Using a *freight absorption pricing* strategy, a seller will quote a product price plus a delivery cost that equals whatever a competitor located nearest to the buyer would charge. Sellers will often use this strategy to try to penetrate a distant market more deeply. As long as sellers' net revenues exceed marginal costs for the product units, they can continue to expand their geographic markets.

Federal Legislation Affecting Pricing

There are many federal regulations affecting pricing. Among the major ones are:

- *Sherman Antitrust Act (1890).* This act made illegal any monopolies, combinations of firms, or any collusion among firms that results in restraint of trade in interstate commerce. When manufacturers, wholesalers, or retailers are involved in interstate commerce, they must adhere to this law. One of the effects of the act was the ban on price fixing.

- *Federal Trade Commission Act (1914).* By this act, the FTC was established as a federal agency to administer the laws designed to protect consumers from unfair competition and promote legal competition. The act prohibited unfair competition.

- *Clayton Antitrust Act (1914).* This act was designed to prohibit discrimination in pricing that could injure competition. Among its restrictions are interlocking boards of directors, tying contracts (in which a manufacturer agrees to sell one product to a middleman only if the middleman will agree to buy another—perhaps undesired—product from the manufacturer), and exclusive dealing (in which a manufacturer forbids its retailers from carrying competing products). The Clayton Antitrust Act was passed because the general wording of the Sherman Antitrust Act made it difficult to enforce. Congress passed the Clayton Antitrust Act to more specifically address the practices it believed led to the creation of monopolies.

- *Robinson-Patman Act (1936).* This act was passed to amend the Clayton Antitrust Act in an effort to strengthen the laws forbidding discrimination in pricing that injured competition. The Robinson-Patman Act held that all price differences must be justified. Price discrimination, the act held, was illegal except under special situations that must be proved by the seller and included:

Grade or quality differences among products

A price difference that resulted in a difference in the cost of selling goods (e.g., selling costs or delivery costs) which would not have occurred without these costs

An attempt to meet competitive prices by lowering prices

Outdated products, which forced the seller to sell the goods at differing prices to different buyers

The Robinson-Patman Act also ruled that if sellers gave promotional materials, advertising allowances, or other services to some buyers, they had to give them proportionately to all buyers.

- *Wheeler-Lea Act (1938).* This act was an amendment to the Federal Trade Commission Act (1914). It increased the power of the FTC by making unfair, deceptive, or misleading practices illegal. The act addressed misleading advertising in particular. Prior to the Wheeler-Lea Act, the Federal Trade Commission was empowered mostly to address unfair practices between competing firms. The Wheeler-Lea Act increased that scope to encompass business' treatment of consumers.

Case Study

What Would You Pay for a Bagel?

In order for a business to reach its objective of maximizing profits on each of its products, it needs to know the shape of the demand curve for those products. When one product in a company's product line dominates the percentage of total sales, a demand curve for that product is a useful tool which can help the company determine how to price the product most profitably.

Marketing professionals can use various tools of marketing research to gather the information they need to plot the points on the demand curve.

Consider the example of a fictitious company that manufactures frozen bakery goods. We'll call the company Boonton Baked Goods. The major product in Boonton Baked Goods' product line is its frozen bagels—Boonton Bagels. Management decided to determine the demand curve for this product.

Had Boonton Baked Goods had enough money, the best marketing research approach would have been to price its bagels differently in various grocery stores in different target market segments to see how the markets responded to different prices. Management could then have gotten accurate sales records and plotted the sales volume against the various price levels to come up with a demand curve for its frozen bagel product. Clearly this would have been a good approach, agreed management, but there were also problems:

1. Such a marketing research endeavor would have been very costly.
2. Boonton Baked Goods would not have had control over which of the supermarkets that carried its products would have agreed to such a test being run in their store.
3. The company would not have been able to control the prices of competing products, ensuring that they were the same from store to store in various market segments.
4. Boonton would have had no control over the numbers or types of brands competing against its product from store to store.

Instead, Boonton Baked Goods decided that it would be more effective to run a simulated experiment. Potential customers would be shown pictures of three bagel products—Boonton Bagels, Sara Lee bagels, and Lender's bagels—stocked in a supermarket freezer case. Prices would be posted underneath each of the products in the picture. The price on the Boonton Bagels would vary from one group of respondents to another. One group would see the price at $1.09 per package, another at 99 cents, another at 89 cents, another at 79 cents, and still another at 69 cents. While these five different prices were tested for Boonton Bagels, the prices of Sara Lee bagels and Lender's bagels would remain fixed at their regular retail prices of 99 cents and 79 cents respectively. The percentage of potential customers in each group responding that they would choose Boonton Bagels was plotted against the price the group saw for the product in the picture. Figure 6-3 shows the results of the test.

Boonton Baked Goods was able to estimate the shape of the demand curve for its bagel product. Management used the results plotted on the graph to determine where the maximum profits on the product could be achieved. The results could be used to

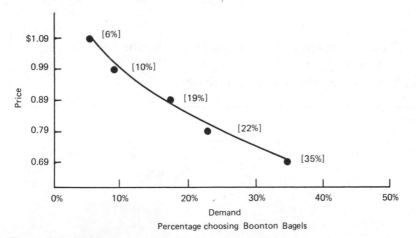

Figure 6-3. Estimating the shape of a demand curve for a product.

evaluate the best price at which to sell Boonton Bagels.

Adapted from James H. Myers, *Marketing*, McGraw-Hill, New York, 1986, pp. 328–329.

CASE REVIEW

1. What further information would you need to know to determine whether changes in the price of Boonton Bagels resulted in an elastic or an inelastic demand for the product?

2. What can Boonton Baked Goods learn from its research on the pricing of Boonton Bagels? How can this information be used as the basis for other pricing analyses of the product?

Lesson Nine Questions

1. What is an oligopoly?

2. What is monopolistic competition?

3. What is price skimming?

4. What is penetration pricing?

5. What is pricing lining?

6. What is leader pricing?

7. What is a noncumulative quantity discount? A cumulative quantity discount?

8. If a product manufacturer quoted a retailer a retail list price of $425 for goods, with trade discounts of 40 and 10 percent, how much would the retailer pay the wholesaler for the goods? How much would the wholesaler pay the product manufacturer?

9. If a buyer receives an invoice dated July 20 for $700 with an offer of terms of 3/10 net 30, what does this mean?

10. What are the three parts to a cash discount?

7
Product Distribution

One of the four P's of the marketing mix is *place*. While "place" is a convenient term to use to fit in with the alliterative phrase "product, price, place, promotion," it actually refers to the *distribution* of product—getting the product into place. Distribution is critical in getting a product to the prospective customer who might purchase it.

Channels of Distribution

Products move from producers to consumers or industrial users through *marketing channels* or *channels of distribution*. The *length* of these channels varies. If the product goes directly from a producer to an end user, for example, it is said to have a *short* or *zero-level* channel. Each time a middleman gets involved in the channel of distribution, another level is added and the channels become longer.

Distribution channels involve transferring ownership of product from producer to ultimate purchaser. While wholesalers or other middlemen never own the product, they are considered part of the marketing channel. Banks and transportation services are not included as part of the distribution channel even though often they play a role in the marketing of the product.

A distribution channel is completed when the final purchaser makes no significant alterations to the product to resell it. If the final purchaser were to change the product and then resell it, a new distribution channel would result.

When cloth is woven and then made into clothing, two separate distribution channels may be involved. The channel for the cloth may be from textile mill to broker to clothing manufacturer. The distribution channel for the finished clothing may be from clothing manufacturer to retail store to consumer.

Channel length indicates how many intermediaries are involved between the producer or manufacturer and the end user. A *short channel* would be one that involved the manufacturer distributing directly to the end user. A *medium channel* might involve the distribution of a product from manufacturer to retailer to consumer. A *long channel* would include distribution channels moving products from manufacturer to wholesaler to retailer to consumer.

Most consumer products move from the producer to the consumer through what are called *channel intermediaries*, which are typically wholesalers or retailers. Wholesalers will usually buy bulk quantities of goods to fill the demand of the retail stores they serve. A smaller percentage of consumer goods are sold directly from the product manufacturer to the ultimate consumer through direct mail, vending machines, telemarketing, or a personal sales force.

Industrial products are usually distributed to customers directly by the producer or through wholesalers who specialize in particular industrial goods.

Major Channels of Distribution

Distribution of Consumer Goods

The methods through which consumer goods can be distributed are limited only by the producer's, distributor's, or retailer's imagination. Cheryl Shuman, for one, found an innovative distribution channel for eyeglasses. Having worked at a California nursing home, Shuman called on residents to fit them for eyeglass frames. Having sensed a market need, she carried the concept further and now travels door-to-door to market eyeglass frames. She used her imagination to create a new distribution channel for a common product.

There are countless channels of distribution for consumer goods, but the five described below are most common. (See Figure 7-1.)

1. *Manufacturer or producer to consumer.* This is the shortest channel. Direct mail and direct sales are common examples of this channel. This channel is used by many catalog companies that do not sell products directly to consumers, but purchase merchandise (either outright or on consignment) to feature in their catalogs. As such, these catalog houses act as retail intermediaries. Because of rising costs, few

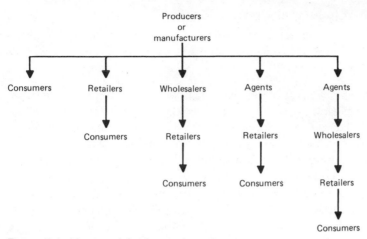

Figure 7-1. Major retail distribution channels.

manufacturers maintain their own sales forces any longer. Companies like Amway, Shaklee, or Mary Kay use sales agents who sell products and earn commissions.

2. *Manufacturer or producer to retailer to consumer.* Retailers buy directly from the manufacturer goods they can sell to consumers. Manufacturers who use this channel may:

- Own their own stores to control retail distribution. (This is called "forward vertical integration.")
- Sell directly to retailers to be able to quickly meet consumer demand.
- Sell perishable goods (foods and dairy products) to ensure freshness.

Companies like Nabisco continue to distribute directly to retailers in spite of rising costs, since it enables them to control shelf space in stores where their products are sold.

3. *Manufacturer or producer to wholesaler to retailer to consumer.* This is by far the most common and cost-efficient channel of distribution for retail consumer products (particularly for small retailers and producers).

4. *Manufacturer or producer to agent to retailer to consumer.* An agent will often be used in place of a wholesaler to reach the retail consumer market. *Food brokers* are a common example of agents that are used to reach the foodstore and supermarket market.

5. *Manufacturer or producer to agent to wholesaler to retailer to consumer.* This is the longest channel of distribution, in which the agent used by the retailer will rely on wholesalers to provide product.

Distribution of Industrial Goods

Producers or manufacturers of industrial goods use four major channels of distribution to reach industrial users, as listed below. (See Figure 7-2.)

1. *Producer or manufacturer to industrial user.* This is the most common distribution channel for industrial goods; it also accounts for the largest dollar volume of industrial goods distributed. Large items like airplanes or construction equipment are typically sold directly from the producer to the end user. This channel is also used when:

- The user is large enough to buy large quantities of goods.
- Products are made to customer specifications (e.g., computer frames manufactured by a sheet metal fabrication company).
- A manufacturer produces its products in a facility located near a high concentration of users making direct distribution convenient and affordable (e.g., a manufacturer located in the middle of a high technology region).
- The manufacturer has invested in branch warehouses to store its products, making direct delivery possible.

2. *Producer or manufacturer to industrial distributor to user.* Where there are many users or users are spread throughout the country, this channel of distribution is very common. Products that frequently move through such a channel include:

- Building supplies
- Small equipment
- Other smaller goods

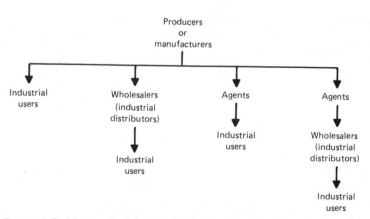

Figure 7-2. Major industrial goods distribution channels.

3. *Producer or manufacturer to agent to user.* This distribution channel is used by many industrial businesses that have no marketing department to market their goods.

4. *Producer or manufacturer to agent to industrial distributor to user.* This channel is also used when a firm does not have the facilities or personnel to sell directly to a user. If large inventories must be kept to meet industrial user demands, firms will often use this channel of distribution to handle the inventory requirements to meet that demand.

Factors Affecting Distribution

When a business establishes its channels of distribution, it must pay careful heed to many considerations, not the least of which are:

- The market
- The product
- The middleman
- The business itself

Market Considerations

Among the market considerations for established channels of distribution are the following:

1. *Size of market.* When considering the marketplace to which a product is to be distributed, the business must have a sense of how many potential customers exist for a product. With industrial products, there is often a limited market for products, which makes designing a distribution channel relatively simple. When there are small numbers of potential customers in the market, a business may decide to directly sell its goods rather than relying on middlemen. With consumer goods, however (and sometimes industrial goods), there are often hundreds of thousands of potential customers, which makes distribution more complex.

2. *Location of market.* The number of potential customers in a market is not the only consideration, however. Where those customers are located will have a significant impact on how easy it is to get the products to the user. If the users are geographically concentrated in one central area, the distribution may be easier to design and less costly to carry out. Even if there are pockets of density within specific geographic re-

gions, a business may find it worthwhile to set up regional warehouses to sell to those pockets and use wholesalers in other areas of the country.

3. *Size of orders.* Another consideration is potentially how large orders might be from various customers in the market. A business may find it cost-efficient to handle customers placing large orders with its own sales force. But if a customer places only small orders, a business might decide that using a middleman to service that company's needs makes more sense.

4. *Consumers versus industrial users.* An obvious market consideration is whether the product is designed for a consumer or industrial user. If it is designed for an industrial user, retailers will not be a necessary feature of the channel design.

Product Considerations

Among the product considerations that will affect channels of distribution are:

1. *Unit value.* When a product is very inexpensive, typically the channels of distribution become longer, unless the product can be sold in mass quantities. When large quantities of inexpensive goods are sold in mass quantities, the channels of distribution can often be shortened.

2. *Perishability.* When a product's design or physical nature could go bad if it doesn't hit the market rapidly, shorter channels of distribution are used to make sure the product hits the market when necessary.

3. *Technical sophistication of product.* For highly technical industrial products, usually the channel of distribution is directly from manufacturer to user. This is partly because the cost of these industrial products is usually high and can warrant shorter channels, and partly because the technical nature of the product makes it difficult for a middleman to perform the presale and postsale selling. As a result, a direct sales force is often more qualified to do the selling.

Distribution of technical consumer products presents a problem for the manufacturer because it is rare that these products are sold directly to the consumer and not through a retailer. To keep the channels of distribution as short as possible, the manufacturer of a technical consumer product will try to sell or distribute directly to a retailer who will sell the product to the consumer. Even using this short channel, the quality of the service that the consumer receives is difficult for the manufacturer to control.

To plan distribution channels effectively, businesses should know the nature of the product they sell. Consumer products can be broadly categorized as follows:

- *Convenience goods.* Consumer goods that are bought often but not typically shopped around for fall into this category. Often products such as shaving cream, blank videocassette tapes, and disposable razors fall into this category. To get the product to the appropriate market, businesses must meet broad distribution needs to satisfy market demand.

- *Shopping goods.* Consumers are willing to shop around for the specific product in this category which they have decided they want. Examples include high-priced clothing, stereo equipment, and household appliances.

- *Specialty goods.* Consumers are willing to go almost anywhere to get the specific specialty product they want. Examples include Rolex watches, Coach pocketbooks, Ben and Jerry's ice cream, Range Rover automobiles, and Joseph Abboud men's suits.

These broad categories don't cover all consumers, simply the majority. Some consumers *will* go from store to store until they find the brand of shaving cream they want, while others will be less fussy about what type of suit they wear.

Middleman Considerations

When a business needs a middleman (a wholesaler or agent), it should look for someone who can provide services that the business could not perform itself. Sometimes the desired middleman is not available because he or she may carry similar products from a competing company.

Middlemen will often represent a manufacturer only if the manufacturer's policies meet his or her needs. These needs might include:

- Territory rights to distributing a line of products
- Specific sales incentives
- Price discounts
- Postsale servicing
- Promotional support

Often smaller businesses will have difficulty finding the middleman they want to represent them. Some wholesalers distribute upward of

30,000 individual items, while some hardware wholesalers distribute more than 50,000 items. It is unlikely that established wholesalers will be clamoring for a minor product to add to their line. As a result, small businesses may have to shop around to find a middleman to represent them.

Business Considerations

Among the chief factors that will determine whether or not a business can successfully distribute its products directly to the customer are:

1. *The financial resources of the business.* A company that is not in a strong financial position may find it needs middlemen to distribute its goods more than a company that is financially strong enough to establish its own sales force and inventory warehouse.

2. *The capability of the business's management.* If a company's management is not seasoned in its marketing skills, it may decide that turning distribution over to a middleman makes the best business sense.

3. *The control that the business feels it must have over its distribution channels.* Even though it may cost more in the long run, some businesses maintain a short distribution channel and distribute directly to the user, or they may distribute to the user through a retailer, because they want control over such factors as product availability, freshness, placement, and appropriate pricing.

4. *The services required by middlemen to distribute a business's products.* Particularly with consumer products, retailers may insist that businesses provide services such as product manufacturer advertising to support sales of products in the retail store. Businesses must decide whether the demands placed on them by middlemen are viable from a financial and a marketing point of view. In some cases, particularly where retail outlets are the only means for distributing a product, businesses may have little choice in whether or not to use this means of distribution.

Multiple Channels of Distribution

Manufacturers may use multiple channels of distribution—*dual distribution* (using two channels) or *multiple distribution* (using three or more channels)—when they are trying to distribute under such circumstances as the following:

- Distributing products to both a consumer and an industrial market (e.g., personal computers or telephones)
- Distributing products that are unrelated (e.g., cookies and motor oil)
- Distributing products that are being purchased by different-size buyers (e.g., a large supermarket versus a corner convenience store)
- Distributing products that are sold directly from the business sales force to buyers in a densely populated geographic region and by middlemen in more diverse regions

One of the unfortunate results of dual distribution techniques is that a business may sometimes find itself using two different channels of distribution to distribute the same product to the buyer. What results is *channel conflict* and the business ends up competing against its own products.

Nevertheless, most companies will use more than one channel of distribution so that they can cover their entire target market and maintain quality distribution even in markets where they cannot find top-notch intermediaries. In the latter case, businesses (if they can afford to) may be forced to set up their own wholesale branches to meet the distribution needs of a particular market segment.

Vertical Channels

Vertical channels are marketing channels through which the product manufacturer integrates its product into the marketplace by owning its wholesaling (e.g., Nabisco) or retailing outlets (e.g., Goodyear Tire, Tile City, or Thom McAn), or both.

The main reason manufacturers use vertical channels is to have more control over product distribution. Presumably, an added benefit would be to gain profits they otherwise would have given away from the retail or wholesale operation. Rarely does the return on invested capital make company-owned stores attractive from a profitability standpoint. And often, because company-owned stores are not owned by individuals who also manage the stores, the thirst for profits by the managers may not be as great as it would be if the managers also owned the stores.

Vertical marketing systems grew out of the concept of vertical channels of distribution. In this system, distribution channels are treated as integrated units. Three common types of vertical marketing systems are:

1. *The corporate vertical marketing system,* in which the same company owns both production and marketing facilities. For example, Benneton sweater company both manufactures clothing and operates its own stores. Corporate vertical marketing systems include the manufacturer-owned retailer and wholesaler as well as corporate retail chains.

2. *The administered vertical marketing system* includes independent wholesalers and retailers who agree to join a manufacturer's marketing program. One of the distribution channel members is powerful enough that the others cooperate with it. Companies like Rolex and General Electric have a strong enough market position that retailers will agree to their requests about advertising, pricing, and display arrangements.

3. *In the contractual vertical marketing system,* independent manufacturers, wholesalers, and retailers join together by virtue of a contract, to get the economic clout and coordination of advertising effort to achieve market share. Examples of contractual vertical marketing systems include:

- *Wholesaler-sponsored voluntary chains.* Independent retailers can elect to join a chain and share a logo, advertising, and the management advice that the wholesaler provides.
- *Retailer-owned cooperative chains.* Retailers own stock either on a one-share-per-store basis or on a volume-purchased basis. These chains can offer product lines under their own label that small convenience stores can stock on their shelves.
- *Franchises.* Perhaps the most commonly recognized and rapidly growing examples of contractual vertical marketing systems, franchises include manufacturer-sponsored retailers like Chrysler, manufacturer-sponsored wholesalers like Pepsi-Cola or Coca-Cola, and service marketers like McDonald's or Jiffy Lube.

These vertical marketing systems all told account for about two-thirds of the market for consumer goods.

The growth in strength of vertical marketing systems has often resulted in a changing role for manufacturers. Often, the systems are larger than the manufacturers which supply them. Corporate chains like K-Mart and behemoth, multibranch wholesalers like McKesson have so much clout in the distribution channel that many have become *channel captains*—the channel members which control the others. McKesson, for example, holds a 28 percent market share of drug wholesaling operations in the United States, the largest in the country. To facilitate sales in the stores that carry its products, McKesson has a computer-based order system which allows major drugstore retailers to press a button on a hand-held computer to reorder inventory. The result is not only ease of ordering for the retailer but assurance that the retailer will buy the products McKesson distributes. McKesson has used its muscle as a channel captain to maintain a strong share of the market.

Because of the strength of channel captains like McKesson, manufacturers or retailers must meet the demands of wholesalers by tailoring their advertising campaigns or distribution policies to be most beneficial to the channel captain. (A channel captain is not always a wholesaler; it can be a manufacturer, retail chain, or wholesaler.)

Traditional nonvertical systems in which wholesalers sell to independent retailers account for most of the remaining one-third of the market for consumer goods. In this relationship, the producer or manufacturer typically maintains the role of channel captain.

Intermediaries

Up to this point in this chapter, we have looked at distribution channels that have involved producers, agents, wholesalers, retailers, and product users. Now let's take a closer look at intermediaries and the role they fill in a company's distribution of products.

Wholesalers and retailers make up the two broad categories of what are referred to as *channel intermediaries*. Wholesalers form a channel between producer and retailers with consumer goods, and between producers and industrial users with industrial goods.

Businesses use marketing intermediaries rather than move the goods themselves when it becomes more cost-efficient or more effective in terms of sales.

Wholesaling Intermediaries

Wholesaling or the *wholesale trade* involves sales of products from one firm to another for business use, not for end use. Even retailers who turn around and sell products to another business can be considered to have taken on wholesaling activities. For example, when Lambert's Rainbow Fruit Market in Dorchester, Massachusetts, sells a head of lettuce to a consumer, it is acting as a retailer. When it sells a box of lettuce to the Puritan Restaurant a few doors down, it has taken on the role of wholesaler, since the owners of Puritan will resell the lettuce to their customers.

All sales, broadly defined, can be considered either wholesale or retail sales. The deciding factor is the end user's use for the product or service.

The term *wholesaling middleman* is used to refer to a business that acts primarily as an intermediary between the manufacturer or producer and the end user. A *wholesaler* (of which there are various types, including jobbers and distributors) is one type of wholesaling middlemen performing wholesaling activities. Other types of wholesaling middlemen include *agents* and *brokers*, who, unlike wholesalers, do not take title to a product. (See Figure 7-3.)

Because most producers or manufacturers in the United States are small, wholesaling middlemen who are knowledgeable about market needs can pool products from a variety of manufacturers and act as intermediaries between buyer and seller. The wholesaling firm can perform distribution tasks for a variety of firms, thus eliminating the need for a number of small firms to duplicate one another's distribution efforts. Wholesaling firms also eliminate the need for some small retailers to go from manufacturer to manufacturer to find the products needed to stock their shelves.

Often, wholesaling middlemen can cut down the cost of transactions for businesses. The cost of having a wholesaler approach 50 different retailers can often be less expensive and is certainly less time-consuming for the manufacturer. When the overall transaction activities of several businesses are considered, the role the wholesaling middleman can play in cutting down transaction costs comes even clearer into view.

Say, for example, that 15 manufacturers each wanted to sell its product to 30 business firms. This effort would involve 450 (15 × 30) sepa-

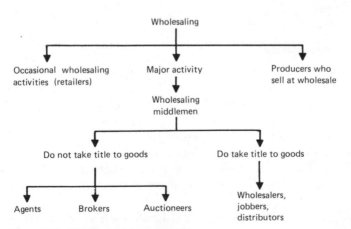

Figure 7-3. Wholesaling intermediaries.

rate sales calls and transactions. If one wholesaler were used by the manufacturers, however, the number of transactions would be cut to 45 (15 sales calls by the manufacturer to the wholesaler plus 30 sales calls from the wholesaler to the business firms). Even if two wholesaling middlemen were used, the number of overall transactions would be dramatically cut from 450 to 90.

The number of wholesaling firms has grown dramatically over the past three decades. In 1954, there were a total of 250,000 wholesaling firms in the United States, accounting for $234 billion in sales. By 1982, the numbers of firms had grown 66 percent to 416,000, and the dollar volume had burgeoned more than 750 percent to almost $2 trillion. (See Table 7-1.)

It is difficult to accurately categorize wholesaling middlemen since they vary greatly in the types of products they carry, the markets they serve, and how they distribute the products they carry to the markets they serve. The Census of Business, the source for the information in Table 7-1, classifies wholesaling middlemen in three broad categories:

1. Merchant wholesalers

2. Agents and brokers

3. Manufacturers' sales branches and offices

It is useful for our discussion of wholesaling to look more closely at these three categories.

Merchant Wholesalers

Merchant wholesalers are usually referred to by marketers as "wholesalers," "jobbers," or "industrial distributors," depending on the

Table 7-1. Wholesale Establishments, 1954–1982

	1954	1958	1963	1967	1972	1977	1982
Total wholesaling establishments	250,000	287,000	308,000	311,000	370,000	383,000	416,000
Establishments with sales of $1 million or more	NA	NA	62,000	75,000	103,000	152,000	190,000
Sales for all establishments (in billions of dollars)	$234.0	$285.7	$358.4	$459.5	$695.2	$1258.4	$1998

SOURCE: U.S. Bureau of the Census, *U.S. Census of Business: 1954*, vol. III; *1958*, vol. III; *1963*, vol. IV; and *1967*, vol. iii. Also *Census of Wholesale Trade: 1972*, vol. I; *1977*, WC 77-A-52; and *1982*, WC 82-A-52. Reported in U.S. Bureau of the Census, *Statistical Abstract of the United States: 1987*, 107th ed., Washington, D.C., 1986, p. 764.

Table 7-2. Wholesale Trade, by Type of Operation and Kind of Business, 1977 and 1982

	Establishments (1000)		Sales (millions of dollars)	
	1977	1982	1977	1982
Wholesale trade	382.8	415.8	$1,258,400	$1,997,895
Merchant wholesalers	307.2	337.9	677,550	1,159,334
Other operating types	75.6	77.9	580,851	838,561
Durable goods*	226.2	256.1	608,756	881,212
Nondurable goods†	156.6	159.7	649,644	1,116,683

*Durable goods include motor vehicles; automotive equipment; furniture; home furnishings; lumber; construction materials; sporting, recreational, and photographic goods; metals and minerals (except petroleum); electrical goods; hardware, plumbing, and heating equipment; machinery; equipment; supplies; and other goods.

†Nondurable goods include paper, paper products, drug, drug proprietaries, apparel, piece goods, notions, groceries and related products, farm-product raw materials, chemicals, allied products, petroleum and petroleum products, beer, wines, distilled alcoholic beverages, and other products.

SOURCE: U.S. Bureau of the Census, *Census of Wholesale Trade, 1977*, Geographic Area Series, WC 77-A-52, and *1982*, Geographic Area Series, WC 82-A-52. Reported in U.S. Bureau of the Census, *Statistical Abstract of the United States: 1987*, 107th ed., Washington, D.C., 1986, p. 767.

function they serve or the industry in which they operate. Merchant wholesalers are typically independently owned, take title to the merchandise they distribute, and account for the bulk of wholesaling firms both in numbers and in volume of sale. (See Table 7-2.)

Merchant wholesalers provide a variety of services to the manufacturer. Among these are:

- *Breaking bulk.* Wholesalers buy large quantities of products from a manufacturer and then break these bulk shipments down into smaller units to be resold.

- *Assorting.* Wholesalers fill orders from retailers who want specific numbers of various products, by sorting the products to match the order.

- *Buying products directly from the manufacturer.* Wholesalers will often buy products directly from a manufacturer, which increases the manufacturer's cash flow.

- *Storing and transporting products.* Wholesalers often store and transport products, which means the retailer needn't worry about inventory control or transportation.

- *Other services.* Wholesalers perform other services, including offering credit to the manufacturer, negotiating between manufacturer and buyer, advising retailers or product buyers what they should buy, and advising on advertising campaigns.

Wholesalers are paid for their services in the form of a discount on the final price of the product. These discounts vary widely. For most products, the discount is between 5 and 15 percent off the final purchase price of the product. Discounts given to retailers are much higher, typically ranging from 15 to 40 percent off the final purchase price, but going as high as 50 or 60 percent with some products like jewelry or books. In spite of the low discounts they get, wholesalers make money because of the volume of goods they handle.

Specific types of merchant wholesalers exist in particular market segments. Usually they get their names based on the function they serve or the industry in which they specialize. Some of the more common ones are mentioned below.

Rack Jobbers.   Originally, *rack jobbers* were merchant wholesalers who supplied food stores with nonfood products. While they still primarily focus on food stores, today rack jobbers supply not only supermarkets, but also drugstores, hardware stores, and other self-service retail stores.

Rack jobbers can supply a grocery store with all the nonfood items it cares to carry. The rack jobbers supply not only the products but the racks on which these products are stocked. Rack jobbers are responsible for keeping the shelves stocked with the fastest-moving items. Essentially the store's function is to provide floor space or shelf space to the rack jobber and to take the money for the products as they are purchased from the store. The rack jobber gets paid only for the items that are sold. Paperback books, magazines, toys, or other merchandise the retailer normally would not know much about are the types of products supplied by the rack jobber. The revolving book racks found in many drug stores or supermarkets are typically the handiwork of a rack jobber.

Limited-Service Wholesalers.   *Limited-service* or *limited-function wholesalers* are merchant wholesalers who do not offer the same services to customers that a full-service wholesaler would offer, nor are their products lines as extensive. Some of the major types of limited-service wholesalers are:

- *Truck jobbers* (sometimes called "truck distributors" or "wagon jobbers," reminiscent of the days when the milk delivery person would deliver via a horse and wagon) are found primarily in the food industry. These specialty wholesalers carry a nationally advertised brand of product and both sell and deliver goods in the same trip. Most frequently their products are perishable, including items such as potato chips, baked goods, fish, dairy products, and tobacco products. Retailers benefit from using truck jobbers since they can buy relatively small numbers of product and, because of the frequency of delivery, be assured of freshness. Because the orders are small and the truck jobbers are unsure of the order sizes until the sales are made, they must often maintain larger stocks in their trucks than will be sold. As a result, truck jobbers have high operating costs which can make their profits slim.

- *Drop shippers* (sometimes called "desk jobbers") take orders from customers which, in turn, are delivered, in the form of drop shipments, directly from the manufacturer to the customer. Like all merchant wholesalers, drop shippers take title to the product (once it leaves the manufacturer). But unlike other wholesalers, they do not physically handle the products. Drop shippers most often deal in products such as coal and coke, lumber, building materials, and some heavy equipment.

- *Retailer cooperative chains* are cooperative warehouses sponsored by a group of retailers who have come together to operate as a wholesale warehouse. While the retailers keep their own identity, the cooperative gives them the ability to buy in large quantities and to warehouse products when necessary. Retailer cooperative chains are common in the grocery industry.

- *Cash-and-carry wholesalers* offer no services (delivery or otherwise) but may carry a wide variety of products. The customers—retail or industrial—send their own trucks to the cash-and-carry wholesaler's warehouse, pay cash for the products, and transport the purchases themselves. Flowers or fresh foods are common products sold on a cash-and-carry basis.

Agents and Brokers

Agents and *brokers* are another category of wholesaling middlemen. Unlike merchant wholesalers, agents and brokers do not take title to the products they distribute, nor do they offer extensive services. Their chief role is to act as intermediaries in transferring the title of ownership of a product from manufacturer to customer (who is sometimes a wholesaler, sometimes a retailer). Commissions for agents and brokers range from 2 to 6 percent, lower than those for merchant wholesalers, who take a more active role in the distribution of products.

Among the more common types of agents and brokers are:

- Manufacturers' agents
- Brokers
- Selling agents
- Commission merchants
- Auction companies

Manufacturers' Agents. *Manufacturers' agents* (sometimes called "manufacturers' representatives") account for the largest number of agents and brokers. As a group, they bring in the largest dollar volume of all agents and brokers. Manufacturers' agents always represent the seller of a product, do not set prices, and are typically independent individuals or businesses (not employees of the manufacturer) which have been assigned a geographical territory in which they can represent a manufacturer's product to prospective customers. They are paid on a commission basis (anywhere from 2 to 20 percent), and can represent more than one manufacturer as long as their products do not compete with one another. The agent usually has an ongoing relationship with the manufacturer.

Manufacturers are particularly useful to small businesses which have no sales force, and to firms that want to enter a new geographic market and so use a manufacturers' agent who is familiar with the territory.

Brokers. *Brokers* do not handle products nor do they work on a year-round basis with manufacturers. They act as intermediaries between buyers and sellers and furnish information on the market, prices, and competing products. Like agents, brokers act chiefly as negotiators and have no power to set prices or to accept or reject an offer to buy. Brokers are most common in the food industry.

Usually a manufacturer which uses a broker has a seasonal production schedule. It will hire a broker (the same one if the relationship has been positive) each year to sell products to buyers. The broker will advise about the market and competing prices, and then the manufacturer will set a price. The broker will sell the product to wholesalers, retailers, and other interested buyers until the product supply is gone, at which point the manufacturer and broker cease to do business until the next season when products are again available.

Because brokers bring buyers and sellers together, they can represent either party. But, for the most part, brokers represent the sellers of goods. In some industries, brokers have developed permanent relationships with the businesses they represent. Strictly speaking, this would make them manufacturers' agents. But many former brokers (particularly food brokers) have chosen to continue to refer to themselves as "brokers."

Other common examples of brokers not used on a permanent basis, but only when a product is bought or sold, are stock brokers and real estate brokers.

Selling Agents.   A *selling agent* is an independent agent that takes the place of a manufacturer's entire marketing department. Selling agents represent all the manufacturer's products and can have a large influence on pricing structure, product offerings, and marketing programs.

Selling agents usually have the most control of all agent wholesaling middlemen. A manufacturer may use several agents or brokers, but will only use one selling agent. Selling agents account for about 1 percent of all wholesaling professionals. They are usually found in the textile and coal industry, although they are also used to some extent in the selling of the following products:

- Clothing and apparel
- Food products
- Lumber
- Metal products

Commission Merchants.   *Commission merchants* (sometimes called "commission men" or "commission houses") are used primarily to market agricultural products. Commission merchants usually operate out of a central market. Producers of goods consign shipments to commission merchants who take responsibility for setting prices and for storing and selling the goods. Commission merchants take their commission and reimbursement for all expenses incurred in selling the products and pass on the rest to the product supplier.

Auction Companies.   *Auction companies* provide a forum in which buyers and sellers can exchange goods. Auction companies provide both the physical place for goods to be displayed and sold, and the auctioneers who will actually sell the products. About 1 percent of all wholesale activity is accounted for by auction companies. They are most commonly used in the selling and buying of agricultural products (e.g., tobacco and livestock) and used cars.

Manufacturers' Sales Branches and Offices

Manufacturers' sales branches and offices are the third type of wholesaling middlemen. While these sales branches and offices are not part of the manufacturing plant, they are owned and operated by the manufacturer. A sales branch carries a manufacturer's inventory, while a sales office does not.

Because of the expense of opening an office and staffing it with salespeople, sales branches and offices are usually owned by larger manufacturers who can afford the expense. The manufacturer gains a greater deal of control over the marketing of its products than if it had used an independent wholesaling middleman, since the sales offices and branches will represent only the products the manufacturer makes.

Lesson Ten Questions

1. What are marketing channels or channels of distribution?
2. How is the length of a channel determined?
3. What is channel length?
4. What are channel intermediaries?
5. What are vertical channels? What is the primary reason manufacturers use them?
6. What are channel captains?
7. What is wholesaling?
8. What is a wholesaling middleman?
9. What are merchant wholesalers?
10. What are agents and brokers?

Retailing Intermediaries

Retailing intermediaries sell goods to ultimate consumers for non-business use. As of 1982, there were close to 2 million retail firms in the United States, more than 200,000 more than in 1954. By 1985, retail trade sales added up to almost $1.4 trillion. (See Tables 7-3 and 7-4.)

The growth in the number of retail outlets from 1954 to 1982 is strong, but nowhere near as dramatic as the growth in population during the same time period (164.6 million in 1955 as compared to 238.2 million in 1985) or the growth in sales of retail firms experienced from 1970 to 1985, an almost fourfold increase.

For government statistics, the category of retailers consists of not just retail stores but all businesses selling directly to the consumer, including:

Table 7-3. Retail Trade, 1954–1982

	1954	1958	1963	1967	1972	1977	1982
Total establishments (in thousands)	1722	1795	1708	1763	1780	1855	1923
Establishments with sales of $1 million or more (in thousands)	NA	NA	NA	NA	74	119	193

SOURCE: U.S. Bureau of the Census, *U.S. Census of Business: 1954*, vol. I; *1958*, vol. I; *1963*, vol. I; and *1967*, vol. I. Also *Census of Retail Trade, 1972*, RC 72-S-1; *1977*, RC 77-52; and *1982*, RC 82-a-52 and RC 82-I-1. Reported in U.S. Bureau of the Census, *Statistical Abstract of the United States: 1987*, 107th ed., Washington, D.C., 1986, p. 755.

Table 7-4. Retail Trade Sales, 1970–1985

	1970	1975	1979	1980	1981	1982	1983	1984	1985
Retail trade total sales (in billions of dollars)	358.4	588.1	899.1	959.6	1041.3	1072.1	1174.3	1293.1	1373.9

SOURCE: U.S. Bureau of the Census, *Current Business Reports*, series BR, *Monthly Retail Trade*. Reported in U.S. Bureau of the Census, *Statistical Abstract of the United States: 1987*, 107th ed., Washington, D.C., 1986, p. 756.

- Mail-order catalog houses
- Vending machines
- Household service providers

More than 95 percent of all retail sales, however, are done through *retail intermediaries*—a unit or store that sells directly to consumers.

Retail Stores. Franchised stores account for roughly 35 percent of all retail stores. Chain stores account for 33 percent, and independently owned stores account for 32 percent. Retailers can be broadly categorized according to the types of products they carry—general merchandise stores and limited-line stores.

General Merchandise Stores. *General merchandise stores* carry a wide variety of products and typically stock all products evenly. Department stores and variety stores fall into this category. *Department stores* carry items ranging from apparel, furniture, and automotive goods to household goods, tools, and home furnishings. In 1982, general merchandise stores accounted for $120.4 billion in sales.

Limited Line Stores. *Limited-line stores* (sometimes called "single-line stores") stock a wide assortment of products by only a few manufacturers in a few related areas. These stores are most commonly referred to by the type of products they carry. Food stores, automobile parts stores, hardware stores, drugstores, liquor stores, bakeries, bookstores, furniture stores, and sporting goods stores are all examples of limited line stores.

Specialty stores is another name used for limited-line stores. Sometimes, particularly in the case of drugstores and food stores, it is no longer possible to identify the line of goods the store carries simply by its descriptive name.

Scrambled merchandising—the practice of adding unrelated lines of products to those carried in the rest of the store—is a growing practice, particularly in food and drugstores.

Ownership of Retailers

Chain Stores. *Corporate chain stores* are owned and managed by the same corporation. *Voluntary chain stores* consist of independent stores that form an association that enables the independent stores to have more economic power in the marketplace.

The stores in a chain typically carry the same lines of products. Corporate chain stores are very common among department stores and drug stores. Chain stores usually can offer lower prices than independent stores because they buy larger volumes of goods from wholesalers. As a result, their unit prices often are lower and they can pass these savings onto their customers.

Franchises. *Franchise systems* operate when a franchisor gives independent franchisees the right to operate or sell the franchisor's service or product. The franchisee usually pays a franchise fee and a royalty on all earnings. Fees for franchise rights range from as low as $500 for a Jazzercise health and fitness franchise to $35,000 and up for franchises like Jiffy-Lube quick oil change centers. Start-up fees can run anywhere from several hundred dollars for a real estate brokerage franchise to upward of $2.5 million for a Super 8 Motels franchise. (Every November, *Venture* magazine publishes "The Franchisor 100," a report on the fastest-growing franchises in the United States.)

Franchises have indeed become big business. According to the U.S. Department of Commerce, the number of franchise units (not different types of franchises, but total units that are part of franchises) has grown from 396,000 (72,000 company-owned; 324,000 franchisee-owned) in 1970 to 476,000 in 1986 (91,000 company-owned; 387,000 franchisee-owned). What's more, sales of products and services by franchises increased from $120 billion in 1970 to $576 billion in 1986. The average sales per franchise unit grew from $302,000 in 1970 to $1,203,000 in 1986. (See Table 7-5.)

Table 7-5. Domestic Franchising, 1970–1986

	1970	1975	1980	1986
Number of franchised units (in thousands)	396	435	442	478
Sales of products and services (in billions of dollars)	120	191	336	576
Average sales per franchise unit (in thousands of dollars)	302	439	760	1203

SOURCE: U.S. Department of Commerce, International Trade Administration, *Franchising in the Economy, 1984–86*. Reported in U.S. Bureau of the Census, *Statistical Abstract of the United States: 1987*, 107th ed., Washington, D.C., 1986, p. 763.

Franchising allows the franchisor company to expand its retail franchise using the capital paid by the franchisee. Franchisees are able to enter a business that has a track record and gain from the market recognition of the franchise and the marketing expertise of the franchisor's management team.

But franchising is not without risk. In 1986, the U.S. Department of Commerce reported that more franchisors had failed than ever before—78 franchisors operating 5667 outlets and accounting for $574 million of sales in 1985. In addition, in 1986, more franchisors than ever before decided to discontinue franchising as a method of doing business—105 franchisors operating 5082 units in 1985, with $2.3 billion in sales.

Operation of Retailers

The four principal types of retailers categorized according to operation are:

- Full-service retailing firms
- Supermarket retailing firms
- Discount retailing firms
- Nonstore retailing firms

Full-Service Retailers.   Full-service in-store retailers are not as prevalent as they were three decades ago. Fine clothing stores and upscale jewelry stores still maintain full service, and they likely will continue to do so, but it is in the area of self-service retailing and nonstore retailing that much of the growth in retailing operations has occurred.

Supermarkets. *Supermarkets* are large retail food businesses that operate on a self-service basis and feature merchandise in aisles typically categorized according to product type. They were begun in the 1930s by independent operators attempting to compete with chain food stores. Supermarkets feature a wide assortment of products, from groceries and meats to produce and dairy products.

While supermarkets have become the dominant food retailers, their average net after-tax profit is only 1 percent of gross sales. The average supermarket has 17,000 square feet of floor space and does gross weekly sales of around $230,000.

Discount supermarkets have developed in recent years to compete at the low end of the supermarket market. These discount supermarkets offer fewer services (consumers even pay for grocery bags) and charge less than the typical supermarket.

Convenience stores are much smaller in scale than supermarkets, but they too compete with supermarkets. Even though the prices at convenience stores are typically higher and the assortment of products (while broader than that of a limited-line store) is not as great, convenience stores have flourished because of the long store hours they keep and because they are often located in or near residential neighborhoods, which makes getting to them easier.

Superstores take the supermarket concept a step further by offering not only the grocery products consumers need but also other products they routinely purchase, such as tobacco products, alcohol, stationery products, and lawn furniture.

Discount Retailing Firms. *Discount houses* are large stores that carry a variety of products, from wearing apparel to appliances and home furnishings, at discount prices (below manufacturers' list prices). Discount houses do not offer much in the way of customer service.

Off-price retailers is a name given to retailers who sell brand-name products below list price. Marshalls and T. J. Maxx, for example, specialize in selling a wide variety of apparel below list price.

Wholesale and warehouse clubs act as wholesalers to small retailers and as retailers to a select group of consumers who meet specific membership requirements, such as being employees of a nonprofit organization or a bank. The consumer usually pays about 5 percent more than a retailer would pay for the same product. While wholesale and warehouse clubs stock the same variety of goods as other discount houses, they usually do not carry as many brands.

Catalog showrooms are discount retail stores that feature a store display of all the retailer's catalog items. When the consumer chooses an item, he or she fills out an order form and gives it to a clerk. The order is filled from the retailer's inventory. The primary attraction to catalog showrooms is that they advertise prices in their catalogs that are far below the list prices of other discounters. Recently, however, as other discounters have been catching up on the discounts, catalog showrooms have been forced to upgrade their image and make shopping easier in their showrooms.

Nonstore Retailing.   Of the almost $1.4 trillion in retail sales in 1985, $31.6 billion came from nonstore retailers. Four broad categories that make up nonstore retailing are in-home personal selling, telemarketing, mail-order selling, and vending-machine selling.

In-home personal selling can involve the door-to-door selling that is associated with the archetypal Fuller Brush man who goes from house to house trying to sell his goods, or the encyclopedia salesperson who often sets up appointments after meeting prospective customers in a store or getting prospects' names from a mailing list and calling them.

The *party-plan* type of selling, of which Tupperware parties are perhaps the most famous, is also a form of personal selling. In the party-plan sales method, one prospect will act as host or hostess, allowing a sales representative to show goods in the host's or hostess's home to a group of friends. Cookware, lingerie, makeup, and toys are all commonly sold through the party-plan method. The commissions paid to a salesperson selling products in homes usually run in the area of 40 to 50 percent of the retail price, which can make it a costly venture for a retail firm.

Door-to-door sales also suffered in the past because of the difficulty of ensuring the quality of salespeople. In spite of this, direct selling establishments grew from 11,000 in 1977, with sales of $7.56 billion, to 12,200 in 1982, with sales of $11.362 billion. Both producers and retailers still use in-home personal selling to distribute their products.

Telemarketing continues to grow at a brisk pace. Buying and selling by telephone is a nonstore sales technique that has been used for a long time. But simply because the number of households with telephone service has practically doubled in the last quarter of a century, the use of telemarketing has ballooned. In 1960, only 78.5 percent of the 52.8 million households then in existence (or 41.45 million households) in the United States had telephone service. By 1986, 92.2 percent of all households, then numbering 88.5 million, had telephone service (81.6 million). It is more convenient than ever for consumers to shop by telephone. And sophisticated computer equipment allows retailers to target their market segment for effective telemarketing.

Mail-order selling includes not just ordering goods through catalogs, but also responding to advertisements or direct mail solicitations. Originally mail-order selling was designed to reach rural areas of the country which had limited access to retail stores. Today, mail-order selling successfully targets urban areas as well.

Shopping by catalog is often more convenient for a consumer than having to go to the store and buy goods. The overhead expense of a physical structure is not incurred if the catalog is the sole means of retail marketing for the retailer. But customers do not have the ability to inspect the goods before they buy them, and so mail-order houses are compelled to have liberal return policies and creative catalog presentations to satisfy customers. Land's End, an outdoor clothing retailer, went so far as to hire well-known writers to write its catalogs in an effort to attract its target market.

Because catalogs are very expensive to prepare and take time to produce, mail-order houses make every effort not to change prices drastically after a catalog is published. Catalogs are also expensive to mail. In response to the 25 percent increase in third-class postal rates in the spring of 1988, many catalog retailers began to seek other methods of distributing their catalogs, including:

- Piggybacking mailings with newspapers and magazines
- Dropping nonactive buyers from its mailing lists
- Printing catalogs on lighter-weight paper

Lillian Vernon, Inc., a mail-order house that sells small gift items, tested an abridged version of its catalog as an insert with the Sunday *New York Times*. Spiegel Inc., another major mail-order house, had its catalog shrink-wrapped in plastic to go out with *Inc.* magazine. And some companies, like J. S. & A., a mail-order house specializing in fitness equipment, have had their catalogs inserted into airline magazines.

Vending machines, according to *Vend* magazine, make up to 1.5 percent of all retail sales in the United States. Cigarettes, candies, sodas, detergents, toiletries, and other items are sold through coin-operated machines. Even videocassettes are now being marketed in vending machines. VideoRated, Inc., a Costa Mesa, California, company, began putting video vending machines into hotel lobbies in 1985, for use with credit cards. The movies rent for an unlimited number of showings over a 24-hour period, or for a blanket weekly price. The company expected revenues of $30 million in 1987.

Most products sold in vending machines have a low unit value, and because there is not much price markup, they are relatively expensive to sell through stores. Vending machines can broaden the availability of some products beyond what retail stores could reach through their distribution efforts.

Physical Distribution

Physical distribution involves moving a product from manufacturer or producer through whatever distribution channels are necessary to get the product to the consumer or industrial user. Physical distribution adds to a business' customer service. If the right products are distributed on time and in good order, customers' needs are met. Without effective physical distribution of products, quality customer service is impossible.

Physical distribution includes the following five chief aspects, each of which is discussed below.

1. Warehousing

2. Materials handling

3. Inventory control

4. Order processing

5. Transportation

Warehousing

Warehousing differs from storage in that it involves not only storing products but also performing a variety of distribution functions, including:

- Assembling
- Bulk breaking
- Getting products ready for shipment from the warehouse

Some companies have chosen to develop large warehousing centers, which are called *distribution centers* and are located near their target markets. At the distribution center, orders are taken, filled, and sent out for delivery to customers. The purpose of distribution centers is to lower the number of warehouses a company needs to fulfill its distribution of products. Companies with distribution centers are able to keep better control of inventories, making sure not to overstock but also not to understock products.

Companies have the option of deciding whether they should operate their own warehouses or use public warehouse services. In public warehouses, companies pay only for the space they actually use.

Materials Handling

It is important that a company choose appropriate equipment for handling its products during the physical distribution process, to cut down on breakage or theft of products. More and more companies have moved toward using one-story warehouses, rather than multilevel warehouses that require elevators and chutes to move products. The workers in the warehouse use forklifts, conveyer belts, or other tools to safely move products. The one-story warehouses are typically located where there is enough land (often in industrial parks) for loading docks where the products can be loaded for distribution.

Containerization has become a more common means of moving products through the distribution process. Large shipments of products are sealed in a container and not opened until the shipment reaches the customer. The use of containerization involves less physical handling of products than other methods of distribution.

Inventory Control

Inventory control involves keeping enough product on hand to fill customers' orders, but not so much that investment costs in inventory and warehouse costs are driven sky-high. Sales forecasts are used to predict how much inventory is necessary to keep on hand. The more accurate the sales forecast, the more effective inventory control can be.

The cost of the inventory includes the costs of making and storing the product, including any losses caused by breakage or theft.

The *just-in-time* concept of inventory-control management involves buying parts in small quantities just in time for use in the production of products and producing products just in time for sale to customers. Just-in-time inventory control can lower the expense of maintaining large inventories and increase a company's ability to inspect its products for quality control, since the production runs will often be smaller than previously.

Order Processing

Businesses must establish some system of *order processing* that allows them to fill product orders efficiently. Procedures for billing, granting credit, sending invoices, and collecting on accounts should all be firmly established, so that a customer will never be served poorly. More and more companies are using computers to process their orders. Software packages have been designed to meet the order-processing needs of many different types of manufacturers and retailers.

Transportation

The major methods of transporting goods from producer to customer include:

- Railroads
- Trucks
- Water vessels
- Pipelines
- Airplanes

Businesses have to decide which means of transportation is most efficient in terms of speed and cost in transporting its products. Table 7-6 compares how much the different modes of transportation are used in the United States for intercity freight transportation. Table 7-7 compares the speed, cost, reliability, flexibility, number of geographic locations served, and products most suitable for the same modes of transportation.

When deciding what method of transportation to use in the physical distribution of products, most companies use a *total cost approach*, which considers all aspects of the distribution, not just the cheapest method of transportation or the best way to get products out of its warehouse.

For example, for a company to decide whether to distribute its prod-

Table 7-6. Volume of Domestic Intercity Freight Traffic by Type and Transport, 1970–1985

	Billions of Ton-Miles			
	1970	1975	1980	1985
Railroads	771.0	759.0	932.0	898.0
Motor trucks	412.0	454.0	555.0	600.0
Oil pipelines	431.0	507.0	588.0	562.0
Inland waterways	319.0	342.0	407.0	348.0
Air carriers	3.3	3.7	4.8	6.4
Total	1936.3	2065.7	2486.8	2414.4
	Percentage Distribution			
	1970	1975	1980	1985
Railroads	39.82	36.74	37.48	37.20
Motor trucks	21.28	21.98	22.32	24.85
Oil pipelines	22.26	24.54	23.64	23.28
Inland waterways	16.47	16.56	16.37	14.41
Air carriers	0.17	0.18	0.19	0.26
Total	100.00	100.00	100.00	100.00

SOURCE: Transportation Policy Associates, *Transportation in America*, Washington, D.C., March 1986, with periodic supplements. Reported in U.S. Bureau of the Census, *Statistical Abstract of the United States: 1987*, 107th ed., Washington, D.C., 1986, p. 579.

Table 7-7. Comparison of Modes of Transportation

Mode	Selection Criteria					Products most suitable
	Speed	Cost	Reliability	Flexibility	Number of geographic locations served	
Rail	Medium	Medium	Medium	*Widest variety*	Very many, but only where track is laid	Long hauls of carload quantities of bulky products
Water	Slowest	*Lowest*	Poor	Widest variety	Limited	Bulky, low value, nonperishable
Highway	Fast	High	Good	Medium	*Unlimited, very flexible*	Short hauls of high-value goods
Pipeline	Slow	Low	*Excellent*	Very limited, very inflexible	Very limited	Oil, natural gas, slurried products
Airways	*Fastest*	Highest	Medium	Somewhat limited	Many	High-value, perishable, where speed of delivery is all-important

SOURCE: William J. Stanton and Charles Futrell, *Fundamentals of Marketing*, McGraw-Hill, New York, 1987, p. 401.

ucts by train or air freight, it must determine whether or not the comparative cheapness of train shipment makes up for its comparative slowness in getting the product to the buyer—taking into account that the slowness makes it necessary for the company to stock more inventory in its warehouse, which raises warehouse costs. Sending the product air freight, in contrast, means that inventory levels can be kept low and that products can get to the customer more quickly. The price of shipping air freight, however, is higher than the price of shipping by train. The company must decide whether the higher warehouse costs outweigh the higher air-freight costs. And all these determinations must be made in light of considerations of which method will be most satisfying to customers.

Case Study

Cutting Out the Middleman

It was only a matter of time before someone caught on to the fact that the office-supply retail business could be revolutionized by applying the same discount retailing concept that had successfully worked for retail apparel sales at places like T. J. Maxx and Marshalls and for the toy business at toyland supermarkets like Child World and Toys 'R Us.

For years, though, the smaller business owner and consumer, who account for between 40 and 60 percent of all office-supply purchases, had not been privy to the same generous bulk discounts that large businesses got on office supplies. It was generally assumed that office-supply buyers were willing to pay a little extra in exchange for the services that traditional office-supply retailers offered—telephone orders, generous credit policies, and free delivery.

By the mid-1980s, the office-supply industry had grown to $108 billion in sales. Along about this time—January 1986, to be exact—the National Office Products Association, an industry trade group based in Alexandria, Virginia, conducted a study in conjunction with the Wharton School at the University of Pennsylvania. The study suggested the traditional assumptions about office-supply stores were incorrect. The study found that price, not service, was the single most important factor in a consumer's buying decision.

Armed with this information, at least four different discount retailers have sprung up in the office-supply business since 1986. Among the most ambitious of these is Staples, Inc., based in Newton, Massachusetts. Not surprisingly, it was founded by former supermarket executive Thomas Stemberg, who, from his supermarket days, knew that price would win out over service. By the spring of 1988, Staples had opened 16 stores. Sales from May 1987 to April 1988 were $40 million.

Staples customers are offered products in warehouse-size buildings for prices that are 50 percent or more off retail list prices. Staples members get an even larger discount off selected items. For example, a box of 10 computer floppy disks, which retails for $29.99, normally sells for $9.49 at Staples. As a "featured product," members can buy the floppy disks for $6.95. Membership in Staples is free.

Others have entered the office-supply discount retailing business with gusto. Venture capitalists have poured $33 million into four different ventures. ($18.5 million of it has gone to Staples.)

Office Club in California opened two stores in 1987 and hopes to have opened 65 by the end of 1991. Members of Office Club pay $10 a year for discounts ranging from 50 to 70 percent on products; nonmembers pay 10 percent more than members do. Also in 1987, Office Depot had opened three stores in Florida and one in Georgia, and Office Stations (a division of Ben Franklin Stores, Inc.) had opened stores in Indianapolis and Omaha.

The new stores promise to change traditional industry practices. First off, overall profits have shrunk for the typical office-supply retailer, who must cut prices in an attempt to compete with these superstores. But more important, stores like Staples may turn the traditional distribution channel for office supplies on its ear.

Rather than buy through wholesaling middlemen, stores like Staples buy in such bulk quantity that they go directly to the manufacturers to buy products, cutting out both the middleman and his cut of the action. As a result, these stores are able to beat the prices of traditional office-supply retailers.

Industry analysts are only slightly exaggerating when they foresee the trend of office-supply discounting as sounding the death knell for wholesaling middlemen in the office-supply industry.

Success in the discount retailing business will be no cakewalk for Staples or others in the field, however. Recognizing consumer demand, general-merchandise discount retailers have already begun to stock up on their office supplies. And the office-supply discount retailers have begun to alter their no-frills approach by offering services like accepting credit cards and cashing business checks. Office Club even goes so far as to offer a Club Plus membership for $50 a year, entitling members to credit privileges, telephone orders, and delivery service.

SOURCE: Reed Abelson, "They Can Get It for You Wholesale," *Venture*, August 1987, pp. 27–28. Additional source: David Mehegan, "Staples: Supermarket for the Office Worker," *The Boston Globe*, March 29, 1988, pp. 25, 32.

CASE REVIEW

1. What has a store like Staples done to the traditional marketing channels in office-supply retailing—shortened them or lengthened them? How might this affect pricing, competition, and customer orientation?

2. What other businesses that have traditionally operated in small retail, high-service settings might benefit from a discount retailing approach?

Lesson Eleven Questions

1. What are retailing intermediaries?
2. What is scrambled merchandising?
3. What is the difference between a corporate chain store and a voluntary chain store?
4. What is a franchise system?
5. What are the advantages of a franchise system to the franchising company? To the franchisee?
6. What are the four principal types of retailing operations?
7. What are the five chief aspects of physical distribution?
8. How does warehousing differ from storage?
9. What is the just-in-time concept of inventory control?
10. What is a total cost approach to distribution costs?

8

Marketing Communications

Marketing communications is the process of developing messages and sending them to a specific receiver. It is successful when the message the sender wants to get across hits the desired target, is understood, and is acted upon. The marketing professional uses various methods of marketing communications to reach the target market.

Communications Model

The process that takes place in marketing communications is similar to the process that takes place in any communications. Figure 8-1 shows the classic communications model and how it applies to a marketing situation.

The Communications Model in Marketing

Here's how the communications process works in marketing:

1. The *source* of the message is the marketer. The marketer (i.e., the company or organization marketing a product or service) must decide what message it wants to send about its product or service and whom it wants to send the message to.
2. The marketer *encodes* the message by deciding what symbols— words, sounds, pictures—will be used to communicate the message.

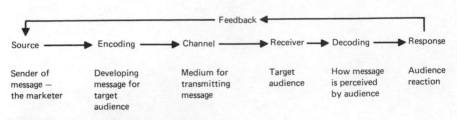

Figure 8-1. The communications model.

3. The *channel* is the medium the marketer decides to use to get the message to the receiver.

4. The *receiver* is the target market that the marketer wants to receive the message.

5. *Decoding* is how the receiver, the target market, understands the message sent by the marketer.

6. The *response* is how the target market reacts to the message, whether by simply acknowledging or by actually buying the product or service.

7. *Feedback* is what the marketer learns, through a variety of methods including sales performance or marketing research, about how the message was communicated.

At any point in the communications process, the sender and receiver may have to deal with *noise*, which is any factor that may distort the message at any point in the process. Feedback can often alert the sender to where the noise occurs or what effect it has. Feedback also allows the marketing professional to know how successful the communication has been or where it has fallen short in getting across the desired message to the target audience.

The communications model can be used in planning all aspects of marketing communications and all elements of the promotional mix, including:

- Advertising
- Personal selling
- Sales promotion
- Publicity

Promotion

Like product, price, and place (distribution), *promotion* is one of the "four Ps" of the marketing mix. Promotion is that aspect of the marketing mix that involves convincing or persuading a target audience about the quality or attractiveness of a company's products or services.

The Promotional Mix

Promotional mix is a term used to refer to the choice of promotional tools that are used to market a product or service. The word "promotional" is used in its broadest sense, to encompass all elements of the marketing communications process. The promotional mix can include:

- Advertising
- Personal selling
- Sales promotion
- Publicity and public relations

Advertising and personal selling are the two most used methods of the promotional mix.

The promotional mix used for one product or service may differ entirely from the promotional mix used to market another. Some products or services require little advertising and a great deal of personal selling. Others require heavy advertising. The makeup of the promotional mix will vary from product to product.

Many people mistakenly consider "marketing" and "selling" to be interchangeable terms. It is important to recognize that selling is only one aspect of marketing, the aspect that involves persuading an audience about a product or service you want it to buy. On the other hand, marketing encompasses the whole scope of planning the product or service, pricing it, distributing it, and promoting it to the target market.

The term "selling" is often used to indicate the act of persuading or influencing a target market about a product or service. While "promotion" is a more accurate term to describe this action, the two terms can be used interchangeably as long as it is clear that promotion involves all the activities that can be used in the promotional mix to persuade the target market. Too often, when using "selling" and "promotion" interchangeably, the user limits the concept of selling to the meaning "exchange of goods." For this reason, promotion is a more appropriate term.

Beyond the specific techniques that make up the promotional mix, many other aspects of marketing can have a promotional side to them. Product differentiation and market segmentation, for example, can be used to promote a product or service to a particular target market in a desired way.

Advertising

Advertising is perhaps the most readily identifiable form of the promotional mix—the form that we encounter every day. It consists of presenting a paid message about a company's services, products, or concepts. Advertising involves the action of calling the public's attention to the product, service, or idea being represented. The advertisement presents a message to a receiver who is part of the intended market for the company's product, service, or idea. The message can be presented in a variety of media and is paid for by an identified sponsor.

Billions of dollars are spent on advertising every year. In 1985 alone more than $94 billion dollars was spent on all types of advertising, including:

- Newspapers
- Magazines
- Television
- Radio
- Direct mail
- Outdoor advertising

Table 8-1 shows just how much money has been invested in advertising in the United States from 1950 to 1985. Over 75 percent more dollars were poured into advertising in 1985 than in 1980. Clearly, advertising is a big business that continues to grow.

The Purpose of Advertising.   Theoretically, the purpose of all advertising, directly or indirectly, is to communicate a message to a target au-

Table 8-1. Advertising—Estimated Expenditures, 1950–1985

Year	Total (in millions of dollars)	National	Local
1950	$ 5,700	$ 3,260	$ 2,440
1955	9,150	5,380	3,770
1960	11,960	7,305	4,655
1965	15,250	9,340	5,910
1970	19,550	11,350	8,200
1975	27,900	15,200	12,700
1980	53,550	29,815	23,735
1985	94,750	53,355	41,395

SOURCE: Reprinted with permission from *Advertising Age*. Copyright, Crain Communications, Inc., 1986. U.S. Bureau of the Census, *Statistical Abstract of the United States: 1987*, 107th ed., Washington, D.C., 1986, p. 537.

dience about a product, service, or idea. More pragmatically, the goal is to create sales of products or services. But since advertising is but one of the many types of promotion that can be used to create a sale, it often plays a more limited role. Often, advertising is used to:

1. *Create awareness.* When a company uses advertising for *brand image* (or *brand personality) advertising*, it is trying to create an awareness of the company's brand name or trade name. The company wants the receiver of the advertising message to become more aware of a new or old product in the company's line.

2. *Spur action.* The goal of all advertising is to get someone to buy the product or service being sold. But while advertising might sometimes cause direct action, more often than not it serves to remind consumers or industrial buyers to buy or order the advertised product the next time they are in need of such a product, or to remind industrial buyers to be willing to meet with product salespeople the next time they call.

3. *Maintain interest.* To keep customers from forgetting particular products even though they may buy them regularly, businesses use *reminder advertising* to keep the product name fresh in the customer's head. This fights the chance that the brand or company will be easily forgotten or lose out to a sea of competitors in the marketplace.

In addition to creating awareness, spurring action, and maintaining interest, advertising can also be used for myriad other purposes, including:

- Promoting events
- Attracting new salespeople or retailers
- Getting sales leads
- Improving a company's image
- Reaching an otherwise untapped audience
- Improving company morale

Classification of Advertising. There are many different types of advertising. Among these classifications are:

- Product advertising
- Institutional advertising
- Primary demand advertising

- Selective demand advertising
- Cooperative advertising
- National advertising
- Local advertising

Product and Institutional Advertising. Advertising can be either product advertising or institutional advertising.

Product advertising is used to inform the target market about a product or to encourage a purchase. Product advertising can be further classified as *direct-action* advertising or *indirect-action* advertising.

- *Direct-action advertising* is designed to get customers to take immediate action; it encourages the prospective customer to make an immediate purchase decision. Coupon advertising is a common form of direct-action advertising. Customers are promised a discount, or a free sample, but only if they act within a certain time period.

- *Indirect-action advertising* is used to build awareness of a product so that when the customer is ready to make a purchase, he or she will be inclined to choose the advertiser's product.

Institutional advertising is not used to sell a specific product, but rather to create an awareness of the company that is doing the advertising. General Electric has done this type of advertising for years, presenting itself as "bringing good things to life," rather than extolling the virtues of any particular product in its product line. Two types of institutional advertising are:

- *Patronage advertising*, which gives specific information about the advertiser's business (e.g., extended department store hours during a holiday season)

- *Public service advertising*, which presents the advertiser in a favorable civic light (e.g., what a company has done to decrease pollution in local rivers; advertisements urging the market not to drink and drive). When McDonald's runs an advertisement about one of its Ronald McDonald Houses, which are set up as lodging for parents of ill children, this is an example of public service advertising.

Primary Demand and Selective Demand Advertising. The purpose of *primary demand advertising* is to create a demand for a broad product group rather than a specific product. There are two chief uses for primary demand advertising:

1. *Pioneer advertising.* Pioneer advertising introduces a new product concept. For example, when videocassette recorders (VCRs) first hit the market, Sony or Zenith may have run advertisements designed to highlight the virtues and uses of VCRs in general.

2. *Trade group advertising.* Trade groups or industry associations for products such as milk, summer produce, meat, other dairy products, coffee, and countless others advertise generically. Some advertisements for sugar, for example, feature a nostalgic look at the times when sugar is used in a person's life.

Selective demand advertising is the opposite of primary demand advertising. Selective demand advertising is used to create a demand for a specific brand of product—for example, Domino sugar or Melitta brand coffee. A form of selective demand advertising is *comparative advertising*, in which a company compares its product with a competing product.

One of the most creative examples of comparative advertising in recent years has been the advertising campaign for Sweet 'N Low, a low-calorie sugar substitute manufactured by Cumberland Packing Corporation in Brooklyn, New York. Facing increasing competition from nonsaccharin products, particularly Equal, another sugar substitute, Kathy Kiely and Karen Larson, creative people in Pedone and Partners (Cumberland's advertising agency) came up with the perfect tag line for the Sweet 'N Low advertisement:

For millions of people, there's just no equal.

Not only does the advertisement emphasize consumer loyalty to the existing product, it cleverly uses a play on the competitor's name to position itself as *the* first choice in sugar substitutes.

Cooperative Advertising. *Cooperative advertising* or *co-op advertising* involves two or more companies sharing the expenses of an advertising campaign. If two companies are sharing the expense, the split is typically fifty-fifty, but it can vary depending on the arrangement between the companies.

Vertical cooperative advertising is done by companies at different points in the channel of distribution, which share advertising expenses. For example, a manufacturer and a retailer sharing advertising expenses is one of the more frequent instances of cooperative advertising.

Manufacturers also may offer what is called a *promotional allowance* (or *advertising allowance*) to a retailer. The promotional allowance may be given in the form of cash or as a discount on the invoice, which the manufacturer offers to retailers to advertise its products. The allowance is used as an incentive to get the retailer to advertise the manufacturer's brand. Because local retailers often get better rates on advertising than do national manufacturers, the manufacturer benefits from issuing a promotional allowance because the retailer may get the lower advertising rates.

Horizontal cooperative advertising involves the sharing of advertising expenses by companies at the same level of the distribution channel. This is a common practice among retailers in shopping malls, which may band together to advertise all the stores and the mall itself.

National and Local Advertising. *National advertising* (sometimes called *general advertising*) is advertising done by product manufacturers. A manufacturer's advertising is considered national even if it is placed in a local or regional publication. *Local advertising* is advertising done by retailers. Even if a retailer is part of a national chain (e.g, K-Mart, J. C. Penney), it is still considered a local advertiser when a particular outlet advertises in local or regional media. More than 56 percent ($53.335 billion) of the total of $94.75 billion advertising done in 1985 was accounted for by national advertising. Local advertising ($41.395 billion) accounted for almost 44 percent of the total.

One of the main differences between national advertising and local advertising is that advertising agencies can collect a commission on national advertising. Manufacturers typically will hire an advertising agency to place their advertisements. The advertising agency will receive a commission from the media in which they place the ad. Retailers, on the other hand, will most often place their own advertisements with the local or regional media, and get a discount on the advertisement in lieu of the commission that would typically go to an advertising agency.

In concept, too, there is a distinction between national and local advertising. National advertising is usually used to develop brand awareness. Maytag runs its national advertisements, for example, to increase prospective customers' perception of the quality of its washing machines. Retailers generally run advertisements to increase store traffic, although some prestigious retailers also advertise to maintain awareness in the market.

Measurement of Advertising

Marketing professionals use marketing research to:

- Learn about the characteristics of their target market
- Measure the performance of brand-name products
- Measure the performance of specific advertisements

The copywriter writing an advertisement must have some facts about the target market in order to write an advertisement that addresses the needs and wants of that target market. The copywriter can use many of the facts derived from the marketing research process to develop an effective advertising piece.

Marketing research techniques can also be used to measure the performance of brand products. Many marketing research techniques—especially consumer surveys and focus groups—can be used to gain an understanding of how the market is perceived in the marketplace.

Pretesting and Posttesting. Advertising can be tested before (*pretested*) or after (*posttested*) it is placed in the media. The advertising can be tested to see how effectively it gains a customer's attention, how well it gets the desired message across, and how well it is remembered. Again, this type of testing is typically done by the marketing research department of a company or by a marketing research firm that is hired to gather these facts.

Readership, Recognition, and Recall Tests. *Readership, recognition,* and *recall tests* are indirect measurements of how effective advertisements have been. Individuals are shown a previously run advertisement to see whether they read the ad, whether they remember it, and whether they remember who sponsored it. The idea is that the greater the number of people who remember the ad and its sponsor, the greater the number of people who will be inclined to follow whatever action is prescribed by the advertisement.

One of the casualties of creativity in advertising is that often the ads are so creative and clever that the product being advertised gets lost in the shuffle. Customers remember the ads, but forget what product was being advertised. Advertisers, as a result, must be careful that their creativity does not obscure the real intent of the advertisement—to market a product or service.

Measuring Response Mechanisms. One simple method of measuring the effectiveness of an advertisement is to record the number of coupons or response mechanisms that were used after they appeared in an advertisement. Since most of these response mechanisms can be coded with a number indicating where they appeared, it is easy for the advertiser to determine which advertisements in which specific media had the best results.

Kemp & George, a Boston-based company that sells home renovation supplies through catalogs, follows just such a procedure. By coding its advertisements and catalogs, it can trace where the sales are coming from. By including its toll-free number in advertisements and on catalogs, it enables customers to place telephone orders. Here too, Kemp & George traces the source by having its operators ask callers where they saw the advertisement or what the code number is on the advertisement or catalog. Ultimately, the company learns which lists work best and where advertising pays off most.

Measuring AIDA. *AIDA* is an acronym used to indicate the stages a person goes through in making a purchase decision, and the letters stand for the following words:

- Attention
- Interest
- Desire
- Action

Ideally, advertising should get the target market to experience all these characteristics. One method of measuring the effectiveness of advertising is to measure how effective the advertisement was at each stage of this process, as follows:

1. To make such a measurement of *awareness*, customers can be asked whether or not they have seen particular advertisements. The following three techniques can be used to perform this measurement:
   a. *Unaided recall*, in which customers are simply asked to remember what ads they remember having seen or heard in a particular medium, whether newspapers, magazines, radio, television, or billboards
   b. *Aided recall*, in which customers are asked such questions as "Do you remember seeing any ads about such and such a product?"
   c. *Recognition*, in which customers are shown a specific advertisement and asked if they remember having seen it
2. Interest can be measured by asking the customer to try to remember:
   a. What was said in the advertising
   b. The message the advertisement was trying to get across
   c. What the customer found interesting about the advertisement
3. *Desire* can be measured by asking a customer how likely he or she was to buy the product or service after seeing the advertising.
4. *Action* can, of course, be measured by asking customers whether they bought the product as a result of seeing the advertisement.

To test the effectiveness of an advertisement, companies will often measure customers' interest in and desire for the product or service both before and after they are shown the advertisement. As a result, the advertiser may get a sense of how persuasive the advertisement was in getting the customer to respond to the product.

Selecting Advertising Media

The basic decision that must be made in selecting which of the many types of media to advertise through involves deciding which will best reach the desired target market. All media outlets, whether they be newspapers, radio stations, television stations, magazines, or any other form, have done demographic studies to indicate how large an audience they reach and what kind of audience they reach, i.e., income, sex, net worth, interests, and so forth.

The advertiser must not only decide which medium best reaches its intended audience or prospective buyer, but also which provider within that medium best presents it with the possibilities for successful advertising, as well as the best exposure with the desired target market.

Of course, once the advertiser determines the type of medium that best reaches the target market (based on the objective of the advertisement and the circulation, viewership, or listenership of the medium), the cost factor must also be weighed. Advertising on national television may reach the target market better than advertising in a regional magazine, but the advertiser may find the cost prohibitive. Cost must be a factor in the decision-making process.

Measuring potential exposure revolves around two important factors:

1. *Reach.* The number of households or prospective customers exposed to the medium during particular times.

2. *Frequency.* The number of times that a household or prospective customer is exposed to an advertisement within a given time period.

All media publish lists of reach and frequency, showing how many people they reach during particular time periods. By multiplying reach times frequency, the advertiser can learn how many exposures it can expect to have to its advertisement in any given time period. In television and radio, these exposures are called "gross ratings points." They give the advertiser information about how many households are listening to or watching a particular medium at a particular time, which is the information needed to choose the media and time for advertising.

Media Scheduling. Companies must decide how often to run particular advertisements in particular media throughout an advertising campaign. This particularly difficult task is called *media scheduling* or *media* *strategy*. A typical strategy is to spread the advertising budget over different media during a several-month period in an attempt to hit the target market as effectively as possible. Advertisers use *media flowcharts* to plan media schedules. Figure 8-2 shows a media flowchart used by Citytrust Bank in Bridgeport, Connecticut. Among other things, this flowchart helps Citytrust to integrate its corporate advertising program with the bank's other promotional efforts.

Characteristics of Major Types of Media.   Figure 8-3 is a pie chart showing how the major types of media accounted for all advertising expenditures in 1985. The major types of media discussed below include:

- Newspapers
- Magazines
- Direct mail
- Radio
- Television
- Outdoor advertising
- Experimental advertising

Newspapers.   Newspapers provide a timely, flexible advertising medium at a relatively low cost. (Costs for advertising medium are typically

Week of:	12/30	January 5 12 19 26	February 2 9 16 23	March 2 9 16 23 30	April 6 13 20 27	May 4 11 18 25 1 8
Daily newspapers		•		•• ••	• •	• •
		††† ††† † † † † †		‡ ‡ ‡ † ‡ ‡ ‡ ‡		‡ ‡
					§ § § § § § § §	
Weekly newspapers		† † † † † †		‡ · ‡	‡ ‡	‡ ‡
Radio					• •	• •
		† † †		† † † † † †	† †	
		‡ ‡ ‡ ‡ ‡ ‡ ‡ ‡ ‡ ‡ ‡ ‡ ‡ ‡ ‡ ‡ ‡ ‡ ‡ ‡			‡ ‡	‡ ‡
		‡			‡ ‡	‡ ‡

Product code: • Corporate   † Passbook Savings   ‡ Mortgage   § Deposit products

Figure 8-2. Typical media flowchart.   (*Adapted from Deborah L. Colletti, Marjolijn van der Velde, and Jeffrey L. Seglin,* Small Business Banking: A Guide to Marketing and Profits, *Bank Administration Institute, Rolling Meadows, Ill., 1987, p. 31. Used with permission.*)

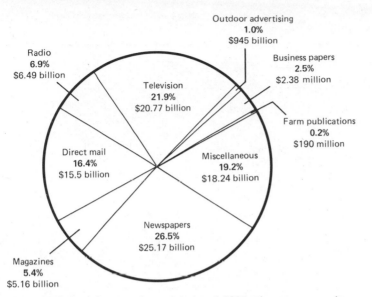

Figure 8-3. Percentage and amount of total 1985 advertising expenditures by category, based on Table 8-2. Dollar amounts are rounded off, and as a result, the total of all expenditures on this pie chart is higher than the total amount in Table 8-2. The total in Table 8-2 is accurate.

expressed in terms of *cost per thousand*. This refers to how much it would cost to reach 1000 prospects using this medium, based on the circulation of the medium.) One of the major drawbacks to newspaper advertisement is that the life of the advertisement is significantly shorter than in other types of media, particularly in daily newspapers. (See Table 8-2.) With an expenditure of $25.17 billion, newspaper advertising accounted for 26.5 percent of all advertising expenditures in 1985.

Magazines. Magazines, particularly those that are published monthly or less frequently, present the advertiser with a medium that gives the advertisement a longer shelf life than do newspapers. The high-quality printing and glossy stock of many magazines also give a good look to the advertising piece, which may be of particular importance to advertisers who need color in their advertisements. Because of the wide variety of magazines available, virtually every type of target market can be reached. Advertisers can choose to advertise in a national magazine, a regional edition, a special-interest magazine, or a regional publication. The cost of reaching a prospective customer through magazine advertising is relatively low.

With an expenditure of just under $5.16 billion, magazine advertising accounted for 5.4 percent of all advertising expenditures in 1985.

Table 8-2. Advertising—Percentage of Estimated Expenditures by Medium, 1970–1985

Advertising medium	Percentages		
	1970	1980	1985
Newspapers	29.2	27.6	26.5
National	4.6	3.7	3.5
Local	24.6	24.0	23.0
Television	18.4	21.3	21.9
Network	8.5	9.6	8.8
Spot	6.3	6.1	6.3
Local	3.6	5.5	6.0
Cable	NA	0.05	0.1
Direct mail	14.1	14.2	16.4
Radio	6.7	6.9	6.9
Network	0.3	0.3	0.4
Spot	1.9	1.5	1.4
Local	4.5	5.1	5.1
Magazines	6.6	5.9	5.4
Weeklies	3.2	2.6	2.4
Monthlies	1.9	1.8	1.6
Women's	1.5	1.5	1.4
Business papers	3.8	3.1	2.5
Outdoor	1.2	1.1	1.0
Farm publications	0.3	0.2	0.2
Miscellaneous	19.7	19.6	19.2
Total	100.0	100.0	100.0

SOURCE: Reprinted with permission from *Advertising Age*. Copyright, Crain Communications, Inc., 1986. U.S. Bureau of the Census, *Statistical Abstract of the United States: 1987*, 107th ed., Washington, D.C., 1986, p. 538.

Direct Mail.   With direct mail it is possible to reach the specific target market the advertiser chooses, by purchasing or creating lists of prospective customers in that target market. There is less wasted circulation than in other types of advertising. Direct mail consists solely of the advertising material the advertiser sends. Unlike ads in newspapers or magazines, those in direct mail are not surrounded with editorial material or other advertisements. While the cost per prospective customer is higher than the cost of most other types of media, direct mail is a more targeted approach and therefore typically garners a higher response rate, particularly when postage-paid return envelopes or cards— referred to as "business reply envelopes" (BREs) and "business reply cards" (BRCs)—are enclosed with the direct-mail advertisement.

In addition to the cost of direct mail—a factor that is off-putting to many advertisers—another problem lies in getting high-quality lists of prospective customers. *List brokers* are in the business of identifying sources of lists and helping advertisers to plan a list selection for a direct-mail campaign. List brokers are typically compensated by taking a commission off the purchase price of the list.

Because of the volume and variety of direct mail, another problem it has had is the perception of it as "junk mail." Other than an advertiser committing to use quality writers and production people to produce quality direct-mail pieces and to sell quality goods and services, this is a problem that is unlikely to be easily resolved.

With an expenditure of $15.5 billion, direct-mail advertising accounted for 16.4 percent of all advertising expenditures in 1985.

Radio.   As television advertising has grown, radio advertising has decreased. Radio advertising no longer plays the dominant role it did in pre-World War II days. But radio advertising presents many opportunities for local and regional advertisers to reach local target markets.

Some developments in radio have presented unique, inexpensive advertising opportunities. Tunnel Radio, for example, is a radio broadcast that can be heard only in the Dewey Square Tunnel in downtown Boston. Hundreds of thousands of cars pass through the tunnel every day. Tunnel Radio has wired the tunnel so that it can broadcast on every AM station while a car is in the tunnel. It can also sell advertising on the station. Because Tunnel Radio is in such a limited broadcast area, the price for advertising is significantly lower than the cost of traditional radio outlets.

With an expenditure of $6.49 billion, radio advertising accounted for 6.9 percent of all advertising expenditures in 1985.

Television.   Television presents the unique opportunity to use both sight and sound to appeal to a target market. It presents a wide possibility of geographic coverage, from local to national markets. While it is perhaps the most sophisticated advertising medium in terms of production (with some advertisements bordering on theatrical quality), it is likewise a very expensive medium, much more expensive than most of the other media available.

The televised message, while appealing to eye and ear, is fleeting, lasting for minutes or less and then gone. To make a distinct impact, unless the advertisement is aired during a heavily watched event like the Super Bowl, an advertisement must be repeated many times to have an effect.

With an expenditure of $20.77 billion, television advertising accounted for 21.9 percent of all advertising expenditures in 1985.

Outdoor Advertising.   Outdoor advertising presents a flexible, low-cost advertising outlet. It is particularly useful for consumer goods that need few words to sell them but instead can rely on the large color graphic that billboards allow. Advertisements that rely heavily on copy or nonconsumer goods are not best suited for outdoor advertising. While the cost of a national advertising campaign using outdoor advertising would be high, it is quite possible to pinpoint specific regions to which the advertiser wants to target its message.

The major criticisms of outdoor advertising are that it clutters the outdoors—ruining views on highways—and that it is offensive in neighborhood areas, particularly when alcohol and tobacco products are advertised in areas trafficked by young children. Many campaigns have been organized against billboards, perhaps the most famous of which was Lady Bird Johnson's attempt to beautify America by ridding the nation's highways of billboards.

With an expenditure of $945 million, outdoor advertising accounted for 1 percent of all advertising expenditures in 1985.

Experimental Advertising. *Experimental advertising* has grown tremendously in the last several years. Experimental advertising includes any new type of advertising, including advertising in places where you'd least expect to see it. While these kinds of advertising have not been tracked by the industry as a whole in terms of expenditures, Campbell Soup Co. alone spends $3 to $5 million a year on experimental advertising. Listed below are some places where experimental advertising has been used.

- Shopping carts
- Miniature billboards in airplane restrooms
- Shopping bags
- Trailers after videocassette movies
- Stall doors in public restrooms

Campbell Soup went so far as to put fish recipes on the backs of Roman Catholic church bulletins during Lent. And a company called The SoftAd Group, based in Sausalito, California, places advertisements on floppy computer disks and sends them via direct mail to target households.

While experimental advertising may not have the proven track record of more established forms of advertising, it does often present advertisers with low-cost, unique opportunities to hit a target market.

Advertising Costs

There are no fixed standards for what percentage of sales a company should spend on advertising. The percentage varies from company to company. If a company must rely on national television for its advertising, it will undoubtedly spend more than a company that is able to rely on a local newspaper.

Advertisers must also weigh the cost of using an advertising agency. Advertising agencies traditionally perform the function of creating and placing advertisements for companies. Advertising agencies usually buy advertising space for their clients at 85 percent of the price of the space. They then bill their clients for 100 percent of the cost. Thus the advertising agency receives a 15 percent commission fee.

Some businesses find the 15 percent commission unacceptable, and therefore many agency clients have established arrangements whereby they pay their advertising agency a smaller commission plus a fixed fee, solely a fixed fee, or some variation.

To get an idea of what the major companies in the United States spend on advertising as a percentage of their earnings, see Table 8-3. Clearly, there is no set standard ratio of advertising revenues to sales. In fact, some of the companies in the country with the highest revenues, like General Motors, spend a relatively low percentage of sales revenues on advertising.

Personal Selling

Personal selling is another aspect of the promotional mix. Companies spend even more money on personal selling activities than they do on advertising. Industrial companies rely almost entirely on personal sales efforts to market their goods.

Personal selling involves personal communications with prospective

Table 8-3. Top Ten National Advertisers, 1986

Company	Advertising expenditures	Sales, 1985	Percentage of sales
Procter & Gamble	$1.6 billion	$15.439 billion	10.4
Philip Morris Cos.	1.4 billion	15.964 billion	8.8
RJR/Nabisco	1.093 billion	16.595 billion	6.6
Sears, Roebuck & Co.	800 million	40.715 billion	2.0
General Motors Corp.	779 million	96.371 billion	0.8
Beatrice Cos.	684 million	11.396 billion	6.0
Ford Motor Co.	614.6 million	52.774 billion	1.2
K-Mart Corp.	567 million	22.4 billion	2.5
McDonald's Corp.	550 million	3.761 billion	14.6
Anheuser-Busch Cos.	522.9 million	7.683 billion	6.8

SOURCE: Percentages calculated by author based on information in *Advertising Age*, Sept. 4, 1986.

customers in hopes of persuading them to buy a product or service. Personal selling differs from advertising, sales promotion, and publicity and public relations in that these are *impersonal* forms of mass communication.

Personal selling can involve either face-to-face communication or communication over the telephone with a prospective customer. Particularly in the case of the face-to-face sale, personal selling allows the seller to be very flexible in response to the needs and wants of the prospect. The salesperson can alter the sales pitch depending upon the reaction of the prospect.

Like advertising, the sales presentation should make use of the AIDA—attention, interest, desire, action—concept to get the prospect to buy a product or service.

Personal selling has an advantage over other aspects of the promotional mix, in that it is better able to influence buyers to move toward an ultimate purchase, or action. Advertising, for example, may arouse interest and create desire but may have more difficulty in causing action, since no one is in the room or on the telephone with the prospect who is reading or seeing the advertisement.

Although more than 12.5 million people in the United States were employed in personal selling in 1985, this approach does have its drawbacks. First, finding good-quality salespeople is often difficult. Second, personal selling can be quite expensive. Table 8-4 shows the cost of an average sales call in 1987 and how much it increased over 1986.

Table 8-4. Cost of Average Sales Call, 1987

	Cost per call	Percentage increase from 1986
Consumer goods	$151.51	28
Industrial goods	207.21	16
Services	193.18	19

SOURCE: Reprinted by permission of *Sales and Marketing Management*. Copyright Feb. 22, 1988, Survey of Selling Costs.

The 5-P Process.   Like many aspects of marketing, personal selling has a procedure that can be remembered by initials. The personal selling process is a "five P's" process, with the letters standing for the following words:

- *Preparation.*   Know everything about the product, the market, and the competition.

- *Prospecting.*   Find the ideal customer for the product or service.

- *Preapproach.*   Find out everything you can about the prospect.

- *Presentation.*   Use the AIDA approach to get the prospect's *attention*, create *interest* in the product or service, create a *desire* for the product or service, and ultimately, persuade the customer to *act* and buy the product or service.

- *Postsale.*   Stay in touch with the customer after the purchase, not only to reduce the person's anxiety about the purchase but also to build good rapport so that he or she will come back to you should a similar product be needed in the future.

Telemarketing.   *Telemarketing,* a form of personal selling over the telephone, has been used for years. As the number of households with telephones has increased, so too has use of telemarketing. Today, technology has made it possible for companies to use computers, television, and the telephone to develop very sophisticated telemarketing programs.

The cost of telemarketing also makes it very attractive as a personal selling tool. According to Ernan Roman in *Telemarketing Campaigns that Work!*[1] the average cost of a industrial market telephone call is $6 to $10; for the consumer market, it's $3 to $5. With the use of scripts and well-trained telemarketers, telemarketing has become more common not only for sales, but also for marketing research.

Sales Promotion

Sales promotion is another part of the promotional mix. It includes all the activities—other than advertising, personal selling, and publicity and public relations—that:

- Spur the prospective customer on to buy a product or service

- Increase customer demand

- Improve the effectiveness not only of a retailer or end seller but also of a wholesaling middleman

Manufacturers or middlemen may sponsor sales promotions. Sales promotion includes a number of aspects, including:

- Coupons
- Free samples

[1]McGraw-Hill, New York, 1983.

- Contests for consumers or middlemen
- Giveaways
- Product demonstrations
- Premiums (gifts)
- In-store point-of-purchase displays
- Trade shows
- Cash refunds
- Free samples
- Sweepstakes
- Trading stamps
- Advertising specialities

Sales promotion is often used as a method of getting from advertising to personal selling. A salesperson may use a sales promotion tool to re-kindle awareness created by advertising and to build a relationship with a prospective customer.

Like advertising and personal selling, the ultimate goal of sales promotion is to:

- Get prospective customers to try a product
- Gain new customers
- Be more attractive than the competition
- Increase impulse buying activity in retail outlets
- Get more cooperation from retailers for middlemen

A company must consider several factors when creating a sales promotion program, including:

- The overall promotional goals of the company
- The appropriateness of the sales promotion for the target market
- The cost of the sales promotion

Types of Sales Promotions. There are many types of sales promotion. Among the major categories are:

- Trade promotion
- Consumer promotion
- Industrial user promotion

- Sales-force promotion

Trade Promotions. *Trade promotions* are commonly used in retail sales when wholesaling middlemen who sell consumer goods want to get retailers to stock a particular product and give it favorable display. *Case allowances* (discounts for ordering case amounts of products) are given to retailers in return for their displaying the product favorably or using point-of-purchase displays for the product. While trade allowances are more important for consumer goods' middlemen because they help to influence retailers, industrial middlemen can also use trade promotions to encourage their industrial distributors to stock a particular product.

Consumer Promotions. *Consumer promotions* are used to persuade consumers to buy a particular brand when they are shopping. Examples of consumer promotion include:

- Coupons
- Price-reduction displays
- Two-for-one packages
- Extra product offered for the same price
- Free samples
- Price rebates
- Trading stamps
- Contests or raffles

It is essential that companies analyze the affordability of promotional campaigns before undertaking them. Sometimes a successful promotion can wind up costing more than a company bargained for. National Convenience Stores, Inc., of Houston, Texas, for example, decided to institute a frequent-shoppers program through which regular customers could earn gifts by buying a set amount of gasoline or merchandise from its Stop 'N Go stores. The company showed losses of $2.1 million in the fiscal second quarter ending December 31, 1988, according to a report in *The Wall Street Journal.*[2] The loss resulted in part from the $7 million spent on the consumer promotion. Though the company is optimistic about the number of new customers the sales promotion brought in, recouping the money it spent to attract them will take quite a while. In the future, the company has decided, it will try to attract new customers by spending fewer promotional dollars. One precautionary

[2]Jan. 18, 1989.

move has been to hire a marketing executive from Coca-Cola to stave off any future potentially losing promotional propositions.

Industrial-User Promotions. *Industrial-user promotions* are commonly designed to create awareness of a product or to get prospective customers to request more information. Because most industrial products are not impulse items, and many are quite expensive, sales promotions targeted at industrial users are usually not designed to create an instant sale.

Advertising Specialities. In industrial-user promotions, small gifts are commonly given by manufacturers or middlemen to industrial prospects. Such gifts include lucite-enclosed clocks, pen-and-pencil sets, umbrellas, letter openers, calendars, and even more creative giveaways like personalized Louisville Slugger baseball bats. All such gifts are imprinted with the company's name and logo, and all of them are *advertising specialities*.

Advertising specialities needn't be limited to industrial-user promotions. They can be used in other sales promotion efforts as well. For example, when the Sears store located in City of Industry, California, wanted to attract more credit-card customers, it bought gold-plated chains from Schmidt-Cannon, Inc., one of many advertising specialty houses. The premium program attracted a record number of credit-card applications. Advertising specialty houses like Schmidt-Cannon, Inc., will work with buyers of the advertising specialities to develop a sales promotion program using the premiums they have to offer.

Sales-Force Promotions. *Sales-force promotions* can include both incentives for the sales force and collateral material (e.g., brochures, catalogs, price lists, videos) for them to use with prospective customers. Trade-show exhibits, another form of sales-force promotion, can be very costly since they include the costs of:

- Renting trade-show floor space
- Building an exhibit
- Hiring personnel to host the booth
- Transportation and lodging for the personnel
- Moving the exhibit material to and from the exhibit hall

Publicity and Public Relations

The final aspect of the promotional mix to be discussed here is *publicity* and *public relations*. Basically, *public relations* is a group's overall effort to create a positive image for a company among its target market or in the community in which it operates. Whereas public relations is the overall plan for getting this positive message across, *publicity* is the tool, used in public relations, that communicates the message.

Matthew Rovner, principal of Ward Rovner Public Relations, Inc., in Boston, Massachusetts, holds that explaining public relations is a lot like explaining freedom. Indeed, the definitions do get slippery, depending on who is doing the defining.

Publicity is unlike advertising, in that the media is not paid to place publicity. Public relations professionals, however, can charge a pretty penny for their services. Typically these firms will insist on several months' retainer of at least $1500 to $2000 a month. Some public relations firms, however, have tried to meet the demand of companies not wanting to spend large sums on public relations efforts. One notable example is Media Syndicate, a public relations firm in New York City. Media Syndicate will do small-scale public relations work on a project-to-project basis. A 1-page press release mailed to 100 top news outlets costs $350, for example.

A *publicity campaign* is a promotional communication that typically is geared for use in a third-party news source, or as the material in a speech or presentation given by a company official. A well-executed publicity campaign can do wonders for a business's sales.

Publicity can be used to promote not only products or services, but also almost every other aspect of a company—e.g., its personnel, environmental track record, commitment to community service, and history of unique product developments.

While publicity can be used to promote a specific product or service, typically public relations is used to promote the organization as a whole.

There are many routes that publicity can take. Among the more common are:

- *News stories.* When a new product is introduced or some event occurs within a company, a press release or news story is often written and sent to area press detailing the news. While most media will not run a press release word for word, many will use it as the basis for an interesting story. Person-to-person communication may also be used to get the news to a newspaper, radio, television, or other outlet. This may take the form of an in-house public relations professional or a public relations firm that is hired to perform the task of calling the media and keeping them up-to-date about the news of the company. For example, when Prince Andrew and his wife Sarah toured the United States in February 1988, part of their mission was to promote British foods through a group called "Food from Britain," a British government–sponsored promotional effort to encourage American consumption of British foods. Not only did their trip make news, but such stores as Vons Pavillions supermarket in Arcadia, California, benefitted from the royal couple's visit to the store.

- *News mentions.* Getting a recognizable brand name mentioned in a story, or photographed or filmed, can also be good publicity for a product. For example, when a medical study showed that aspirin decreased the likelihood of a heart attack, one of the benefactors of the publicity was Bufferin aspirin (made by Bristol-Myers Co.), since it was this brand of aspirin that had been used in the study. Mentions of the brand name were featured in various media throughout the country.

  Some companies have managed to make news mentions really pay off by including their locations as part of their names. When Ed and Joe Kane decided to open a seafood restaurant in Hingham, Massachusetts, they wanted to attract clientele from as far away as Boston. So they named the restaurant "Stars on Hingham Harbor," letting nearby Bostonians know just where the restaurant was located. Some newsletter publishers have used this same technique, making the town and zip code part of the official name of the publication; thus, whenever the newsletter is cited in the press, readers have the address and can easily send for more information.

  Sometimes news mentions can have unexpected results. When *Chicago Tribune* columnist Bob Greene mentioned Canfield's Diet Chocolate Fudge soda in a January 1985 column, the response was so overwhelming that Canfield Co. management was at wit's end trying to meet demand. Ultimately the company did meet demand and learned what a positive news mention can do for sales.

- *Television displays.* Product displays on television may vary from showing a sports figure like Jim McMahon of the Chicago Bears wearing an Adidas headband, to giving away particular brands of products and services as prizes on shows like *Wheel of Fortune.*

- *Speeches.* Speeches by company officials are good publicity for the company. Not only can the official give information about the company, but by providing speakers for events ranging from community meetings to professional trade shows, the company can build goodwill.

- *Movies.* Showing branded products featured in films has become a good publicity technique. While many companies have moved toward paying to have their products used, other companies can benefit from some free publicity given their product by a star in a hit movie. Rayban Wayfarer sunglasses, for example, got an excellent dose of publicity when Tom Cruise wore a pair in the movie *Risky Business.*

Case Study
Finding the Right Advertising Look

When Weston Financial Group, a Wellesley, Massachusetts, financial planning firm, wanted to launch an advertising campaign in 1983, it was leery. Few if any other financial planning firms had launched successful advertising campaigns—ones that both built awareness and got clients in the door.

Enter Harry Washburn, a principal in Walsh & Washburn, a marketing consulting group. In fact, Washburn—who had been an ad executive with several advertising agencies before forming his own company—approached Weston Financial on the basis of a tip from a friend who had told him that Weston was in need of help.

Weston, formed in 1978 by Rich Horowitz and Doug Biggar (who were later joined by partner Joe Robbat, Jr.), had already been advertising with limited success. But its efforts to attract more of the upscale professional clientele it catered to were meeting with limited results. What Weston wanted was to differentiate itself from the other financial planning firms marketing to the same target market.

The series of ads developed in conjunction with Washburn attempt to differentiate Weston with an innovative, informative approach. The first series of ads had the look of columns in *The Wall Street Journal*. Clearly labeled as advertisements, the ads still drew readers' attention. The body of the ad, rather than selling Weston's services, presented information about a variety of financial topics—tax reform, limited partnerships, financial planning, and so on.

What Washburn wanted to do was to come up with an advertising campaign that would be interesting and professional, not boring like some competitors' advertising had become. Washburn didn't feel he needed to create an image for Weston since the firm had already done a solid job of creating a positive image in its first 5 years of existence. What he wanted to do, however, was to get the message across about what Weston is, what it does, how it thinks. His ads created awareness and built interest among readers.

As a second series of advertisements, Washburn designed ads to look like cartoons in *The New Yorker* magazine, with editorial copy beneath them that resembled *The New Yorkers*' typeface. One *New Yorker*-type ad ran the headline "This Little Piggie." The cartoon, as drawn by John Mahoney, showed two men at a cocktail party, chatting. One says to the other, "Pork bellies will never be lower, Bill, it's the chance of a lifetime. And if worse comes to worse, you can always eat your losses." *The New Yorker* advertisements may be funnier than the ones in *The Wall Street Journal*, but they haven't gotten as much response.

Weston still runs roughly one advertisement a month in *The Boston Globe* (paying about $2500 per ad for 10 column-inches) and perhaps one or two a year in *Boston* magazine (which charges about $1000 per ad for two-thirds of a page).

Weston uses no set percentage of its annual sales revenues as a basis for its advertising budget. According to Horowitz, the firm decides what it wants to do in terms of advertising, plays with the numbers, and determines whether the cost is affordable within the overall budget.

Washburn holds that advertising should never be expected to generate direct business dollar for dollar, and that 50 to 80 percent of all new business for professional services like financial planning will and should come from referrals of satisfied customers or other professionals. Advertising should, however, create awareness and generate legitimate leads at a reasonable cost.

To get a rough idea of how much money to devote to advertising, Washburn says that he estimated how many employee-hours it would have taken management to bring in a client. He then multiplied these hours by the hourly rate such an employee would have earned, and decided to devote a portion of that money to advertising. The result was to shift some of the burden of getting new clients from management to advertising. Washburn estimates that half the money invested in advertising goes to creating awareness and building interest; the remaining 50 percent goes to getting the prospective client in through the door.

Weston receives about 50 or 60 responses from an advertisement in *Boston* magazine. Of these, Horowitz estimates that one turns into a new client, which more than pays for the ad. But Horowitz, like Washburn, is quick to point out that it's difficult to measure all the side benefits of advertising—things that go beyond getting clients to sign up with the firm, including benefits like name recognition.

SOURCE: Adapted from Jeffrey L. Seglin, *Marketing Financial Advisory Services: A Hands-On Guide*, Prentice-Hall, Englewood Cliffs, N.J., 1988, p. 133; and from Jeffrey L. Seglin, "Grabbing Attention," *Financial Planning*, December 1985, pp. 218–221.

Case Review

1. How might a company like Weston Financial Group use other aspects of the promotional mix to make itself known in its marketplace?

2. Does Weston run the risk of being too creative in its advertisements? Might prospects remember the ads, but not the company name? Are there advertisements you can recall as being so creative that you remember them but forget the company? How might a company try to achieve a balance of creativity and company name recognition?

Lesson Twelve Questions

1. What is marketing communications? When is it successful?
2. What is promotion?
3. What is a promotional mix? What might it include?
4. What is the difference between direct-action advertising and indirect-action advertising?
5. What is the difference between primary demand advertising and selective demand advertising?
6. What is AIDA?
7. What three techniques can be used to measure customers' awareness of advertising?
8. What is media scheduling?
9. What are the five P's of personal selling?
10. What is the difference between public relations and publicity?

Answers to Lesson Questions

Lesson One Answers

1. Exchange is the process of trading something of value (e.g., money, time, goods) to someone who voluntarily offers you something of value (e.g., ideas, goods, or services) in return.

2. For the marketing process to occur, there must be marketers; the goods, services, or ideas being marketed; and potential markets.

3. A utility is that feature in something that causes it to be able to satisfy people's needs and wants.

4. The four types of utilities that are created by marketing are time, place, possession, and image utility. Marketing also helps to support form utility.

5. Form utility, or "production," as it is referred to in business, consists of the changes that make a product more valuable than it had been before. Marketing may impact form utility as a result of marketing research that might indicate a variety of production issues—e.g., what weight, design, typeface, quantity, color, or fabric a product should be.

6. The four phases in the evolution of marketing are the production-oriented phase, the sales-oriented phase, the marketing-oriented phase, and the marketing and social-oriented phase.

7. Most firms today are still in the third phase in the evolution of marketing—the marketing-oriented phase. Few have deigned to progress into the marketing and social-oriented phase.

8. The marketing concept at its core holds that businesses exist, economically and socially, to fulfill consumers' wants and needs and, over the long term, to make a profit.

9. The three basic tenets at the heart of the marketing concept are customer orientation, profitable sales volume, and organizational coordination.

10. While the marketing concept holds that businesses exist to fulfill consumers' wants and needs and, over the long term, to make a profit, the

selling concept has at its heart the desire to sell a product that the business has made. Rather than matching consumer demand, the business following the selling concept seeks to make consumer demand match the products it has produced.

Lesson Two Answers

1. A strategic plan is a plan developed to help a business formulate a direction and a focus for the future. The business evaluates its resources and capabilities and decides how it should plan for opportunities in the future.

2. Strategic planning goes beyond the marketing concept by insisting that the business look at all external factors that may affect the company. The marketing concept becomes one of many factors that management seriously considers in its planning process.

3. The process of strategic planning involves:
    a. Developing a mission statement for the business
    b. Setting objectives for the business to meet its goals
    c. Planning with and evaluating strategic business units (SBUs)
    d. Choosing the strategies that allow the business to meet its goals

4. A mission statement is a formal statement about what a company's mission is in business. It answers the following questions:
    a. Given our resources and expertise, what business are we now in?
    b. What business should we be in?

5. To plan for and manage more efficiently, many large companies have divided into major product or market divisions, which have become known as "strategic business units." To be considered an SBU, the division (or product group) should:
    a. Be in a distinctly different business from the rest of the company's division or products.
    b. Have its own mission statement.
    c. Have its own competitors.
    d. Have its own management and financial responsibility.
    e. Have its own strategic plan.
   SBUs developed because some businesses that were large and diversified in their product or service offerings found it impractical or impossible to strategically plan for the entire business.

6. Once a corporation has set up its SBUs, the business can be examined as a portfolio consisting of separate business units. One of the goals of strategic planning becomes to evaluate the performance of each of these SBUs. The evaluation is known as "business portfolio analysis." The end result of the business portfolio analysis is to examine each SBU and:
    a. Determine its effectiveness within the overall corporation.

    b. Determine what changes can be made to improve its effectiveness.

    c. Determine what role it should play in the company.

7. A strategic marketing plan details the marketing objectives of a business firm that fit in with the overall strategic objectives of a company. The strategic marketing plan usually can help the business focus on the most profitable market segments and market opportunities available.

8. The annual marketing plan:

    a. Lists the objectives of the marketing effort.

    b. Pinpoints the target markets.

    c. Details the strategies that will be used to attract those target markets including the marketing mix being used.

    d. Identifies how much money is available to perform these marketing tasks.

9. A strategy involves the plans through which an organization hopes to reach its objectives. Tactics, on the other hand, are the specific means through which strategies are to be carried out. Tactics are more specific, task-oriented actions than are strategies. Tactics are also usually more relevant to short-term goals, while strategies encompass the big picture, long-term goals.

10. A policy is a plan adopted by a business that serves as a guide to indicate the decisions and actions that business will make.

Lesson Three Answers

1. Marketing research is the gathering, recording, and analyzing of data that relates to a specific problem in marketing products or services.

2. Marketing analysis is used to analyze market-segment factors to determine how much market potential a given product or service has. The marketing researcher gathers data and analyzes the factors that affect possible sales within a given market segment.

3. Economic analysis is used:

    a. To determine how actively a company should market in a given market segment

    b. To determine how much money the company should invest in marketing to that segment

    c. To determine how much it may have to produce to fulfill the needs of the market segment

4. Product concept tests are used when a new product is being developed to see how customers might react to it. Marketing researchers verbally describe or visually depict the prospective product to a group of potential customers in the target market. Once the product has been accepted during the concept-testing stage, a business may move on to develop a prototype of the product. The marketing research department may

then conduct product use tests, in which potential customers are given the new or modified product—be it industrial or consumer—to try.

5. Content research measures how the desired content of an advertisement comes across to an audience sample.

6. By pretesting and posttesting customers, marketing researchers can determine whether the desired message is getting across in a positive manner.

7. Marketing research departments do a sales analysis by studying customer records and other available data to determine where marketing opportunities lie among potential target markets. In doing selling research, on the other hand, the approach used by the person selling the product or service is analyzed to determine whether the sales presentation is effectively piquing the interest of the customer and allowing him or her to understand the product.

8. A marketing information system provides a continuous flow of marketing information that management can use to make marketing decisions. It is made up of data that can be generated, stored, and retrieved for use in the marketing decision-making process.

9. The three basic types of marketing information systems are data banks, statistical banks, and model banks. The data bank is an extensive computerized collection of raw data. The statistical bank lets marketing professionals create what-if scenarios, using the information available in the marketing information system. The model bank lets the marketing professional determine what the best solutions to marketing problems might be, based on information stored in the marketing information system.

10. The five basic parts of any marketing information system are: hardware, software, information, procedures, and personnel.

Lesson Four Answers

1. The five major steps of the marketing research process are as follows:
    a. Define the marketing objective.
    b. Design the marketing research study.
    c. Collect the necessary data.
    d. Analyze and interpret the collected data.
    e. Present the findings of the marketing research study to company management.

2. The purpose of a situation analysis is to get a sense of the situation in which the marketing problem exists, by analyzing the business, the market, the competition, and the type of business being done.

3. Using the survey method, the researcher gathers data by interviewing a

sample (limited number) of people selected from a larger target market group. The survey interview can be conducted in person, over the telephone, or through the mail.

4. The observation method of collecting primary data for marketing research involves observing the respondent doing something. No interviewing is involved until perhaps after the action has been observed and the researcher wants to follow up.

5. The experimental method of gathering primary data for marketing research involves setting up a controlled experiment in which real market situations are simulated. By analyzing the results of this smaller-scale experiment among a market sample, researchers can use the results to develop a market program to hit the larger target market.

6. Market sampling involves randomly selecting a sample—a smaller number of items from a universe—from a larger number of items, with the premise that the characteristics of the sample will be proportionately the same as the characteristics of the universe.

7. In a random (probability) sample, the survey units are selected so that each unit in the overall universe has the same probability of being chosen for the sample.

8. The top-down method of forecasting sales involves forecasting overall economic trends to determine the industry's market potential for a product, and measuring the market share the firm is already getting. The company then uses these figures to arrive at a sales forecast for the product.

9. The buildup method of forecasting sales involves estimating the future demand for a product within particular segments of the overall marketplace. To get an overall sales forecast, the researcher then adds together all the individual segment forecasts.

10. The market potential for a product or service is the total market within the industry for that product or service. The sales potential (or market share) is the specific company's estimate of how much of that market it can capture.

Lesson Five Answers

1. In the market demand for any given product or service, the following three factors come into play:
    a. People or groups with needs to satisfy
    b. The purchasing power of these people or groups
    c. The buying patterns and behavior of these people or groups

2. The four elements of the marketing mix are:
    a. Product
    b. Price

    c. Place
    d. Promotion

3. Market definition is the measurement of the characteristics of an organization's actual or prospective buyers.

4. The two broad areas measured by market definition are:
    a. Who the buyers and prospective buyers are
    b. How the buyers and prospective buyers buy

5. A target market is that segment (or segments) of the market to which an organization has chosen to direct its primary marketing efforts.

6. Using a market aggregation strategy, a company views the market as an entirety, as one large, aggregate market.

7. Market segmentation involves viewing a market as being composed of several smaller segments within that market and targeting one of these segments.

8. Market segments are groups of prospective buyers with similar needs who will respond favorably to a given marketing mix.

9. Four methods of doing business internationally are:
    a. Franchising
    b. Exporting
    c. Joint ventures
    d. Direct investment

10. Ultimate consumers are those who buy a product or service for their own nonbusiness use; industrial users include institutional organizations that buy products or services either to use in their own businesses or to use in making other products or services.

Lesson Six Answers

1. Demography is the statistical study of human populations. It is one of the marketing approaches most widely used in segmenting consumer markets.

2. The three groups of metropolitan areas classified by the U.S. government are:
    a. Metropolitan Statistical Area (MSA)
    b. Primary Metropolitan Statistical Area (PMSA)
    c. Consolidated Metropolitan Statistical Area (CMSA)

3. The term "psychographics" is most commonly used in marketing to describe people's activities, interests, opinions, motives, personalities, personal values, attitudes, and lifestyles. It is often used by marketing researchers to encompass the psychological variables and personal values that can affect a buyer's (or a potential buyer's) decision making.

4. A motive involves a need that has been stimulated and that the individual or organization is seeking to satisfy.

5. Biogenic needs include needs for food and physical comfort, and arise out of physiological states. Psychogenic needs include the need for appreciation and self-esteem, and arise out of psychological states.

6. Maslow's five levels of human needs involve:
   a. Physiological needs
   b. Safety and security
   c. Belongingness and love
   d. Esteem
   e. Self-actualization

7. For a product not to fall within the selectivity and perception of a potential buyer would mean that buyer would fail to see the product as an option to buy.

8. When a marketer attempts to change a consumer's attitude about a product, the process is often called "repositioning."

9. A reference group is a group of people who influence an individual's attitudes, values, and behavior patterns.

10. The three things marketing professionals must pay close attention to in trying to understand prospective buyer's buying habits are:
   a. When the potential buyer buys a particular product or service
   b. Where the potential buyer decides to buy a product
   c. How the potential buyer buys a product or service

Lesson Seven Answers

1. *Products* can be broadly defined as tangible or intangible items that are offered for sale or barter to individuals or institutions.

2. Unique products are those products that have never been offered before to customers. Unique products include products newly developed to meet a market need that has never been fulfilled before; they can also be products that innovatively meet needs that have been met before but in a way that is more attractive to the customer.

3. Parity products are competing products that customers perceive to be similar.

4. Augmented products are products that provide something extra to the buyer—something that goes beyond what is normally expected when such a product is purchased.

5. The six steps of product development are:
   a. Producing new product ideas
   b. Evaluating new product ideas

     c. Business analysis
     d. Product development
     e. Test marketing
     f. Commercialization

6. The five categories of product adopters are:
     a. Innovators
     b. Early adopters
     c. Early majority
     d. Later majority
     e. Laggards

7. A product line is a group of related products or services offered by a business to its customers.

8. All the products and product lines a business offers make up its product mix.

9. The four periods of a product's life cycle include:
     a. Introduction
     b. Growth
     c. Maturity
     d. Decline

10. A brand distinguishes competitor's products from one another. When a name, phrase, symbol, or graphic design, or some combination of these, is used to designate the products or services of a seller, they are said to be a brand.

Lesson Eight Answers

1. A price is what some individual or organization pays for a product or service. It is the monetary value of a product or service that is set when its utility and value have been determined. It is usually expressed in terms of money—dollars and cents in the United States, other denominations in other countries. It is also one of the four elements (the four P's) of the marketing mix.

2. Value is a quantitative measure of the product's or service's worth in terms of its ability to attract something in exchange for it. Usually value is determined in terms of money.

3. In the supply-and-demand approach to pricing, prices are based on estimates of how much market demand there will be for the product as well as how much of the product will be available. The costs of marketing and production must be determined to use this approach.

4. In the competitive pricing approach, prices are determined based on what competitors are charging for their products or services. Using this approach, when a firm enters the market with a product or service that

is at a mature stage in its growth, it may simply match the market price that has already been established in the marketplace.

5. $7.15

6. The break-even point on a product occurs when the revenue it earns equals the total costs that have been incurred, assuming a given selling price.

7. Demand is measured as the total amount of product or service bought (in monetary amount or units sold) in a given time period.

8. A positively sloped demand curve suggests that, as prices rise, demand increases. A negatively sloped demand curve suggests that, as prices rise, demand decreases.

9. The situation in which a business raises its prices and sales increase is called "inverse demand"; as the price is increased, there is also an increase in the units of product sold. Once a product reaches an appropriate price level, inverse demand stops and the usual demand curve begins. At this point, demand begins to go down as prices go up.

10. Elasticity measures the change in total revenue (price multiplied by the number of product units purchased) that results from a change in the price of a product. Demand for a product is said to be "elastic" when reducing the product's unit price causes an increase in total revenue or raising it causes a decrease in total revenue. Conversely, demand is said to be "inelastic" when a cut in the price causes total revenues to decline or raising it results in an increase in total revenue.

Lesson Nine Answers

1. An oligopoly exists when a few product sellers control all or almost all the supply of a particular product. These leading companies protect their market-share position by moving in concert with one another on price cuts and increases.

2. Monopolistic competition occurs when many sellers for a product exist, but each tries to differentiate itself enough to give the appearance of offering a unique product in the marketplace. Because their products are highly differentiated or they are separated by geographical distances, these companies do not necessarily gain or lose market share in response to a competitor's price cuts or increases.

3. Price skimming takes place when a company prices a product high in the expected price range. The strategy is used frequently when a new product is introduced because a company hopes to quickly recover the money it invested in development costs.

4. Penetration pricing is the strategy of setting a low initial price on a product with the objective of immediately reaching the mass market.

5. Pricing lining, a strategy used by some retailers, is choosing a set number of prices and then pricing goods within those categories.

6. Leader pricing involves a retailer's cutting the prices of a handful of popular items to attract customers. The items that are offered at these special prices are called "loss leaders." This strategy holds that customers will come to the store to buy not only the advertised loss leader but also nonsale items. As a result, the retailer hopes to experience an overall increase in sales volume as well as an increase in net profits.

7. A noncumulative quantity discount is based on a one-time order for a quantity of a product. This discount strategy encourages large orders. A cumulative quantity discount is based on the total volume purchased by a buyer over an agreed-upon period of time. The strategy is used to build a relationship between buyer and seller in which the buyer becomes closely dependent upon the seller for goods.

8. The retailer would pay $255 for the goods. The wholesaler would pay the product manufacturer $229.50.

9. If the buyer pays the bill by July 30 (10 days after the invoice date), he or she may take a 3 percent discount ($21) off the total due. If the bill is not paid by July 30, the entire bill must be paid by August 19 (within 30 days of the invoice date).

10. The three parts to a cash discount are:
    a. The percentage discount being offered
    b. The time frame for which the discount is offered
    c. An indication of the date after which the bill becomes overdue

Lesson Ten Answers

1. Distribution channels involve transferring ownership of product from producer to ultimate purchaser. A distribution channel is completed when the final purchaser makes no significant alterations to the product to resell it.

2. Each time a middleman gets involved in the channel of distribution, another level is added and the channels become longer.

3. Channel length indicates how many intermediaries are involved between the producer or manufacturer and the end user. A short channel would be one that involved the manufacturer's distributing directly to the end user. A medium channel might involve the distribution of a product from manufacturer to retailer to consumer. A long channel would include distribution channels moving products from manufacturer to wholesaler to retailer to consumer.

4. Channel intermediaries are the people or business who move products

from the producer to the consumer or industrial user. They are usually wholesalers or retailers.

5. Vertical channels are marketing channels through which a product manufacturer integrates its product into the marketplace by owning its wholesaling or retailing outlets, or both. The main reason manufacturers use vertical channels is to have more control over product distribution.

6. Channel captains are members of a distribution channel that is strong enough to have control over the other members of the channel.

7. Wholesaling involves sales of products from one firm to another for business use, not for end use.

8. The term "wholesaling middleman" refers to a business that acts primarily as an intermediary between the manufacturer or producer of a product and the end user.

9. Merchant wholesalers are usually referred to as "wholesalers," "jobbers," or "industrial distributors," depending on the function they serve or the industry in which they operate. Merchant wholesalers are typically independently owned, take title to the merchandise they distribute, and account for the bulk of wholesaling firms both in numbers and in volume of sales. The provide a variety of services to the manufacturer, including:
    a. Breaking bulk
    b. Assorting
    c. Buying products directly from the manufacturer
    d. Storing and transporting products

10. Agents and brokers are another category of wholesaling middlemen. Unlike merchant wholesalers, agents and brokers do not take title to the products they distribute, nor do they offer extensive services. The chief role of an agent or broker is to act as an intermediary in transferring the title of ownership of a product from manufacturer to customer. (The customer is sometimes a wholesaler, sometimes a retailer.)

Lesson Eleven Answers

1. Retailing intermediaries sell goods to ultimate consumers for nonbusiness use. They are often stores that sell directly to consumers.

2. Scrambled merchandising is the practice of adding unrelated lines of products to those carried in the rest of a store. It is a growing practice, particularly in food stores and drugstores.

3. Corporate chain stores are owned and managed by the same corporation. Voluntary chain stores consist of independent stores that form an association that enables the independent stores to have more economic power in the marketplace.

4. In a franchise system a franchisor gives independent franchisees the right to operate or sell the franchisor's service or product. The franchisee usually pays a franchise fee and a royalty on all earnings.

5. Franchising allows the franchising company to expand its retail franchise using the capital paid by the franchisee. Franchisees are able to enter a business that has a track record and gain from the market recognition of the franchise and the marketing expertise of the franchisor's management team.

6. The four principal types of retailing operations are:
   a. Full-service retailing firms
   b. Supermarket retailing firms
   c. Discount retailing firms
   d. Nonstore retailing firms

7. The five chief aspects of physical distribution are:
   a. Warehousing
   b. Materials handling
   c. Inventory control
   d. Order processing
   e. Transportation

8. Warehousing differs from storage in that warehousing involves not only storing products but also performing a variety of distribution functions including assembling, bulk breaking, and getting products ready for shipment from the warehouse.

9. The just-in-time concept of inventory control involves buying parts in small quantities just in time for use in production, and producing products just in time for sale to customers. Just-in-time inventory control can lower the expense of maintaining large inventories and increase a company's ability to inspect its products for quality control, since the production runs will often be smaller than previously.

10. The total-cost approach to distribution considers all aspects of distribution (customer satisfaction, safe handling procedures, etc.), not just the cheapest method of transportation or the best way to get products out of its warehouse.

Lesson Twelve Answers

1. Marketing communications is the process of developing messages and sending them to a specific receiver. It is successful when the message the sender wants to get across hits the desired target, is understood, and is acted upon.

2. Promotion is that aspect of the marketing mix that involves convincing or persuading a target audience about the quality or attractiveness of a company's products or services.

3. The term "promotional mix" refers to the choice of promotional tools that are used to market a product or service. The promotional mix can include advertising, sales promotion, personal selling, publicity, and public relations.

4. Direct-action advertising is designed to get customers to take immediate action; it encourages the prospective customer to make an immediate purchase decision. Indirect-action advertising is used to build awareness of a product so that when the customer is ready to make a purchase, he or she will be inclined to choose the advertiser's product.

5. The purpose of primary demand advertising is to create a demand for a broad product group rather than a specific product. Selective demand advertising is the opposite of primary demand advertising; it is used to create a demand for a specific brand of product.

6. AIDA is an acronym used to indicate the stages a person goes through in making a purchase decision:
   Attention
   Interest
   Desire
   Action

7. To make such a measurement of awareness, customers can be asked whether or not they have seen particular advertisements. Three techniques that can be used to perform this measurement are:
   a. *Unaided recall*, in which customers are simply asked to remember what ads they have seen or heard in a particular medium
   b. *Aided recall*, in which customers are asked such questions as "Do you remember seeing any ads about such and such a product?"
   c. *Recognition*, in which customers are shown a specific advertisement and asked if they remember having seen it

8. Media scheduling is the process companies go through to decide how often to run particular advertisements in particular media throughout an advertising campaign.

9. The 5-P process of personal selling consists of:
   a. Preparation
   b. Prospecting
   c. Preapproach
   d. Presentation
   e. Postsale

10. Public relations is a group's overall effort to create a positive image about a company among its target market or the community in which it operates. Publicity is the tool used in public relations to get the message across.

Index

Abstracts, 31
Accessory equipment, 89
Administered vertical marketing system, 138
Advertising, 52, 163, 164
  brand image, 165
  classification of, 165–166
  comparative, 167
  cooperative, 167–168
  costs of, 176–177
  direct-action, 166
  experimental, 176
  general, 168
  horizontal cooperative, 168
  indirect-action, 166
  institutional, 166
  local, 168
  measurement of, 168–171
  national, 168
  outdoor, 175–176
  patronage, 166
  pioneer, 167
  primary demand, 166–167
  product, 166
  public service, 166
  purpose of, 164–165
  reminder, 165
  selective demand, 167
  trade group, 167
  vertical cooperative, 167–168
Advertising allowance, 167
Advertising effectiveness research, 27
Advertising media, selecting, 171–176
Advertising research, 26–27
Advertising specialities, 180, 182
Age composition of population, 63–64
Agents, 140, 144–145
AIDA (attention, interest, desire, action), 170–171, 178, 179
Aided recall, 170

AIO (attitudes, interests and opinions), 73–74
American Management Association (AMA), 1, 3
Apple Computer, 64
Area samples, 39
Art museum, marketing of, 2
Assembling, 154
Assorting, 142
Attitude, 72
Attitudes, interests and opinions (AIO), 73–74
Auction companies, 146
Augmented product, 83–84
Average markup, 105

Baby-boom market, 60
  effect of, on marketing, 63–64
Bait-and-switch pricing, 120
Beliefs, 72
Belongingness, 70
Bidding system, 55–56
Biogenic needs, 69
Blumenblatt, Robert, 82
Brand, 94
  classification of, 95
Brand image advertising, 165
Brand label, 99
Brand loyalty, 77
Brand mark, 94
Brand name, 94, 96
  functions of, 96
Brand strategies, 96–98
  family, 97
  manufacturers', 96–97
  middlemen's, 97
  multiple-, 97–98
Branding, 94
BRCs (business reply cards), 174
Breakdown method, 42–43

Break-even analysis, 104, 106–107
Break-even point, determining, 106–107
Breaking bulk, 142
BREs (business reply envelopes), 174
Bristol-Myers Co., 184
Brokers, 140, 144–146
Buildup method, 43
Bulk breaking, 154
Business, importance of marketing in, 3
Business analysis, 84
Business charter, 53
Business considerations and distribution, 136
Business entities, 2
Business firms and marketing, 2
Business portfolio analysis, 16
Business purpose, 53–54
Business reply cards (BRCs), 174
Business reply envelopes (BREs), 174
Buyer's market, 6
Buying, decision-making process in, 77–78
Buying behavior:
  cultural influences on, 74–75
  lifestyle influences on, 73–74
Buying habits, 77
Buying patterns, 69

Cash-and-carry wholesalers, 144
Cash discounts, 122–123
Cash refunds, 180
Catalog, shopping by, 153
Catalog showrooms, 151–152
Chains, 149
  retailer-owned cooperative, 138
  wholesaler-sponsored voluntary, 138
Channel captains, 138–139
Channels of distribution, 129–130, 162
  conflict in, 137
  intermediaries in, 130, 139
  length of, 130
  multiple, 136–137
Clayton Antitrust Act (1914), 125
Cluster sampling, 40
CMSA (Consolidated Metropolitan Statistical Area), 62, 63
Coca-Cola, 95, 138
  and strategic planning, 20–22
Cognitive theories, 71
Collateral materials, 27
Commercialization, 84
Commission merchants, 146
Communications model in marketing, 161–162
Comparative advertising, 167

Competition:
  evaluating prices of, 114–117
  meeting prices of, 109–110
  monopolistic, 116
  nonprice options in response to, 116–117
  pricing below or above, 117
  types of, 116
Competitive pricing approach, 104
Computerized Information Technologies, Inc., 82
Concept testing, 83
Consolidated Metropolitan Statistical Area (CMSA), 62, 63
Conspicuous consumption, 75
Consumer(s):
  and distribution, 134
  versus industrial users, 56–57
  and marketing, 2
  ultimate, definition of, 57
Consumer buying behavior, 57–58
Consumer demographics, 58–59
  age composition, 63–64
  family life cycles, 67–68
  household size and structure, 65
  income and expenditures, 65–67
  population location, 60–63
  population size and growth rates, 59–60
  sexual composition, 64–65
  spending patterns, 65–67
Consumer goods, 86
  distribution of, 130–131
Consumer market, growth of, 66–67
Consumer product, classification of, 86–87
Consumer promotion, 180–182
Consumer psychographics, 69
  attitude, 72
  buying habits, 77
  cultural influences on buying behavior, 74–75
  decision-making process in buying, 77–78
  influences of lifestyle on buying behavior, 73–74
  learning, 71–72
  and motivation, 69–70
  perception, 70
  reference groups, 76–77
  social class, 75–76
Containerization, 155
Content research, 26–27
Contests, 180, 181
Contractual vertical marketing system, 138

Convenience goods, 86
  distribution of, 135
Convenience stores, 151
Cooperative advertising, 167–168
Corporate chain stores, 149
Corporate vertical marketing system, 138
Correlation analysis, 43, 44
Cost factors, 105–106
Cost-plus pricing, 104, 107
  drawbacks to, 105
  by middlemen, 104–105
Coupons, 179, 181
Cruise, Tom, 184
Cues, 71
Cultural influences on buying behavior,
  74–75
Culture, definition of, 74
Cumberland Packing Corporation, 167
Cumulative discount, 122
Curtis Publishing Company, 23
Customer, product adoption by, 84–86
Customer-intention surveys, 44
Customer orientation and marketing
  concept, 9
Customer reaction, gauging, 110–111

Data:
  collecting necessary, 40–41
  quality of, 31
Data banks, 29–30
Decision-making process in buying, 77–
  78
Decision support system, 27–28
Decoding, 162
Demand, 110
  determining, 110–114
  elasticity of, 112–114
  methods of forecasting, 42–45
Demand curve, 111–114
  kinked, 116
  knowing shape of, 112
Demographic makeup, 53
Demographic studies, 58–59
Demography, 58
Department stores, 148
Descriptive label, 99
Desk jobbers, 144
Direct-action advertising, 166
Direct costs, 106
Direct derivation, 43–44
Direct investment, 56
Direct mail, 52, 174–175
Discount(s), 121
Discount retailing firms, 151–152
Discount supermarkets, 151

Distribution, 52
  of consumer goods, 130–131
  factors affecting, 133–136
  major channels of, 130–133
Distribution centers, 154
Door-to-door sales, 152
Drive, 71
Drop shippers, 144
Dual distribution, 136–137
Dual-income families, 66
Duncan, C. S., 23

Early adopters, 85
Early majority, 85–86
Economic analysis, 25
Economic forecasting, 25
Economists and marketing, 2
Ego, 72
Elasticity of demand, 112–114
Encoding, 161–162
Esteem needs, 70
Evaluations, 72
Exchange, importance of, to marketing,
  1
Expected price, determining, 111
Experimental advertising, 176
Exporting, 56
Express warranties, 100
External environment, 20
"Exurbia," 62

Fabricating materials and parts, 88–89
Fair Packaging and Labeling Act, 100
Family brand strategy, 97
Family life cycles, 67–68
Family packaging, 98
Farm population, 60–61
FDA (Food and Drug Administration),
  labeling regulations of, 99–101
Federal legislation:
  on labeling, 99–101
  on pricing, 125–126
Federal Trade Commission (FTC),
  labeling regulations of, 99–101
Federal Trade Commission Act (1914),
  99, 125
Feedback, 162
Filene's Basement, 105
Fitzgerald, Sue, 19
5-P process, 178–179
Fixed costs, 106
FOB point-of-production pricing, 124
Focus group, 35
Food and Drug Act (1906), 99
Food and Drug Administration (FDA),
  labeling regulations of, 99–101

Food, Drug, and Cosmetics Act (1938), 99
Form utility, 3–4
Forward dating, 123
Forward vertical integration, 131
Franchised stores, 148
Franchising, 56, 138, 149
Free samples, 181
Freight absorption pricing, 125
Frequency, 171
Freud, Sigmund, 71–72
FTC (Federal Trade Commission),
    labeling regulations of, 99–101
Full-service retailers, 150
Fuller Brush, 152
Functional discounts, 122
Fur Products Labeling Act (1951), 99
Futrell, Charles, 67

General advertising, 168
General Electric, 8, 166
General merchandise stores, 148
Generic name, 96
Geographic factors in pricing, 123–125
Giveaways, 180
Goals:
    profit-oriented, 108
    sales-oriented, 109
    status quo, 109–110
Goodyear Tire, 137
Government market, 55–56
Grade label, 99
Greene, Bob, 184
Gross ratings points, 171

Hardware, 30
Hierarchy of needs theory, 70
High-involvement purchases, 73
Honda, 78–79
Horizontal cooperative advertising, 168
Household service providers, 148
Household size and structure, 65
Hudson Industries, 15

IBM, marketing concept of, 10–12
Id, 71
Image utility, 4, 103
Imitative products, 82
Imperfect competition, 116
Implied warranties, 100
Index, 31
Indirect-action advertising, 166
Indirect costs, 106
Industrial distributors, 141
Industrial goods, 86
    classification of, 88–90

Industrial goods (Cont.):
    distribution of, 132–133
Industrial user promotion, 180, 182
Industrial users:
    versus consumers, 56–57
    definition of, 57
    and distribution, 134
Inelastic, 112
Informal investigation, 33
Information, 30
In-home personal selling, 152
Innovators, 85
In Search of Excellence (Peters and
    Waterman), 10–11
Installations, 89
Institutional advertising, 166
In-store point-of-purchase displays, 180
Intermediaries, 139
    agents, 144–145
    auction companies, 146
    brokers, 144–146
    cash-and-carry wholesalers, 144
    commission merchants, 146
    drop shippers, 144
    limited-service wholesalers, 143–144
    manufacturers' agents, 145
    manufacturers' sales branches and
        offices, 146–147
    rack jobbers, 143
    retailer cooperative chains, 144
    retailing intermediaries, 147–149
    selling agents, 146
    truck jobbers, 143–144
    wholesaling, 139–144
Internal environment, 20
International market, 56
Inventory control, 155
Inverse demand, 111

J. S. & A., 153
Jiffy Lube, 138
Jobbers, 141
Joint ventures, 56
Junk mail, 175
Just-in-time inventory-control manage-
    ment, 155

Kemp & George, 169–170
Kentucky Fried Chicken, 56
Kiely, Kathy, 167
Kinked demand curve, 116
K-Mart, 138, 168
Kurzina, Klaus, 82

Labeling, 99
    regulations on, 99–100

Laggards, 86
Larson, Karen, 167
Late majority, 86
Layered samples, 40
Leader pricing, 120
Learning, 71–72
Lifestyle:
  definition of, 73
  influences of, on buying behavior, 73–74
Limited-function wholesalers, 143
Limited line stores, 148–149
Limited-service wholesalers, 143–144
List brokers, 174–175
Local advertising, 168
Long channel, 130
Long-range planning, 13–14
Love needs, 70
Low-involvement purchases, 73
Lower-lower class, 76
Lower-middle class, 75–76
Lower-upper class, 75

McDonald's, 56, 95, 99, 138, 166
McKesson, 138–139
McMahon, Jim, 184
Magazines, 173
Magnuson-Moss Consumer Product Warranty-Federal Trade Commission Act (1975), 100–101
Mail interviews, 36
Mail-order catalog houses, 148
Mail-order selling, 152–153
Management, 18–20
Manufacturers' agents, 145
Manufacturers' representatives, 145
Manufacturers' sales branches and offices, 146–147
Manufacturers' strategies, 96–98
Marginal costs, 112
Marginal revenues, 112
Market(s):
  definition of, 49–50, 53
  and distribution, 133–134
  location of, and distribution, 133–134
  potential, 2
  size of, and distribution, 133
Market aggregation, 54
Market analysis, 25
Market demand, 110
Market factor, 41–42
Market-factor analysis, 43–44
  sales-force composite method of, 45
Market index, 42
Market opportunity, 54

Market position, 115
Market potential, 25, 42
Market research, 110
  and advertising research, 26–27
  collecting necessary data, 40–41
  data analysis and interpretation, 41
  defining marketing objective, 32
  definition of, 24
  designing study for, 33–40
  development of, 23–24
  performance of, 45–46
  and pricing research, 26
  and product research, 25–26
  relationship between, and marketing information systems, 28–29
  and sales research, 27
  types of applications, 25–27
  use of, to measure advertising, 168–169
Market segmentation, 54–55, 60
  demographic bases for, 68–69
Market share, 42
Market tests, 26
Marketers, 2
Marketing:
  communications model in, 161–162
  and creation of utilities, 3–4
  definition of, 1–3
  evolution of, 4–8
  external factors affecting, 20
  importance of, in business, 3
  importance of exchange to, 1
  internal factors affecting, 20
  marketing-oriented phase of, 7
  production-oriented phase of, 5–6
  sales-oriented phase of, 6–7
  setting for, 2
  social-oriented phase of, 8
Marketing communications, 161
  advertising, 164–177
  communications model in, 161–162
  definition of, 161
  personal selling, 177–179
  promotion, 162–163
  promotional mix, 163
  publicity and public relations, 182–184
  sales promotion, 179–182
Marketing concept, 8–10
  distinction between selling concept and, 9
  implementation of, 9–10
Marketing forecasts, 41–42
Marketing information systems, 24
  definition of, 27–28
  design of, 30–31
  operations of, 31

Marketing information systems (*Cont.*):
  relationship between market research
    and, 28–29
  sources of data for, 29
  types of, 29–30
Marketing mix, 50–53, 103, 129
Marketing objectives, defining, 32
Marketing-oriented phase of business, 7
Marketing-oriented philosophy, 8
Markup, 105
Marshalls, 151
Maslow, Abraham H., 70
Materials handling, 154–155
Maximum profits, 108
Maxx, T. J., 151
Media flowcharts, 172
Media research, 27
Media scheduling, 171–172
Media strategy, 171–172
Media Syndicate, 183
Medium channel, 130
Megalopolis, 63
Merchant wholesalers, 141–143
Metropolitan Statistical Area (MSA),
    62–63
Middlemen, 89, 96
  branding strategies of, 97–98
  cost-plus pricing by, 104–105
  and distribution, 135–136
Mission statement, developing, 14–15
Model banks, 29–30
Monopolistic competition, 116
Motivation, 69–70
  Maslow's theory of, 70
Motive, 69, 71
Movies, 184
MSA (Metropolitan Statistical Area),
    62–63
Multiple-brand strategy, 97–98
Multiple distribution, 136–137
Multiple packaging, 98–99
Muppets, 95

Nabisco, 137
National advertising, 168
National brand, 95
National Convenience Stores, Inc., 181
Natural Choice Industries, Inc., 101–102
Needs, 69, 70
  belongingness and love, 70
  biogenic, 69
  definition of, 50
  esteem, 70
  physiological, 70
  psychogenic, 69

Needs (*Cont.*):
  safety and security, 70
  self-actualization, 70
New products, 81–82
News mentions, 184
News stories, 183–184
Newspapers, 172–173
Nielsen, A. C., 27
Noise, 162
Noncumulative discount, 122
Nonprice options in response to competitors' pricing, 116–117
Nonprobability samples, 40
Nonresponse bias, 36
Nonstore retailing, 152
Not-for-profit organizations, 2
  marketing by, 3
  marketing mix for, 52–53
Nystrom, Paul H., 23

Objective, 18
Observation method of data collecting,
    36–37
Odd-even pricing, 121
Off-price retailers, 151
Oligopoly, 116
Operating supplies, 90
Opinion leader, 77
Order processing, 155
Orders, size of, and distribution, 134
Organizational coordination and marketing concept, 9
Outdoor advertising, 175–176
Overproduction, 6

Packaging, 98
  strategies for, 98–99
Parity products, 82–83
Parlin, Charles Coolidge, 23
Party-plan type of selling, 152
Past sales analysis, 45
Patronage advertising, 166
Penetration, 118–119
Penney, J. C., 168
Pepsi-Cola, 138
Perception, 70
Perishability and distribution, 134
Personal interviews, 35
Personal selling, 52, 163, 177–179
Personnel, 31
Peters, Thomas J., 10
Physical distribution, 154–158
Physiological needs, 70
Piggybacking mailings, 153
Pioneer advertising, 167
Place, 51, 52, 129

Place utility, 4, 103
Planning activities, scope of, 13–16
PMSA (Primary Metropolitan Statistical
    Area), 62, 63
Policy, 19–20
Political parties, 2
Possession utility, 4, 103
Postpurchase behavior, 77
Postsale, 179
Posttesting, 169
Potential market, breakdown of, 55
Preapproach, 179
Premiums, 180
Preparation, 178
Presentation, 179
Prestige pricing, 121
Pretesting, 169
Price, 51, 52, 103
Price rebates, 181
Price-reduction displays, 181
Price segments served, 115
Price sensitivity, 115
Price stabilization, 109
Pricing:
    bait-and-switch, 120
    below or above competitive levels,
        117
    and cash discounts, 122–123
    and discounts, 121–123
    federal legislation on, 125–126
    FOB point-of-production, 124
    forward dating, 123
    freight absorption, 125
    geographic factors in, 123–125
    leader, 120
    objectives, 107–110
    and odd-even, 121
    and penetration, 118–119
    prestige, 121
    and pricing lining, 119–120
    psychological, 121
    and quantity discounts, 121–122
    and seasonal discounts, 123
    and skimming, 118
    target return, 108
    and trade discounts, 122
    uniform-delivered, 124
    and unit, 119
    zone-delivered, 124
Pricing lining, 119–120
Pricing research, 26
Primary data, 34–40
Primary demand advertising, 166–167
Primary Metropolitan Statistical Area
    (PMSA), 62, 63
Private brand, 95
Probability samples, 40

Procedures, 31
Product(s), 51, 52, 103
    augmented, 83–84
    definition of, 81
    distribution of, 129–130, 134–135
    imitative, 82
    new, 81–82
    parity, 82–83
    replacement, 82
    technical sophistication of, and
        distribution, 134
    unique, 82
Product adopter, categories of, 85–86
Product adoption by customer, 84–86
Product advertising, 166
Product benefits, 81
Product classification, 86–90
Product concept testing, 25
Product demonstrations, 180
Product development, 84
Product differentiation, 82, 115–116
Product life cycle, 92
    decline, 93–94
    growth, 93
    introduction, 92–93
    length of, 94–98
    maturity, 93
Product lines, 90–91
    positioning of, 91
    trade downs, 91
    trade ups, 91
Product mix, 90–91
Product planning and development,
    stages in, 83–84
Product positioning, 91
Product research, 25–26
Product use tests, 25–26
Production-oriented marketing, 5–6
Profit-oriented goals, 108
Profits, maximizing, 108
Promotion, 51–53, 103, 162–163
Promotional allowance, 167
Promotional mix, 163
Prospecting, 178
Psychoanalytic theory, 71–72
Psychogenic needs, 69
Psychographic profiles, 73–74
Psychographics, 69
Psychological pricing strategies, 121
Public relations, 182–183
Public service advertising, 166
Publicity, 52, 182–183
Publicity campaign, 183

Quality, 117
Quantity discounts, 121–122
Quota samples, 39–40

Rack jobbers, 143
Radio, 175
Raffles, 181
Random-dialing approach, 36
Random sampling, 40
Raw materials, 88
Reach, 171
Readership tests, 169
Recall:
  aided, 170
  unaided, 170
Recall tests, 169
Receiver, 162
Recognition, 170
Recognition tests, 169
Reference groups, 76–77
Reinforcement, 71
Reminder advertising, 165
Replacement products, 82
Repositioning, 72
Response, 71
Response mechanisms, measuring,
  169–170
Retail stores, 148
Retailer cooperative chains, 144
Retailer-owned cooperative chains, 138
Retailers:
  operation of, 150–153
  ownership of, 149
Retailing intermediaries, 147–149
Reuse packaging, 98
Robinson-Patman Act (1936), 125–126
Roman, Ernan, 179
Rovner, Matthew, 183

Safety and security needs, 70
Sales analysis, 27
Sales force, prestige of, in business, 6
Sales-force composite method of market-
  factor analysis, 45
Sales-force promotion, 181, 182
Sales forecast, 42–43
  methods of, 42–45
Sales-oriented goals, 109
Sales-oriented marketing, 6–7
Sales potential, 42
Sales promotion, 52, 179–180
  types of, 180–182
Sales research, 27
Sales volume, profitable, and marketing
  concept, 9
SAMI (Selling Areas-Marketing, Inc.), 74
Samples, 34, 179, 180
  area, 39
  free, 181
  layered, 40

Samples (*Cont.*):
  nonprobability, 40
  planning of, 39
  probability, 40
  quota, 39–40
  simple room, 39
  stratified, 40
Sampling, 39
SBU (strategic business units), 14–16
Scientific sampling, 23
Scrambled merchandising, 149
Seasonal discounts, 123
Secondary data, 34
Selective demand advertising, 167
Selectivity, 70
Self-actualization needs, 70
Selling, 1, 163
  personal, 177–179
Selling agents, 146
Selling Areas-Marketing, Inc. (SAMI), 74
Selling concept, distinction between, and
  marketing concept, 9
Service, 81, 117
Sexual composition, 64–65
Sherman-Antitrust Act (1890), 125
Shopping goods, 87
  distribution of, 135
Shopping-mall intercept method, 35
Short channel of distribution, 129, 130
Short-term planning, 14
Shulz, Charles, 95
Simmons, W. R., and Company, 27
Simple random samples, 39
Single-line stores, 148–149
Singles, 68–69
Situation analysis, 33
Skimming, 118
Social class, 75–76
Social-oriented marketing, 8
SoftAd Group, 176
Software, 30
Sony, 167
Specialty goods, 87
  distribution of, 135
Specialty stores, 149
Speeches, 184
Spending patterns, 65
Spiegel Inc., 153
Stanton, William, 67
Statistical banks, 29–30
Status quo goals, 109–110
Stimulus-response theories, 71
Strategic business units (SBU), 14
  planning with, 15–16
Strategic environment, 20
Strategic marketing planning, 16–18

Strategic planning:
 definition of, 13
 development of mission statement in,
   14–15
 and environment, 20
 and management, 18–20
 scope of planning activities, 13–16
 setting objectives to meet goals, 15
 use of strategic business units in, 15–16
Strategy, 18
Stratified sampling, 40
Subcultures, 74–75
Suburban growth, 62
Sunbelt, 60
Superego, 71–72
Supermarkets, 151
Superstores, 151
Supply and demand approach, 104
Surplus, 6
Survey method of collecting primary data,
   34–36
 mail interviews, 36
 personal interviews, 35
 telephone interviews, 35–36
Sweepstakes, 180
Swift and Company, 23
Systematic sampling, 40

Tactics, 18–19
Target markets, 54–57
Target return approach, 108
Target return net sales, 108
Target return pricing, 108
Taylor, William, 84
Telemarketing, 52, 152, 179
Telephone interviews, 35–36
Television, 175
Television displays, 184
Tendency to act, 72
Test marketing, 44–45, 84, 111
Textile Fiber Products Identification Act
   (1958), 99–100
Thom McAn, 137
Tile City, 137
Time utility, 4, 103
Top-down method, 42–43
Total cost approach, 156
Trade discounts, 122
Trade group advertising, 167
Trade promotion, 180, 181
Trade shows, 180
Trading down, 91
Trading stamps, 180, 181
Trading up, 91
Trademark, 94

Trademark licensing, 94–95
Transportation, 155–158
 comparison of modes of, 157
Trend analysis, 45
Truck distributors, 143
Truck jobbers, 143–144
Tunnel Radio, 175
Tupperware, 152
Two-for-one packages, 181

Unaided recall, 170
Uniform-delivered pricing, 124
Unique products, 82
Unit pricing, 119
Unit value and distribution, 134
United States Rubber Company, 23
U.S. Trademark Act (1946), 94–95
Universe, 39
Unsought goods, 87
Upper-lower class, 76
Upper-middle class, 75
Upper-upper class, 75
Utilities, 103
 creation of, 3–4
 definition of, 3
 form, 3–4
 image, 4, 103
 place, 4, 103
 possession, 4, 103
 time, 4, 103
 types of, 3–4

VALS (values and lifestyles), 74
Value, 74, 103
Values and lifestyles (VALS), 74
Variable costs, 106
Vending machines, 148, 153
Vernon, Lillian, Inc., 153
Vertical channels, 137–139
Vertical cooperative advertising, 167–168
Vertical marketing systems, 137–139
VideoRated, Inc., 153
Voluntary chain stores, 149

Wagon jobbers, 143
Warehouse clubs, 151
Warehousing, 154
Warranties, 100–101
 express, 100
 implied, 100
Waterman, Robert H., Jr., 10
WATS (Wide-Area Telephone Service),
   36
Wheeler-Lea Amendment (1938), 99, 126
Wholesale clubs, 151
Wholesale trade, 139

Wholesaler, 140–144
Wholesaler-sponsored voluntary chains,
    138
Wholesaling intermediaries, 139–144
Wholesaling middleman, 140
Wide-Area Telephone Service (WATS),
    36
Wild, L. D. H., 23
Wine, Barry, 73
Women in work force, 66
Wool Products Labeling Act (1940), 99

Working class, 76
World War I and evolution of marketing,
    6
World War II and evolution of market-
    ing, 7

Young unmarried couples, 68–69

Zenith, 167
Zero-level channel of distribution, 129
Zone-delivered pricing, 124

About the Author

Jeffrey L. Seglin is a frequent contributor to *Venture, Inc.*, *Personal Investing, Financial Planning, Marketing Week*, and other publications. He is also the author or coauthor of ten business books. He runs Seglin Associates in Boston, a consulting group specializing in writing, editing, and marketing projects.

Final Examination

The McGraw-Hill 36-Hour Marketing Course

Name _____

Address _____

City _____ State _____ Zip _____

If you have completed your study of *The McGraw-Hill 36-Hour Marketing Course*, you should be prepared to take this final examination. It is a comprehensive examination, consisting of 100 questions.

Instructions

1. You can treat the exam as an open-book test if you like, referring to this and other textbooks while taking it. That approach will help to reinforce your learning and to correct any misconceptions. On the other hand, if you prefer to establish a superior understanding of the subject matter, you may choose to take the examination without reference to any textbook.

2. Answer each of the test questions directly on the examination sheets. Do so by circling the letter that corresponds to the answer you choose.

EXAMPLE

0. The AMA defines *marketing* as "the process of planning and executing the conception, pricing, promotion, and_____ of ideas, goods, and services to create exchanges that satisfy individual and organizational objectives."
   a. selling   *c.* wholesaling
   b. manipulating   *ⓓ* distribution

3. The questions are either multiple-choice, with four alternative answers to choose from, or true-false. Always select the answer that represents in your mind the *best* among the choices.

4. Each correctly answered question is worth 1 point on a scale of 100 percent. You must answer 70 questions correctly to have a passing grade of 70 percent (70 ÷ 100). A passing grade entitles you to receive a *certificate of achievement*. This handsome certificate, suitable for framing, attests to your proven knowledge of marketing.

5. Carefully fill in your name and address in the spaces provided at the beginning of this exam, and send your completed examination to:

Alison Spalding—Certification Examiner
36-Hour Marketing Course
Professional & Reference Division
McGraw-Hill Book Company
11 West 19th Street
New York, NY 10011

---

1. Marketing research is the
   a. pricing, packaging, and labeling of product offerings.
   b. long-term analysis of a product's chance for survival in the market.
   c. gathering, recording, and analyzing of data that relates to a specific problem in marketing products or services.
   d. creation, application, and adaptation of products as they become needed in the market.

2. To see how customers might react to a new product, companies use
   a. professional actors.
   b. strategic business units (SBUs).
   c. product concept tests.
   d. tamper-proof packaging.

3. For the marketing process to occur, there must be marketers; the goods, services, or ideas being marketed; and
   a. break-even analyses.
   b. potential markets.
   c. strategic business units.
   d. warranties.

4. The "selling concept" and the "marketing concept" are interchangeable terms.
   a. True
   b. False

5. The process companies go through to decide how often to run particular advertisements in particular media throughout an advertising campaign is called
   a. response engineering.
   b. graphic design.
   c. market analysis.
   d. media scheduling.

6. Parity products are
   a. competing products that customers perceive to be similar.
   b. consumer durable goods.
   c. products unacceptable to the target market.
   d. unique to the marketplace.

7. _____ is the process of trading something of value (e.g., money, time, goods) to someone who voluntarily offers you something of value (e.g., ideas, goods, or services) in return.
   a. Returning
   b. Price lining
   c. Exchange
   d. Marketing

8. In the market demand for any given product or service, the following three factors come into play: (1) people or groups with needs to satisfy, (2) the purchasing power of these people or groups, and (3) the buying patterns and behavior of these people or groups.
   a. True
   b. False

9. The aspect of the marketing mix that involves convincing or persuading a target audience about the quality or attractiveness of a company's products or services is called
   a. product.
   b. price.
   c. place.
   d. promotion.

10. The three basic tenets at the heart of the marketing concept are
    a. people, place, things.
    b. price, promotion, product.
    c. distribution orientation, product orientation, price orientation.
    d. customer orientation, profitable sales volume, organizational co-ordination.

11. In a random (probability) sample the survey units are selected so that
    a. each unit in the overall universe has the same probability of having been chosen for the sample.
    b. spoilage is likely to occur in at least 10 percent of the sample.
    c. all demographic and psychographic groups will be represented.
    d. costs of marketing research are kept in check.

12. The just-in-time concept of inventory control management involves buying parts in small quantities just in time for use in production, and producing products just in time for sale to customers.
    a. True
    b. False

13. The four types of utilities that are created by marketing are
    a. time, place, possession, image.
    b. electric, gas, telephone, propane.
    c. usability, marketability, durability, replaceability.
    d. primary, secondary, penultimate, final.

14. The four elements of the marketing mix are
    a. production, marketing, technological, social.
    b. advertising, personal selling, promotion, publicity.
    c. product, price, place, promotion.
    d. capital, inventory, quality control, delivery.

15. The 5-P process of personal selling includes
    a. preparation, prospecting, preapproach, presentation, postsale.
    b. producing, pricing, placing, presenting, promoting.
    c. preparation, paving, placating, presenting, postsale.
    d. preparation, pricing, presentation, public relations, post mortem.

16. Market sampling involves testing products for spoilage.
    a. True
    b. False

17. AIDA is an acronym used to indicate the stages a person goes through in making a purchase decision. It stands for
    a. attention, interest, desire, action.
    b. attitude, interest, desire, action.
    c. attention, inclination, declaration, action.
    d. attention, interest, decision, acceptance.

18. The three basic types of marketing information systems are

    a. word processing, spreadsheet analysis, communications module.
    b. radio, television, newspaper.
    c. linear, algebraic, geometric.
    d. data banks, statistical banks, model banks.

19. A strategic plan is a plan developed to help a business
    a. determine how best to make a profit.
    b. formulate a direction and focus for the future.
    c. evaluate marketing research results and make decisions accordingly.
    d. weigh which products should be taken off the market.

20. A utility is that feature in something that causes it to be able to satisfy needs and wants.
    a. True
    b. False

21. The five chief aspects of physical distribution are
    a. warehousing, materials handling, inventory control, order processing, transportation.
    b. warehousing, retailing, purchasing, inventory control, delivery.
    c. inventory control, retailing, purchasing, processing, ordering.
    d. retailing, wholesaling, pricing, discounting, delivery.

22. Using the cost-plus pricing method, how much would you charge for each unit of a product if your total cost for producing 4000 units were $21,000 and you wanted a 40 percent profit?
    a. $7.35
    b. $7.15
    c. $6.95
    d. $7.25

23. The four phases in the evolution of marketing are
    a. primitive, developmental, mature, declining.
    b. fertilization, incubation, hatching, launching.
    c. production-oriented, sales-oriented, marketing-oriented, marketing and social-oriented.
    d. industrial-based, service-based, technology-based, service- and technology-based.

24. The marketing concept at its core holds that businesses do not exist, economically and socially, to fulfill consumers' wants and needs, but rather to make a profit at any cost.
    a. True
    b. False

25. To plan and manage more efficiently, many large companies have divided into major product or market divisions, which have become known as

      a. marketing support groups (MSGs).

      b. strategic business units (SBUs).

      c. profit accountability center clusters (PACs).

      d. division product groups (DPGs).

26. The promotional mix can include
      a. product, price, place, promotion.
      b. attention, interest, desire, action.
      c. advertising, sales promotion, personal selling, publicity and public relations.
      d. wholesaling, retailing, discounting.

27. What some individual or organization pays for a product or service is
      a. test marketing.
      b. demographics.
      c. price.
      d. repositioning.

28. The annual marketing plan (1) lists the objectives of the marketing effort; (2) pinpoints the target markets; (3) details the strategies that will be used to attract those target markets, including the marketing mix being used; and (4) identifies how much money is available to perform these marketing tasks.
      a. True
      b. False

29. Three techniques that can be used to measure customer awareness of particular advertisements are
      a. cost analysis, economic analysis, situational analysis.
      b. focus groups, price discounts, free samples.
      c. unaided recall, aided recall, recognition.
      d. questionnaires, quantitative analysis, qualitative analysis.

30. Maslow's five levels of human needs are
      a. physiological needs, safety and security, belongingness and love, esteem, self-actualization.
      b. physiological, psychological, economic, social, spiritual.
      c. primal, tribal, relational, dimensional, self-actualization.
      d. lower, upper-lower, lower-middle, middle, upper-middle.

31. Strategic planning goes beyond the marketing concept by
      a. removing all unprofitable products from the business' offerings.
      b. considering the wishes of management and production workers.
      c. insisting that the business look at *all* external factors that may affect the company.
      d. determining how best to beat competitors to market.

32. Marketing communications is the process of developing messages and sending them to a specific receiver. It is successful when the message the sender wants to get across hits the desired target, is understood, and is acted upon.

    a. True
    b. False

33. A reference group is a group of
    a. research librarians who aid marketing professionals.
    b. periodicals that pertain to marketing research activities.
    c. people who influence an individual's attitudes, values, and behavior patterns.
    d. marketing researchers who share ideas and strategies.

34. A mission statement is a formal statement about a company's mission in business.
    a. True
    b. False

35. Intermediaries who sell goods to ultimate consumers for nonbusiness use are called
    a. wholesaling intermediaries.
    b. landlords.
    c. functional intermediaries.
    d. retailing intermediaries.

36. The five categories of product adopters are
    a. lower, upper-lower, lower-middle, middle, upper-middle.
    b. unique adopters, copycats, trailblazers, innovators, adapters.
    c. innovators, early adopters, early majority, later majority, laggards.
    d. primary adopters, secondary adopters, posttesters, pretesters, approvers.

37. A strategic marketing plan details the marketing objectives of a business firm that fit in with the overall strategic objectives of a company. The strategic marketing plan usually can help the business focus on the most profitable market segments and market opportunities available.
    a. True
    b. False

38. When a business raises its prices and finds that sales increase, the result is called
    a. "marketing."
    b. "inverse demand."
    c. "pricing."
    d. "strategic planning."

39. The four principal types of retailing operations are
    a. mom-and-pop, variety, grocery, retail.
    b. clothing, food, grocery, automotive.
    c. discount, prestige, mall, freestanding.
    d. full-service, supermarket, discount, nonstore.

40. Market analysis is used to analyze market segment factors to determine the market potential of a given product or service.
    a. True
    b. False

41. How the desired content in an advertisement comes across to an audience sampling is measured by
    a. content research.
    b. situational analysis.
    c. applause meters.
    d. demographics.

42. The practice of adding unrelated lines of products to those carried in the rest of a store is called
    a. "scrambled merchandising."
    b. "intrusive interloping."
    c. "disjointed intermediary tactics."
    d. "quick-fix marketing."

43. Demand is measured as the total amount of product or service bought (in monetary amount or units sold) in a given time period.
    a. True
    b. False

44. There is no distinguishable difference between primary demand and selective demand advertising.
    a. True
    b. False

45. To determine whether the desired message is getting across to customers in a positive manner, marketing researchers
    a. pretest and posttest.
    b. use speciality advertising.
    c. prepare and postpone.
    d. use direct response mechanisms.

46. The sales of products from one firm to another for business use, not for end use, is called
    a. "retailing."
    b. "free enterprise."
    c. "wholesaling."
    d. "vending."

47. In the competitive pricing approach, in-house marketing personnel bid on price structures.
    a. True
    b. False

48. The member of a distribution channel who is strong enough to have control over the other members of the channel is called
    a. a marketing strongman.
    b. a channel captain.

    c. a distribution controller.

    d. an advertising executive.

49. Augmented products include something extra that is provided to the product buyer—something that goes beyond what is normally expected when such a product is purchased.

    a. True

    b. False

50. In a franchise system, a franchiser gives independent franchisees the right to operate or sell the franchiser's service or product. The franchisee usually pays a franchise fee and a royalty on all earnings.

    a. True

    b. False

51. A positively sloped demand curve suggests that

    a. customers have positive feelings about a product.

    b. customers have negative feelings about a product.

    c. as prices rise, demand increases.

    d. as prices rise, demand decreases.

52. Economic analysis is used to figure out how much a competitor's product costs.

    a. True

    b. False

53. Marketing channels through which the product manufacturer integrates its product into the marketplace by owning its wholesaling or retailing outlets, or both, are called

    a. "marketing straits."

    b. "focus groups."

    c. "vertical channels."

    d. "horizontal channels."

54. Marketing research departments do sales analyses by studying customer records and other available data to determine where marketing opportunities lie among potential target markets.

    a. True

    b. False

55. Corporate chain stores and voluntary chain stores have exactly the same type of ownership and management.

    a. True

    b. False

56. Using the survey method, the marketing researcher gathers data by

    a. studying the psychographic makeup of the consumer market.

    b. preparing an on-site engineering study of the prospective market's dwelling.

    c. interviewing a sample of people selected from a larger target market group.

    d. consulting the marketing information system.

57. A marketing information system provides a continuous flow of marketing information that management can use to make marketing decisions. It is made up of data that can be generated, stored, and retrieved for use in the marketing decision-making process.

    a. True

    b. False

58. When reducing a product's unit price causes an increase in total revenue or raising the unit price causes a decrease in total revenue, demand for the product is said to be

    a. "elastic."

    b. "inelastic."

    c. "stagnant."

    d. "kinetic."

59. The purpose of a situation analysis is to get a sense of the situation in which the marketing problem exists by analyzing the business, the market, the competition, and the type of business being done.

    a. True

    b. False

60. The people or businesses who move products from the producer to the consumer or industrial user are called

    a. "channel intermediaries."

    b. "movers."

    c. "marketing researchers."

    d. "operational engineers."

61. Market definition is the measurement of the characteristics of an organization's actual or prospective buyers.

    a. True

    b. False

62. The three parts to a cash discount are

    a. the percentage discount being offered, the time frame for which the discount is offered, an indication of the date after which the bill becomes overdue.

    b. situational, optional, compulsory.

    c. the amount of cash due, the product liability, the product warranty.

    d. the percentage discount being offered, the product warranty, the inventory location.

63. The five basic parts of any marketing information system are hardware, software, information, procedures, and personnel.

    a. True

    b. False

64. The experimental method of gathering primary data for marketing research involves setting up
    a. a controlled experiment in which real market situations are simulated.
    b. a laboratory where products can be chemically tested.
    c. databases with customer information.
    d. a marketing research department.

65. The term "wholesaling middleman" is used to refer to a business that acts primarily as an intermediary between the manufacturer or producer of a product and the end user.
    a. True
    b. False

66. Estimating the future demand for a product within particular segments of the overall marketplace and then adding together all the estimates to get an overall sales forecast is an example of
    a. top-down sales forecasting.
    b. economic analysis.
    c. the marketing concept.
    d. buildup sales forecasting.

67. A target market is that segment (or segments) of the market that an organization has chosen to direct its primary marketing efforts.
    a. True
    b. False

68. Each time a middleman gets involved in the channel of distribution, another level is added and the channels become
    a. more expensive.
    b. more static-prone.
    c. longer.
    d. more tedious.

69. Market segmentation involves viewing a market as being composed of several smaller segments, and targeting one of the segments.
    a. True
    b. False

70. If a product manufacturer quotes a retailer a retail list price of $820 with trade discounts of 45 percent and 10 percent: (1) How much would the retailer pay the wholesaler for the goods? (2) How much would the wholesaler pay the product manufacturer?
    a. (1) $451.00; (2) $369.00
    b. (1) $369.00; (2) $332.10
    c. (1) $451.00; (2) $405.90
    d. (1) $451.00; (2) $332.10

71. There is no difference between an ultimate consumer and an industrial user.

a. True

b. False

72. Demography is
    a. the use of demonstrations to market products.
    b. the statistical study of human populations.
    c. the analysis of buying decisions.
    d. the technique of selling display models at reduced prices.

73. Value is a quantitative measure of the worth of a product or service, in terms of its ability to attract something in exchange for it.
    a. True
    b. False

74. Using a market aggregation strategy, a company views the market as
    a. an oligopoly.
    b. a monopoly.
    c. an entirety.
    d. a megalopolis.

75. Forecasting overall economic trends to determine the industry's market potential for a product, and measuring the market share the firm is already getting for a product is an example of
    a. economic analysis.
    b. top-down sales forecasting.
    c. buildup sales forecasting.
    d. the marketing concept.

76. The term "psychographics" is most commonly used in marketing to describe people's activities, interests, opinions, motives, personalities, personal values, attitudes, and lifestyles.
    a. True
    b. False

77. The practice, indulged in by some retailers, of choosing a set number of prices and then pricing its goods within those categories is called
    a. "pricing lining."
    b. "leader pricing."
    c. "penetration pricing."
    d. "price skimming."

78. Merchant wholesalers usually take title to the merchandise they distribute, while agents and brokers do not.
    a. True
    b. False

79. The two broad areas measured by market definition are
    a. (1) who the buyers and prospective buyers are and
        (2) how the buyers and prospective buyers buy.
    b. (1) the incomes of the prospective buyers and
        (2) their social backgrounds.

     c. (1) the occupations of the prospective buyers and
     (2) their group status symbols.
     d. (1) price resistance and (2) product acceptance.

80. Distribution channels involve transferring ownership of product from producer to ultimate purchaser. A distribution channel is completed when the final purchaser makes no significant alterations to the product to resell it.
     a. True
     b. False

81. The three groups of metropolitan areas classified by the U.S. government are
     a. cities, townships, villages.
     b. shopping malls, hotels, convention centers.
     c. Metropolitan Statistical Areas (MSAs), Primary Metropolitan Statistical Areas (PMSAs), Consolidated Metropolitan Statistical Areas (CMSAs).
     d. Quintile Metropolitan Areas, Secondary Metropolitan Areas, Progressive Metropolitan Areas.

82. The number of intermediaries involved between a producer or manufacturer and an end user is indicated by
     a. the marketing researcher.
     b. primary markets.
     c. elastic demand.
     d. channel length.

83. Setting a low initial price on a product with the objective of immediately reaching the mass market is called
     a. "pricing lining."
     b. "leader pricing."
     c. "penetration pricing."
     d. "price skimming."

84. A company's product mix consists of
     a. the ingredients used to make a product.
     b. all the products and product lines a business offers.
     c. product, price, place, and promotion.
     d. demographics and pyschographics.

85. When a marketer attempts to change a consumer's attitude about a product, the process is often called "repositioning."
     a. True
     b. False

86. Four methods of doing business internationally are

    a. commercial airlines, shipping lines, postal services, telegraph lines.
    b. bilingual swap arrangements, multilingual purchasing agreements, primary language directorates, pluralistic commitments.
    c. franchising, exporting, joint ventures, direct investment.
    d. franchising, situational analyses, economic analyses, strategic planning.

87. The observation method of collecting primary data for marketing research involves observing the respondent doing something.
    a. True
    b. False

88. When a company offers a product and prices it high in the expected price range, the result is called
    a. "pricing lining."
    b. "leader pricing."
    c. "penetration pricing."
    d. "price skimming."

89. Biogenic needs include needs for food and physical comfort, and arise out of physiological states, while psychogenic needs include the need for appreciation and self-esteem, and arise out of psychological states.
    a. True
    b. False

90. When reducing the price of a product causes total revenues to decline or raising the price results in an increase in total revenue, demand for the product is said to be
    a. "elastic."
    b. "inelastic."
    c. "stagnant."
    d. "kinetic."

91. "Product line" is a phrase used to hype a product.
    a. True
    b. False

92. The four periods of a product's life cycle are
    a. introduction, growth, maturity, decline.
    b. entry, arrival, purchase, decline.
    c. unique, parity, decline, extinct.
    d. primary, late primary, early secondary, secondary.

93. A *product* can broadly be defined as a tangible or intangible item that is offered for sale or barter to individuals or institutions.
    a. True
    b. False

94. A negatively sloped demand curve suggests that
    a. customers have positive feelings about a product.
    b. customers have negative feelings about a product.

     c. as prices rise, demand increases.
     d. as prices rise, demand decreases.

95. The break-even point on a product occurs when the revenue it earns equals the total costs that have been incurred, assuming a given selling price.
     a. True
     b. False

96. When a few product sellers control all or almost all the supply of a particular product, the situation is referred to as
     a. "market share."
     b. "elastic demand."
     c. "an oligopoly."
     d. "capitalism."

97. "Sales potential" and "market potential" are synonymous terms in marketing.
     a. True
     b. False

98. The practice, followed by some retailers, of cutting the prices of a handful of popular items to attract customers, is called
     a. "pricing lining."
     b. "leader pricing."
     c. "penetration pricing."
     d. "price skimming."

99. In the supply-and-demand approach to pricing, prices are based on estimates of how much market demand there will be for the product as well as how much of the product will be available.
     a. True
     b. False

100. If a buyer receives an invoice dated May 9 for $1250 and is offered terms of 2/10 net 30, what does this mean?
     a. Two percent of the bill ($25) is due within 10 days of the invoice; the remainder of the bill is due within 30 days of the invoice.
     b. If the buyer pays the bill by May 19 (10 days after the invoice date), he or she may take a 2 percent discount ($25) off the total due. If the bill is not paid by May 19, the entire bill must be paid by June 8 (within 30 days of the invoice date).
     c. The items can be returned within 10 days for 2 percent less than the billing price; otherwise, the balance must be paid within 30 days.
     d. The biller has had a bad payment experience with the buyer.